THE SEARCH FOR INCOME

AN INVESTOR'S GUIDE TO INCOME-PAYING INVESTMENTS

BY MAIKE CURRIE

Hh

HARRIMAN HOUSE LTD

3A Penns Road
Petersfield
Hampshire
GU32 2EW
GREAT BRITAIN

Tel: +44 (0)1730 233870
Fax: +44 (0)1730 233880
Email: enquiries@harriman-house.com
Website: www.harriman-house.com

First published in Great Britain in 2011

ISBN: 978-0-85719-034-5

British Library Cataloguing in Publication Data
A CIP catalogue record for this book can be obtained from the British Library.

Set in Minion, Bebas Neue and FrutigerMW Cond.

Printed and bound in the UK by CPI Group (UK) Ltd, Croydon, CR0 4YY.

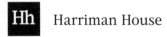

Hh Harriman House

To Piet

CONTENTS

ABOUT THE AUTHOR

As an experienced personal finance writer, Maike Currie writes about income for a living. She has worked across the Financial Times Group as a reporter and editor covering the fundamentals of income investing in its various forms.

Maike started her journalism career in South Africa's tumultuous newspaper industry writing about everything from politics and education to the antics of the Springbok rugby team, finding her niche in financial journalism. She moved to the UK just in time to witness the excesses of the boom years descend into an environment of low interest rates, high debt levels and the culling of dividends. She is in no doubt that the age of austerity has arrived but maintains that there is still income to be found – provided you look in the right places.

ACKNOWLEDGEMENTS

A huge thank you to my contacts in the industry – your thoughts and expertise have been invaluable and accordingly feature throughout the book. The *Investors Chronicle* magazine (part of the Financial Times Group) which has in many ways been an 'alma mater' in investments, and in particular my colleague and friend, Robert Ansted, for helping with the number crunching. My publisher, Craig Pearce – it has been a pleasure working with you. To my family and friends who have been enormously supportive and encouraging. Thank you all.

RISK WARNING

No responsibility for loss incurred by any person or corporate body acting or refraining to act as a result of reading material in this book can be accepted by the Author or the Publisher.

The information provided by the Author is not offered as, nor should it be inferred to be, investment advice or recommendation to readers. The financial circumstances of individuals will vary greatly and investment behaviour which may be appropriate for one reader is unlikely to be appropriate for others. Specific investment vehicles and products are included as illustrative examples only.

If in doubt on any investment issue, consult a financial advisor.

PREFACE

The search for income is not new. It is as old as the history of money, and money's older counterpart, credit. During ancient times income was generated by loaning out wheat and silver at an interest while arable land was leased for income in the form of agricultural produce or metallic money. In ancient Babylonia, laws were established to avoid an abuse of usury, an exorbitant or unlawful rate of interest. Loans were secured with property, or even wives and children, serving as collateral. The ancient world even had its own banking system with temples used to facilitate banking operations similar to those we know today – deposits, transfers and loans while the sun god acted through priests and priestesses as chief banker[1].

Today our bankers are not gods (although some might beg to differ) and the systems used to generate income have become more regulated and refined. Now, income can legally be earned in two main ways:

1. You can exchange your labour, skills, knowledge, talent or time for money.
2. You can have your money earn money for you by investing it.

The former, if you're lucky and provided you can budget, will pay your bills. The latter, if you do it right, will provide cover for a rainy day, assist you in achieving your financial goals and help you to have financial security in your retirement.

It is astonishing, then, how few people pay heed to this second method of generating income or know little about it. This second method of generating income is the focus of this book; this is a guide to those concepts, vehicles and strategies that can be utilised to earn an income from investing. It is about where to find income, how to grow income and of course, once you have income, how to make sure you keep hold of it. We look at the concept of income, the role different investment vehicles play in an income portfolio and the methods that can be employed to effectively draw an income from your aggregated investments.

[1] S. Homer and R. Sylla, *A History of Interest Rates* (John Wiley & Sons, 4th edition, 2005).

When approaching the concept of investment income there are two separate but related issues which should be noted. These are:

1. The preservation of capital.
2. The search for the best income.

The ability to get good income into the future (2) depends on preserving capital (1). To adequately cover the concept of income within an investment context both issues need to be addressed. So while the core focus of the book is on how investors should search for the best income, the importance of preserving and growing capital, whether by protecting against risks such as inflation or by reinvesting income returns, will also be covered.

The ultimate intention is to show you how to use the financial assets and capital which you have to build an investment portfolio, in line with your risk appetite, with the aim of generating income to supplement your personal needs.

This book is for, among others, retirees looking for ways to supplement their pensions, parents who want to generate an income stream to fund their child's education or another family need, individuals seeking to draw an income from their accumulated wealth whether this is to cover basic living costs, a period of redundancy or illness, or to improve their overall standard of living. Whether a knowledgeable investor or a novice at the investing game, if you want to earn an investment income for the long term, you will find this book useful.

How this book is structured

In Part A we place the search for income into context by defining just what constitutes income from an investment perspective. This section covers the essential basics of income, including interest rates, inflation and yield. The intention is to demystify investing jargon while building the reader's basic theoretical knowledge about income.

Those who already have some investing experience and are well-versed in the concepts covered in Part A might be inclined to move straight to Part B. This delves into different asset classes such as cash, fixed interest, equities and property, looking at how these can be utilised to generate income. Investments discussed in this section are classified according to their perceived investment risk. Part B starts by discussing the relatively safe investments, such as cash and bonds, and then moves on to more risky asset classes, such as shares, funds and property. This section concludes by discussing the role alternative investment vehicles can play in generating an income.

The knowledge built up in the first two parts of the book is then applied in Part C, where the focus shifts from the theoretical to the practical. Part C looks at how you may construct an income-producing investment portfolio by using the different investment strategies at your disposal. In this section we discuss:

- How you should blend different investments together to ensure a secure and consistent income stream.
- How to manage your investment portfolio's holdings as your income needs and circumstances change.
- Model income portfolios suited to the different life stages including worked examples of how different investors may go about building an income portfolio.

Part C concludes by discussing the most effective ways to draw an income from your pension pot, as well as tax efficient investment strategies and vehicles which you can employ to ensure you hold on to as much of your income as possible.

Having read all three parts of the book the intention is that you will be equipped to produce and carry out an investment plan fit for your individual income purposes.

INTRODUCTION

A lot of investment advice is centred on how you should save money and accumulate wealth, rather than how you should take out money from your investments. When you are able to draw money out from your investments this is an income you have earned from them. The amount of income generated by an investment, whether in the form of dividends, interest or realised capital gains, is known as the investment's income return. Generating an accumulative income return from a portfolio of different investments, in line with your risk appetite and individual income needs, is what this book is about.

Throughout the history of investing authors have written about income in one form or another and while economic cycles may fluctuate, the fundamentals of income investing remain the same. This is the case whether investors find themselves in a high-growth, high-return environment or in a deep and severe recession, although under the latter circumstances traditional income sources do come under pressure.

The aftermath of the 2007-2009 economic downturn is a case in point. Following the widespread credit expansion leading to this downturn, an environment of low interest rates, unreliable dividend payments and variable yields emerged. This state of affairs sparked an unprecedented search for income. Investors had to work much harder to seek out alternative income-generating investments as traditional channels such as bank savings accounts could no longer be relied upon to produce an adequate income. Income investing in the 21st century is not more important than it was in the past but, as the situation since the financial crisis has shown, more thought and planning is now required by investors to secure the income they desire.

Your investment choices will directly affect the income you receive. Let's look at a couple of examples.

Imagine you had £10,000 in 1980. Say you used this money to buy shares in the oil giant, British Petroleum (BP), and say you made your purchase on 1 January that year. Based on the share price taken on 1 January 1980, and assuming you sold your BP shares on the last day of trading that year, reinvesting any income earned over that that period, by the end of the year you would have received an annual dividend payout (the slice of business profits a company pays to its shareholders) of £2888. Your pot of money would have grown from £10,000 to £12,888 – an increase of almost 30% – leaving you with a significant income return of £2888.

Had you instead in 1980 decided to put the £10,000 into a bank savings account you would have earned £1600 in interest by the end of the year, based on the Bank of England's base rate of 16% at the end of the year. Thus, the safest of all investments – cash – would have rendered you with an income return of £1600.[2]

Now let's fast forward to 2010, and say you adopted a similar strategy at the beginning of that year. An oil spill disaster in the Gulf of Mexico in April 2010 saw BP's share price plummet and the company's dividend payout was suspended in June. As a consequence, the £10,000 investment would be worth £7877 by the end of the year, equating to a loss of over 20%.

Figure A shows BP's dividend payment per share owned from 1980 through to the well publicised dividend cut experienced in 2010.

Figure A – BP's dividend payment per share from 1980 to 2010

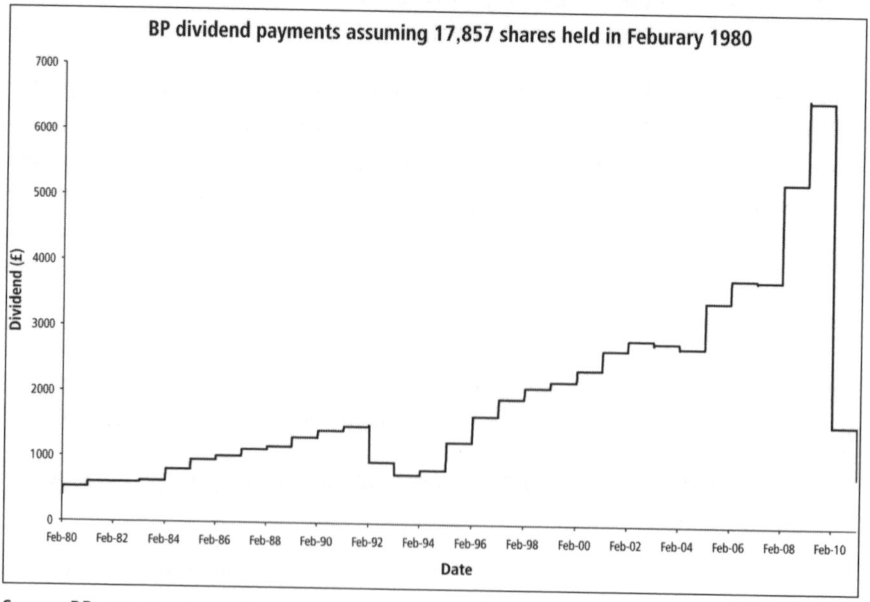

Source: BP company accounts

---

[2] Calculation methodology: Share price taken on first day of first month, assuming you sold on the last day of trading at the end of the given year (1980). Includes income reinvested over that period. Base rate for given year based on the rate on the last day of the year in question.

What if you had opted for the low risk option in 2010 and placed your money into a bank savings account? Based on the bank base rate at the time, £10,000 invested in a savings account on 1 January 2010 would have returned just £50 – a return of 0.5%[3]. Figure B shows the bank rate over the last 40 years in the UK and the dramatic falls in rates from March 2009 to an all-time, extended low.

Figure B – the UK bank rate from 1970 to 2011

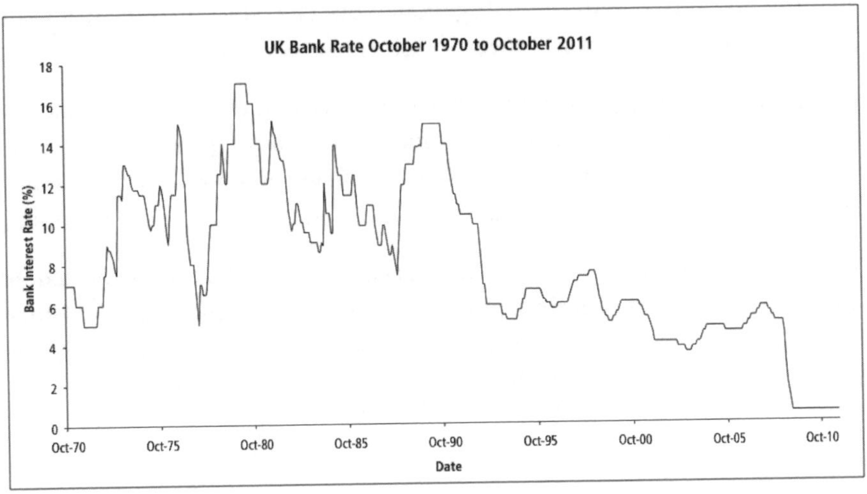

Source: Bank of England

Regardless of which of the two investment routes was chosen in 2010, had you been hoping to draw an income from your £10,000, you would have been left bitterly disappointed.

This is not to say that it would have been better to leave the £10,000 under the mattress.

Despite record low interest rates and dividend cuts by a number of companies in 2010, there were other investment options that could have delivered a more generous income return than an investment in the shares of BP or leaving the £10,000 in a savings account. Had you, for example, invested £10,000 in the

[3] Calculation methodology: Share price taken on first day of first month, assuming you sold on the last day of trading at the end of the given year (2010). Includes income reinvested over that period. Base rate for given year based on the rate at last day of the year in question.

global telecommunications company BT, you would have enjoyed an income return of £4019. Alternatively, had you put the same amount in FTSE 100 company Electrocomponents, your income return would have been £7188; a 72% return.

The above examples illustrate the impact different investing choices and the timing of these can have on income. While it is impossible to control the timing of dividend cuts and interest rate falls, if you understand how investing for income works, what the risks are, and how best to use different investments and blend these together, you can start to construct an investment portfolio that will meet your income requirements.

As we progress through the book you will also see that it is important to hold a diversified spread of investments and to have a long-term investment horizon when investing for income. This book will guide you through these important issues and the steps and strategies to building an income portfolio.

Whether you are a pensioner, parent, working professional, sophisticated or novice investor, understanding how to tap into income from sources other than your salary can go a long way in helping you meet your financial goals. It can also make a significant difference to your quality of life.

PART A:

WHAT IS INCOME?

1

INCOME MATTERS

A definition of income investing

It is important that we start by defining exactly what we mean by income and some of the key concepts related to income investing. For this reason, the following pages contain a lot of basic definitions – you should spend some time getting to grips with these before moving on through the book.

As a starting point, the *Dictionary of Investing*,[4] defines income as:

1. *Personal or business revenues received for a stated period.*
2. *Funds received from an investment as either interest or dividend.*

This means that salaries and wages, the profits from selling property, and returns from trading the financial markets – such as those generated by placing the occasional spread bet – can all be classed as income. Most people's main income will be a salary or wage but income can also be earned through making investments and releasing the capital tied up in assets by selling them.

Income, in short, is a financial gain (money), earned or unearned, accrued over a given period of time.

Keeping this in mind, but breaking the definition down further, income can be split into three broad categories:

1. *Active income*, which is actively earned or generated by working, such as wages, tips, salaries and commissions.
2. *Passive income*, which is income derived without being actively involved, such as receiving rent from leasing a property, or a silent business partnership.
3. *Portfolio income* (or investment income), which is derived from different investment vehicles, ranging from cash deposits to bonds and company shares. This is the classification of income that will be focused on in this book.

Portfolio income can come in many different guises such as *interest*, *capital gains*, *yield* and *dividends*: it is important to understand why these matter to the income investor. You also need to understand how factors such as *inflation* and *interest rate* movements impact investment income in its various forms. All of these concepts will be explained as we progress through Part A.

Let's start by clarifying a basic yet often misunderstood distinction.

---

[4] Jerry M. Rosenberg, *Dictionary of Investing* (John Wiley & Sons, 1993).

THE DIFFERENCE BETWEEN SAVING AND INVESTING

Deposit-based investments such as cash held in a savings account are often referred to as savings, suggesting that investments and savings are sometimes the same thing. So what then is the difference between investments and savings?

Sometimes investments are thought of as savings' "riskier cousin"[5]. Alternatively, savings might be defined as regular investments of small sums of money while investments relate to larger, lump sums. Of course by regularly saving small sums a larger lump sum will eventually be built up, which can then be invested. Clearly the two concepts are closely related and the terms *saving* and *investing* can at times be interchangeable.

There is, however, an important distinction: increasing your savings does not necessarily always equate to an increased income. If you leave your savings stashed away under a mattress there is no chance that those savings will produce an income. As we will see, generating a consistent income stream that grows with time depends on building up your savings and then investing this capital effectively.

THE IMPORTANCE OF INVESTING FOR THE LONG TERM

Of course, to be in a position to make an investment you need to have put some funds to one side, which is why building up your capital through saving and then preserving this capital is so important.

Unless you are lucky enough to come into money through inheritance, winning the lottery or some other windfall, increasing your pot of money for investment purposes takes time. Similarly, to get to a position where you can comfortably draw income from an investment portfolio, without prematurely depleting the capital you invested, cannot be done over night. You need time to grow your capital to ensure the income you eventually draw from your investment is enough to meet your needs.

You should therefore think of income investing as fundamentally a long-term activity – this is not anything like making short-term trades for a quick profit. You should be looking at an investment time horizon – that is the amount of time you expect to hold investments – of at least five years, ideally even longer at anywhere between 10 and 20 years.

---

[5] P. Lewis, *Beat the Banks* (Age Concern Books, 2008), p. 3.

This brings us to another important distinction – there is a difference between saving money, investing to increase your capital, and investing in order to draw an income. Let's look at this now.

Income versus capital gains

The point of investing is to make money and there are two ways in which this can be done:

1. Your investment grows in size and you make a capital gain.
2. Your investment pays you an income.

Say you decide to buy a property for £500,000 as an investment. The property grows in value from the day you bought it and eventually you sell it at a higher price than what you initially paid for it, at £600,000. You have made a *capital gain* of £100,000 from your investment. You have earned a return by adopting the basic premise of selling at a higher price than you originally bought for.

A return could also have been earned by holding on to that property, leasing it out to a tenant and receiving a rental income in return. For instance, you might earn £2000 per month in rental fees from the tenants. In this case your investment is paying you an income.

The same principles can apply when investing in company shares. If you buy a Vodafone share at 100p and sell it at 150p, you will make a 50p *capital gain* on your investment. If instead you choose to hold on to that share, you may receive a dividend payout (a percentage of the company's profits) for each share that you own, for instance 2p per share paid twice annually. In this case you will be earning an *income* from your investment while still maintaining ownership of the share.

INVESTING FOR GROWTH AND INVESTING FOR INCOME

When you seek investments that grow in size this is referred to as *investing for growth* while if you seek investments that pay an income this is *investing for income*. The two investment techniques are different but ultimately both strategies are a way of generating an income.

Typically, younger investors seeking to accumulate wealth will be interested in capital growth – i.e. growing their funds so that their capital pot is large enough to enable them to earn sufficient income from it in later years. Generally they tend to have longer-term considerations, for example purchasing a home or generating money for their child's education, and will look for investments that will grow and preserve their capital to meet this need.

Older investors, on the other hand, are more likely to be on the lookout for an investment which generates a constant income stream. In this case it is their income need that drives the investment. Retirees might require regular income payments from their investments, whether in the form of share dividends, interest paid on a cash deposit or rental income from a leased property which they can use to supplement insufficient pension income.

While age can play a determining role in whether an investor seeks income to live off now or wants to store up capital wealth to draw on in the future, there are no hard and fast rules. For example, a younger investor might be out of work or suffer from a long-term illness and as such not have a wage or salary to live on. To cover for such an eventuality they might prefer to invest for income. Table 1.1 provides a summary of the differences between income and growth investors.

Table 1.1 – the differences between income and growth investors[6]

Income investors	Growth investors
Less active investor	Active investor
Yield is priority	Price/earnings ratio is priority
Spend dividends	Reinvest dividends

Related to both growth and income investing is the concept of *total return*.

[6] R. Hobson, *How to Build a Share Portfolio* (Harriman House, 2011), p. 39. (Based on this table.)

TOTAL RETURN

Total return is the return made on an investment and is the yardstick by which one should assess an investment. It is the combination of income generated from dividends and interest, together with the underlying capital growth of the investment over a given period of time.

```
total return = income + capital appreciation (or depreciation)
```

Let's take the example of the Vodafone share mentioned before and assume you held the share for a year. Your total return from this investment will be the income from the share: 2p x 2 = 4p (the 2p dividend paid twice annually) plus the capital appreciation, i.e. the 50p *capital gain* on your investment. So 2p plus 50p gives a total return of 52p.

As total return is a measure of the performance of an investment, income cannot exist without taking account of capital growth, and vice versa. If either of the two is ignored when making investment decisions the consequences can be detrimental. For example, if you are drawing income without keeping an eye on your capital you run the risk of ending up with a severely depleted pot of money, making it impossible to generate the income returns you desire in the future. This brings us back to the dual focus of this book: the ability to get good income in the future depends on preserving and growing your capital.

A COMBINED INCOME AND GROWTH STRATEGY

Capital and income investing need not be two separate strategies – in fact many investors prefer to classify themselves as *total return* investors as opposed to growth or income investors.[7] These investors typically reinvest the income they earn from investments with the goal of increasing their capital through both income *and* growth (capital appreciation). By reinvesting the income return from an investment, such as share dividends, you can significantly boost the growth of your initial capital amount invested.

To illustrate this, let's think back to the BP example cited in the Introduction to this book. Had you invested £10,000 in BP shares at the start of 1980 and

[7] R. Norton, *Investing for Income: A Bond Mutual Fund Approach to High-Return, Low-Risk Profits* (McGraw-Hill, 1999).

left it there rather than disinvesting at the end of the year, ploughing any dividend payouts back into your original investment each year, the compound effect of the reinvested dividends would have seen your original investment grow to a staggering £373,375 by the end of 2010. Had you not reinvested dividends your investment would have been worth markedly less – around £76,759 at the end of 2010.

A growth-orientated portfolio, in turn, can still be used to produce an income stream by way of regular or ad hoc income withdrawals. You might combine income and growth strategies by investing in a range of asset classes, some of which are oriented toward income and some of which are oriented to growth.

Focusing solely on one of income or capital growth can produce at best a partial or at worst a misleading picture. Both styles of investing have a role to play in generating a healthy total return, and a successful investment strategy will take account of both.

How much income and capital should you hold to be classified as rich?

Here's a question to get you thinking: When, in income terms, can you be defined as *rich*?

Andrew Gadd, an investment expert from the UK-based Lighthouse Group, defines individuals as rich when they do not live off the income payments from their capital, because if they do then there is always the risk of them completely eroding their capital. Rather, a rich individual is one who is able to live off of the income from the income drawn on their capital.

Here's an example. You have £100m of capital. Say the return generated from this capital is 5% of the total, which comes to £5m per year (£100m/100 x 5 = £5m). You are rich according to Mr Gadd's definition if you are able to live on the income payout generated on that £5m. Let's say this is also 5%, making the income that you live on £250,000 per annum (£5m/100 x 5 = £250,000). You are living off 5% of £5m, i.e. the income from the income from your capital.

We will now move on to look at the main types of asset classes that can be used to generate income.

Asset classes

There are a variety of investment options available to those who are looking to invest for income. Different investment assets pay income in different ways and as such are used for different purposes by investors.

For example, you might have a single investment such as a holding of Vodafone shares which pays you an income in the form of a twice yearly dividend, usually in February and August. A dividend is paid for each share, so the amount you receive will depend on the number of shares you own. Shares are one variety of investment asset and dividends from them are a form of income.

Alternatively, you might draw an income from a lump sum of cash held in a bank deposit account which pays you an annual or monthly interest return. Cash held in a savings account is another type of investment asset, and it also delivers an income by paying interest.

There are three main types of investment assets and these are categorised based on their income return potential and their risk to the investor. These three categories are called *asset classes* and they are:

1. *Cash* – savings in a deposit account.
2. *Fixed interest* – bonds, either government or corporate.
3. *Equities* – company shares, selected either for income or growth.

THE RISK/REWARD RATIO

Each of the three asset classes, even cash, comes with a certain degree of *investment risk*. This is the risk that the return from the investment will not meet the investor's expectations.

Uncertainty in the outcome of an investment is directly related to the investment's *volatility*. Volatility is a measure of an investment's stability, so the greater the volatility, the more likely the return from the investment is to fluctuate and hence the higher the risk accompanying the investment. As well as making returns uncertain, volatility can also result in a loss of the investor's initial investment capital.

With the most risky investments, for example equities, there is a danger of an investor losing all of their capital. To compensate for this, higher risk investments hold the possibility of more lucrative income returns. Conversely, lower risk investments such as cash come with lower but more stable returns. This balance between high risk and high reward against low risk and low reward is known as the risk/reward ratio. It is a measure of the *reward* (the income return) of an investment corresponding to the amount of *risk* taken by investing in the asset class.

The risk/reward ratio lies at the heart of investing and successful portfolio construction: the risk built into a portfolio needs to be at a level at which the investor is comfortable while the reward needs to be matched to the investor's income goals. Thus the risk/reward balance is the most important guideline when building and managing an income portfolio. Before an investment is made you should always understand the risk of the investment and the reward it offers in return for this.

It is worth noting that the three asset classes given above are not the only asset classes available. There is also a range of alternative asset classes and investments which can be used to generate income depending on the amount of risk an investor is willing to take. These will be discussed in greater detail in Part B.

Figure 1.1 presents the asset classes we cover in this book and should act as a directory to their level of investment risk.

Figure 1.1 – different assets and their levels of investment risk

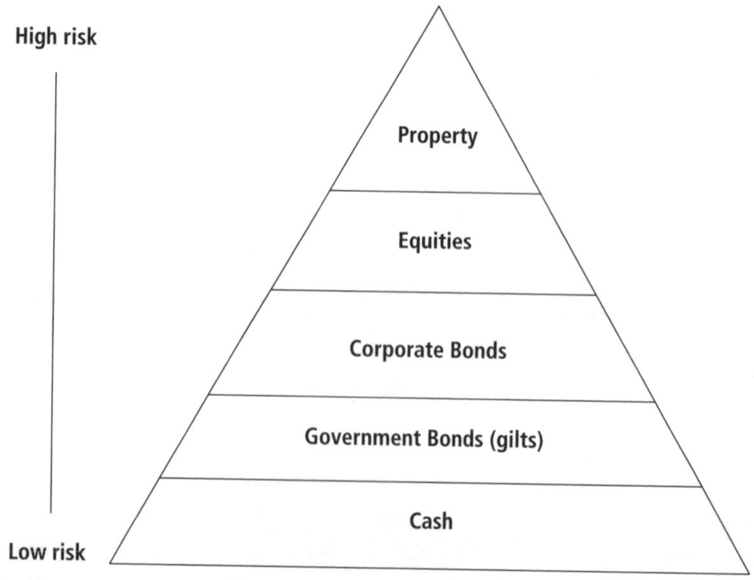

Now that we have defined the main asset classes let's move on to look at the different types of income that these asset classes generate.

Types of income

To construct an income portfolio successfully, we have to know about the different types of income provided by different asset classes.

There are primarily three ways to categorise the types of income that investment assets produce. The income can be:

1. Variable over time and under certain economic conditions: *variable income.*
2. Fixed from the outset: *fixed income.*
3. Definite, with a schedule of obligatory payments and backed by a third party: *guaranteed income.*

Each of these three forms of income has a role to play within an investment portfolio. An individual's income needs will dictate how their portfolio is weighted to the different incomes and the investments that generate these.

Let's take a closer look at these three forms of portfolio income.

1. VARIABLE INCOME

Variable income is income which cannot be predicted ahead of time and will fluctuate depending on factors such as interest rate changes, inflation rate movements or the profitability of a company. A savings account which pays a variable rate of interest linked to a country's bank rate or in line with the prevalent inflation rate would be classed as providing a variable income (the bank rate and inflation will be explained later in Part A).

Dividend income paid by company shares can also be seen as a variable form of income as this will depend on the company's results and profits over a given period of time. Rental income from a property investment will also vary over time depending on factors such as demand and supply within the property market.

Variable income is usually generated by higher-risk investments prone to greater volatility. Given the higher risk associated with these investments, they tend to offer the possibility of higher returns and the potential of growing the capital invested.

As a rule, a longer time horizon is needed for more volatile investments as this allows time for the risk of fluctuating returns to be smoothed out. For example, if an investment pays a good income in years 1, 3, 5, 7 and 8, but a low income in years 2, 4 and 6, the income from all of the years will average out to give a reasonable income return over the period.

2. FIXED INCOME

Fixed income is the polar opposite of variable income – it is set when the investment is made and stays at this level. This form of income is generated by investments that yield pre-determined income payments, usually on the basis of a fixed schedule. Fixed income investments tend to be bond investments and cash deposit accounts which pay out a fixed rate of income every month.

Another form of fixed income comes in the form of permanent interest bearing shares (Pibs). These are special shares, issued mostly by building societies, that pay a fixed rate of interest (although under exceptional circumstances these payments can be missed). Given their predictable nature, investments such as cash and bonds which promise fixed income form the *safe* part of an investment portfolio.

Sometimes *fixed income* assets are defined as those with a schedule of obligatory income payments, but in this book we refer to investments with obligatory income payments as *guaranteed income*. An investment paying a guaranteed income, as explained below, can qualify as a fixed or variable income paying investment.

3. GUARANTEED INCOME

As the name indicates, *guaranteed income* is the most certain form of income. This income is guaranteed or backed by a third party such as the government or an insurance company.

Examples of investments which generate a guaranteed income include certificates of deposit issued by government-backed institutions such as National Savings and Investments (NS&I), bonds which are backed by their issuer and annuities purchased in retirement, in which case the insurance company issuing the annuity guarantees an income payment.

For investors in retirement who no longer have active income at their disposal, securing a guaranteed income can provide important security, although it is important to note that the strength of the guarantee will depend on the party backing the investment.

Investments offering a guaranteed income can usually pay that income in either a fixed or variable form. For example, annuities can pay a variable income or a fixed income depending on the type of annuity purchased; index-linked annuities will vary income payments depending on the rate of inflation while fixed rate annuities pay a predetermined income based on the interest rates at the time the annuity is purchased (these are explained in greater detail in chapter 12).

Similarly, bonds can pay fixed income or, if you are purchasing index-linked bonds where the income payment is linked to the rate of inflation, variable income. NS&I savings certificates also pay variable and fixed income depending on whether you are buying index-linked savings certificates (also known as inflation-beating savings) or fixed interest savings certificates.

Table 1.2 summarises the three different types of income and some examples of assets that can provide these.

Table 1.2 – a summary of different income types and the investments that generate them

Fixed income	Variable income	Guaranteed income
Bonds	Equities	NS&I certificates
Gilts	Funds and ETFs	Annuities
Fixed term cash deposits	Property and property funds	Bonds
Sovereign Bonds	Infrastructure funds	Pensions (provided the scheme holds up)
Pibs	Structured products	Inflation linked bonds
	Timber funds	Gilts

BUILDING AN INCOME PORTFOLIO

When constructing an income investment portfolio and blending together different investment vehicles you should be aiming to achieve a mix of asset classes that fits with your risk profile and generates an income that meets your needs. This blending process is known as *asset allocation* and is the bedrock of portfolio construction.

If you have investments in more than one type of asset class, for example holdings of shares, a savings account paying interest and some exposure to bonds, the aggregation of these different income streams is your *portfolio income.*

Within a single asset class you can find a range of investments with different risk/return profiles and hence different income-generating capacities. For example, within the fixed-interest class you can find high-yielding bonds, investment grade bonds and inflation-linked bonds, to name just a few. Each of these has a different risk-return profile which will influence the size of the income return in line with the level of risk taken.

Of course, if you can meet your income requirements by adopting a cautious investment approach there is no reason why you would or should want to take additional risk. But it is highly unlikely that most people will be able to meet their income requirements by staying solely invested in cash or similarly low-risk investments. The approach that is required, therefore, is to build a portfolio that encompasses a spread of investments from different asset classes. This is known as *diversification.*

DIVERSIFICATION

In simple terms, diversification means not putting all your eggs in one basket. Asset allocation and diversification are often (and wrongly) used interchangeably. Even if you are 100% invested in cash this is still a form of asset allocation. It is not, however, diversification.

No single asset class can be the top performer all the time and in all economic conditions. By holding a mix of the different asset classes you reduce the risk of the overall performance of your income portfolio being damaged by unexpected or severe falls in any single investment.

Diversification is also based on the principle that different asset classes are to an extent uncorrelated – in other words, their prices and performance move independently of each other. So by holding a range of different assets that are not correlated with each other, the positive performance of some of the investments should balance out the negative performance of the others, smoothing out overall portfolio returns.

We will discuss asset allocation and diversification in more detail in Part C when we use these concepts to construct an income portfolio.

For now, let's consider briefly the circumstances that might cause problems for investors when they are seeking a diversified portfolio of assets that pay an income.

Searching for income

The role different types of income and the investments that generate them play in an income investment portfolio has not changed fundamentally over time. However, income investments can come under pressure, leaving investors struggling for consistent and reliable sources of investment income. For example:

- An interest-paying deposit account has little use for an income-seeking investor if the interest rate offered on the account, and thus the income return, is at a low level.
- If inflation is rising rapidly and the income from an investment is not keeping pace this will erode the worth of the capital invested along with the worth of future income returns.
- For an investor relying on share dividends companies suffering falling profits and weak balance sheets is bad news as it is likely to lead to dividend cuts and an eventual fall in income payouts.
- If there is an increased risk that companies and even governments might go bankrupt, fixed-income investments such as bonds and gilts lose their low-risk status.
- Even guaranteed income investments, the lowest risk investment option available, can disappoint if the economic situation deteriorates far enough.

A situation where all sources of investment income come under severe pressure simultaneously might sound highly unlikely, but in the wake of the 2007-2009 financial crisis this is exactly what happened. In March 2009 interest rates fell to their lowest level in the Bank of England's 317-year history, dropping to just shy of zero at 0.5% and remaining stagnant at this level for more than two years.

At the same time, many companies, most notably banks, cut or suspended their dividends as profits and balance sheets came under pressure. The safe-haven status of corporate bonds and gilts was called into question as the risk of companies and certain governments falling into bankruptcy became a frightening possibility. Investments generating guaranteed income, such as NS&I Savings Certificates, were withdrawn from sale in mid-2010 and again in 2011 while at the same time annuity rates fell to their lowest level in 20 years.

The aftermath of the financial crisis led to an unprecedented search for income but irrespective of the broader economic circumstances, whether interest rates are low, or the state of the stock market, income investing remains important.

In order to ensure a consistent income stream without prematurely depleting your capital pot it is important that you understand how investing for income works and the ways to preserve and protect your capital invested.

A good place to start is with a look at interest rates.

2

INTEREST RATES

Interest is the amount charged or paid, at a particular rate, for the use of money – it is charged when money is borrowed and paid when money is loaned. Depositing cash with a financial institution such as a bank or building society for an interest is one of the simplest ways for investors to earn an income.

The notion of using one's assets to generate an income return in the form of interest is as old as the history of man. The Bible talks of interest, the most well-known incidence perhaps being the New Testament story of the rich man who went on a journey, entrusting three slaves with his property, or talents (which in biblical terms is a large unit of money). When the master returned he rewarded two of the slaves for putting his money to work and growing the initial income they received but he lashed out at the third slave who decided instead to dig a hole in the ground and bury the money entrusted to him. The rich man's angry words to the slave were: "You should have deposited my money with the bankers and on my return I would have received my money back with interest."

Interestingly, one of the distinguishing practices in Islamic Sharia law is that the lending of money should be interest-free. Charging interest – i.e. making money from money – is regarded as usury and therefore is not permitted. Rather, the Islamic financial model works on the basis of risk-sharing. For example, in banking the customer and the bank will share the risk of any investment on agreed terms and divide any profits between them.

In the next section we will look at how the different interest rates work, and their impact on financial markets and investments.

What is an interest rate?

An *interest rate* is the percentage of a sum of money charged for its use. This means the interest rate is also the income return or payment in return for depositing or loaning that money. Interest rates can be traced as far back as 3000 B.C. to Sumer, the earliest known civilisation. In ancient Sumer, a historical region in southern Mesopotamia (today the country of Iraq), grain and silver were the two standards of value – the return on a loan of barley was one-third per year, while a loan of silver would earn its lender an income return of 20%.[8]

---

[8] S. Homer and R. Sylla, *A History of Interest Rates* (John Wiley & Sons, 4th edition, 2005).

Moving forward to the present, when depositing a cash investment of £10,000, a 2% interest rate means the income return you receive is 2% of the money deposited: it is 2% of £10,000, which is £200. By convention interest rates refer to an annual calculation.

HOW TO CALCULATE SIMPLE INTEREST

To calculate the interest earned on a cash deposit you need to know:

- The amount deposited with the bank, known as the *principal.*
- The interest rate offered, known as the *rate.*
- The *time*, in years, the money will be left on deposit.

The formula for calculating interest is:

```
interest = principal x rate x time
```

The tricky part of this equation is the time, which must be in years. If this is given to you in months, divide it by 12 (as there are 12 months in a year). If it is given to you in days, divide the amount by the number of days in the given year (this will usually be 365, or 366 in a leap year).

Remember that interest rates are expressed as a percentage, and a percentage is a ratio of a number to 100. You will need to divide the interest rate on offer by 100 to express it as a decimal (a fraction out of 100). So if the interest rate is 10%, dividing it by 100 will give you a decimal of 0.1

Let's say you have £1000 that you would like to put into a savings account for 18 months and the interest rate on offer is fixed at 10%.

Your interest calculation will be:

```
£1000 (principal) x 0.1 (interest rate = 10/100) x 1.5 (time
18/12) = £150
```

Note that the £150 is known as simple interest. This is the interest paid only on the original amount invested. It is a one-off, fixed amount. Interest which builds up from one period to the next is known as compound interest. The merits of compound interest and how to calculate it will be explained later in this chapter.

Interest rates are one of the most powerful forces in financial markets. Banks pay interest on money deposited and then use these deposits to make loans, on which loanees must pay interest. This is the essence of the modern day banking system. Getting the balance between loans and deposits right is pivotal to any bank's financial health.

For an important topic, interest rates are the source of some confusion for many investors. This is due to the range of different interest rates that are referred to.

Different types of interest rates

When interest rates are referred to it will usually be in one of the three following ways:

1. Bank deposit rates
2. The bank rate or base rate
3. The London interbank offered rate (LIBOR)

These are all interest rates and it is important to understand the differences between them.

1. BANK DEPOSIT RATES

Let's assume a bank is offering a deposit rate of 3% on one of its savings accounts. How do they arrive at that figure?

Banks and building societies are free to set whatever rate of interest they like, but they will be influenced by:

- The Bank of England bank rate.
- Supply and demand in the market. Banks will raise interest rates to attract more deposits by savers, while lower interest rates will discourage savers from depositing their money. Getting the right level can be tricky – if the bank sets rates too low it won't attract many depositors but if it sets them too high this will squeeze its profit margin.

2. THE BANK RATE

Interest rates offered or charged by high street banks change as a result of changes in policies from a country's central bank. The rate of interest a country's central bank uses to steer monetary policy is also the rate at which it is prepared to lend to the commercial banks, including the high street banks everyone uses daily. This rate is known as the *bank rate* or the *base* interest rate.

The bank rate is a critical measure. Not only does it affect interest rates throughout the whole banking system but it is also used to influence macroeconomic factors such as the inflation rate and the money supply of a country. To understand how all of this works, it is important to have a grasp of how and why central banks go about setting the bank rate.

In the UK the central bank is the Bank of England. Once a month, the Bank of England's Monetary Policy Committee (MPC) holds a meeting to decide the bank rate for that month. The Bank of England's core objective is to achieve price stability for the pound and meet the government's inflation target. This stability is usually achieved by making changes to the interest rate – a process referred to as *monetary policy.*

Monetary policy

If the Bank is concerned that the present rate of inflation is too high above target, the bank rate may be increased – or otherwise put, monetary policy will be tightened. An increased bank rate means higher interest rates throughout the banking system. This generates more public interest in saving money, as deposit-based accounts will now earn better interest returns. Borrowing, on the other hand, will become more expensive as the interest on loans also increases and so spending becomes less attractive. In this way, interest rate changes are used to control how much money is spent and, so, keep inflation under control.

The opposite is also true. If the economy requires a boost from more spending and borrowing, the MPC may lower the bank rate and so loosen monetary policy. A reduction in interest rates means saving becomes less attractive as the interest return on cash-based investments will be lower. Borrowing and spending money become more attractive, as people now face lower interest payments on their loans and mortgages, and hence have more disposable income on hand. As spending increases, prices will once again be driven up, and eventually inflation will result. This is why inflation rates and interest rates tend to move together.

Figure 2.1 shows the correlation between interest rate movements and inflation over time. We can see that from beginning 2010 these two measures diverge: while interest rates remain low, inflation is edging up. This is because the MPC resisted putting up the bank rate in fear that it would curtail economic growth and put pressure on indebted consumers at a time when the UK economy was emerging out of the deep recession of 2008/2009.

Figure 2.1 – the bank rate and inflation as measured by the RPI over the last 40 years in the UK

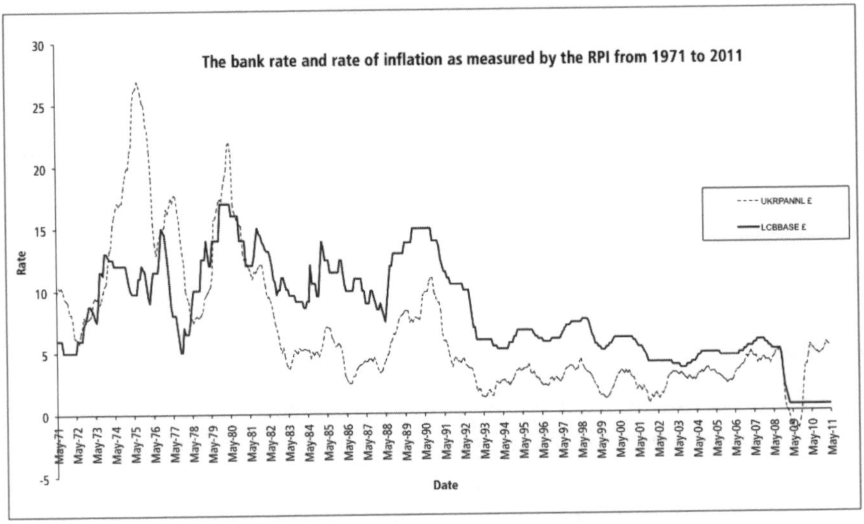

Source: Bank of England and Office of National Statistics

The historic bank rate

Figure 2.2 shows the bank rate for the last 40 years in the UK. We can see that since September 1990, when the bank rate stood at nearly 15%, the rate has been systematically coming down, and with it interest rates offered by banks. This means the interest paid on deposits in savings accounts has reduced drastically over the last 20 years. By September 2008 the bank rate stood at 5%. As the brunt of the credit crunch set in, marked by the collapse of Lehman Brothers in that same month, the bank rate fell every month from September 2008 until reaching an all time low of 0.5% in March 2009. It was at this lowly level nearly three years later in September 2011.

Figure 2.2 – the bank rate over the last 40 years in the UK

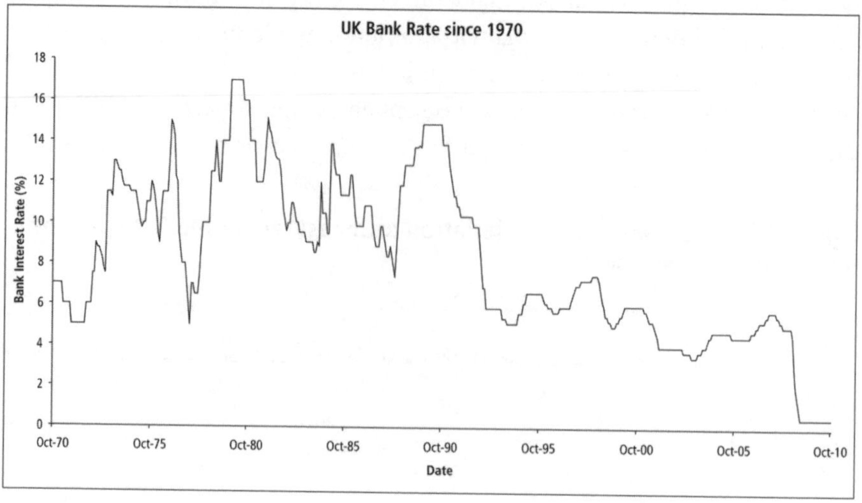

Source: Bank of England

3. LIBOR

As well as borrowing from the Bank of England at the base rate set by the MPC, high street banks can also borrow money from each other. In the UK, the London Interbank Offered Rate (LIBOR) is the interest rate at which banks can borrow money (in different currencies) from other banks in the London wholesale money market (or interbank market) over the short term.

The rate came into existence in the 1980s as demand grew for an accurate measure of the real rate at which banks globally would lend money to each other.

The LIBOR rate can be fixed for different maturities (time spans) and currencies. The British Bankers' Association (BBA) publishes LIBOR rates ranging from overnight to one year, and these are denoted by abbreviations such as s/n, o/n and 1w, 1m. There are 15 different time spans for ten different currencies. The shortest is overnight (o/n), 1w stands for one week and 1m stands for one month. The longest maturity for which the LIBOR rate is fixed is 12m (12 months).

One of the most important measures is the sterling three-month LIBOR rate. This rate influences the level at which lenders set some interest rates on loans, especially mortgages, to consumers and to businesses. It also influences the amount they are willing to lend.

The three-month LIBOR rate is also seen as a good indicator of how willing banks are to lend to each other – the wider the gap between three-month LIBOR and the base rate, the more nervous banks are about lending to each other.

SUMMARY OF THE DIFFERENT INTEREST RATES

Table 2.1 provides a summary of the current deposit rate of a typical bank account, the base rate and LIBOR as at April 2011.

Table 2.1 – summary of the different interest rates

Interest rate	Rate in April 2011 (%)
Base rate	0.5
Bank deposit rate	0.92
LIBOR (3m, Sterling)	0.82

From Table 2.1 you can see that while the bank deposit rate tends to reflect the base rate, at 0.92% it is still slightly higher than the 0.5% base rate so as to attract depositors.

The three-month LIBOR rate in April 2011 was around 0.32% higher than the base rate. Under normal banking conditions LIBOR should be around 10 to 20 basis points higher than the base rate. While 32 basis points is a wider gap than you would expect under normal conditions, it is still nowhere near credit crunch levels where the gap peaked at 130 points; a reflection of banks' reluctance to lend to each other.

The LIBOR rate is generally regarded as a good reflection of short-term swings in interest rates while the bank deposit rate is seen as a reflection of longer-term interest rate trends. This is because the bank rate is changed relatively infrequently, and only to reflect changes in the base rate by the government. The LIBOR rate on the other hand is a constantly changing measure of the cost of money in large amounts for the banks themselves.[9]

[9] M. Brett, *How to Read the Financial Pages* (Random House Business Books, 2000).

Interest rates and the credit crunch

The start of the credit crunch, defined as a severe shortage of money or credit, in the latter part of 2007, and the global financial crisis that followed, led to an environment of low interest rates in many of the world's developed economies.

Central banks from America to Australia cut interest rates to historic lows in the wake of the financial crisis to help ease the cost of the debt burden on individuals and financial institutions, get economies moving again and encourage consumers to spend.

In the UK, interest rates were cut to an all time low of 0.5% for more than two years. At no time prior to this had interest rates in the country fallen below 2%, the level at which they were held following the Great Depression of the 1930s. In America and Japan interest rates were pushed down to similar low levels. While lowering interest rates was seen as essential monetary policy in order to avoid complete economic meltdown, it meant that the income returns on cash investments suffered.

Figure 2.3 shows the bank rate in the UK since 2004. It is notable how the rate dropped in late 2008 and early 2009, staying at a low level as the Bank of England attempted to deal with the financial crisis.

Figure 2.3 – the bank rate since 2004

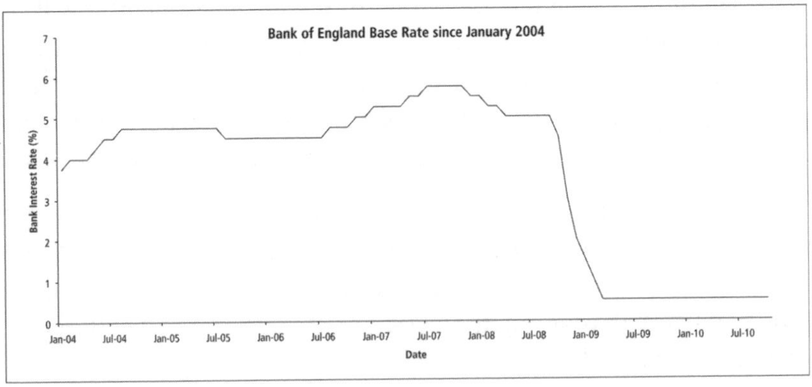

Source: Bank of England

The power of compound interest

THE GREATEST FORCE IN THE UNIVERSE?

There is some dispute over whether it was indeed Albert Einstein who labelled *compound interest* "the greatest force in the universe", "the eighth wonder of the world", and "the greatest mathematical discovery of all time", but all three are epigrams regularly attributed to the physicist. There is little doubt, though, over the merits of this phenomenon.

Before looking further, it is worth noting that compound interest might seem slightly at odds with our focus in this book. Our concern is mainly on taking income from investments, whereas compounding interest is about re-investing income back into your investments rather than withdrawing it. However, compound interest – which is interest earned on interest when reinvested – is a very important topic for the income investor. It can help to significantly grow your income returns in the future.

HOW COMPOUND INTEREST WORKS

What you do with the income gains from your investment(s) will have a significant impact on the accumulation of value within that investment. If you draw the income out from your investments regularly you will be left with your original capital – the *principle*. If, however, you put the income back to work, in other words, you reinvest it, you take advantage of *compounding*.

Compounding means the income return is added to the original investment so that in the following year you will be earning interest on your original investment, plus the earlier interest earned. The year after that, you will be earning interest on your original investment, plus the interest of the preceding years, and so forth. The snowball effect of compounding interest can make a significant difference to your investment's total return. The benefits of compound interest manifest themselves over the long term.

Let's say you are looking to draw an income from a lump sum of £10,000 deposited for 30 years at an interest rate of 6%. If the interest rate remained fixed at 6%, you could draw £600 in interest each year and after the 30 years you could recover the initial £10,000 invested. Here you have not taken advantage of compounding. Your total return would be £600 x 30 (£600 each year for 30 years), which equates to £18,000. You would also still have your original £10,000.

However, if you decided not draw to the £600 income each year and instead allowed it to roll-up alongside the initial £10,000 invested, earning interest on the accumulated amount each year, you would not only grow the £10,000 initially invested but also the income return which you can eventually draw from it.

Figure 2.4 shows how a lump sum investment of £10,000 can grow over time if the interest earned is compounded. We are again assuming that the interest rate remains constant at 6% for the 30-year period.

Figure 2.4 – the growth of a £10,000 lump sum with a 6% interest return compounded over 30 years

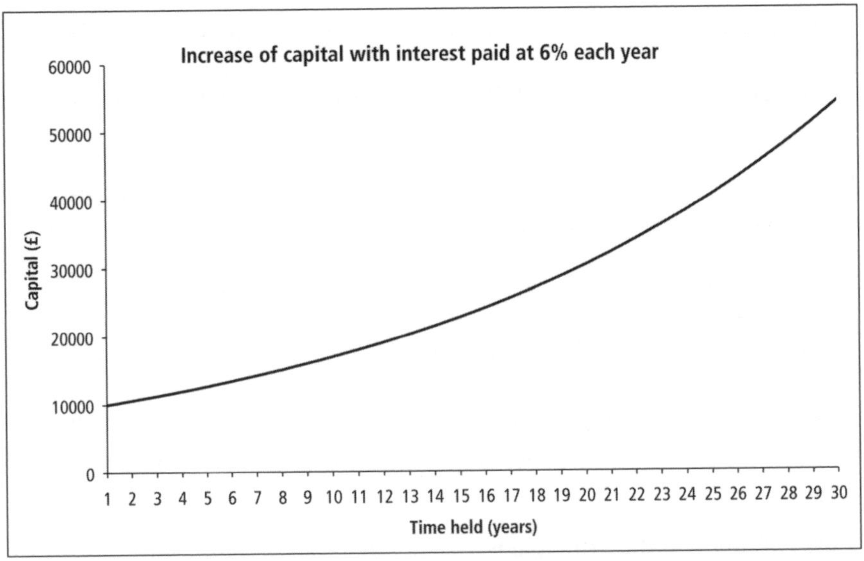

At the end of the 30-year period the initial £10,000 has grown to more than £54,000. This is a return of £44,000, which is clearly better than the £18,000 income that would have been earned by drawing £600 interest each year.

The extent to which you can benefit from compounding will depend on how long you can afford to delay drawing an income from your investment and instead leave the interest return to accumulate. The longer interest is compounded, the more your investment's capital value will grow and so too the income payments you will eventually draw from it.

The power of compound interest can be seen as further testament to the interdependence of capital gains (growing an original investment) and the income payments drawn from an investment.

CALCULATING COMPOUND INTEREST

To calculate compound interest earned on a deposit you will need to know the following:

- The *principal* (the amount deposited with the bank).
- The *rate* of interest offered by the bank.
- The *time*, in years, the money will be left on deposit.

The formula for calculating the total your investment will grow to using compound interest is:

$$\text{total investment} = \text{principal} \times (1 + (\text{interest rate}/100))^{\text{time in years}}$$

The interest rate should be divided by 100 to express it as a decimal (i.e. a fraction out of 100).

Let's say you have £1000 that you would like to put into a savings account for five years. The interest rate on offer is 6%.

The calculation will be:

$$£1000 \times (1 + (6/100))^5 = £1338.23$$

This is the total amount your investment will grow to. The compound interest earned can be calculated by taking this amount and subtracting the principal from it.

Total amount less the principal is:

$$£1338.23 - £1000 = £338.23$$

Therefore £338.23 is the compound interest accumulated.

If you have access to a computer and the spreadsheet program Microsoft Excel, the formula for calculating compound interest is:

```
=principal*POWER(1 + interest rate/100, time in years)
```

So the Microsoft Excel formula for £1000 compounded over 5 years at an interest rate of 6% will be:

```
=1000*POWER(1.06,5)
```

When you hit return the result 1338.23 will show in the cell.

There is also a compound interest calculator provided by the Motley Fool (**www.fool.co.uk/school/calculators/calc1.asp**).

THE RULE OF 72

The Rule of 72 is a quick method that can be used to get an idea of how long it will take to double your cash investment using the power of compounding. The rule states that to find the number of years needed to double your initial investment at a given interest rate you need to divide 72 by the interest rate on offer.

For example, at a fixed interest of 8%, it will take nine years to double your money as 72/8 = 9. You can also run the calculation backwards. Say you need to double your money in eight years, then divide 72 by 8, and you will find the interest rate (9%) which you must receive on your investment to achieve this.

It is interesting to note that at an interest rate of 0.5% (the historical low to which the bank rate in the UK fell in March 2009), it would take a staggering 144 years to double your money.

While the Rule of 72 is fairly accurate, it is best used as a rough guideline. It tends to only work if the interest rate is less than 20%. At higher rates, the error margin starts to become significant.

Also, unless you are leaving your money on deposit in a long-term investment offering a fixed interest rate, you will hardly ever have the benefit of an interest rate that remains constant.

* * *

As an investor you do not just look at the interest you are earning on a given investment in a particular asset – this does not allow you to compare investments in different asset classes or work out if you could invest for a better return elsewhere. The way to work this out is to look at the yield an investment delivers.

Yield

The yield is the income return on an investment compared to the price paid for that investment or the amount of the initial investment – it tells you how hard your invested capital is working to earn you an income. It is expressed as a percentage. One of the income investor's main aims is to secure a high yield on their capital without putting that capital at too great a risk.

Here are some examples of yield:

- If you have £1000 invested in a savings account and you earn a rate of 5% interest in one year, your £1000 investment has an income of £50 (£50/£1000 x 100). The yield in this instance is 5%.
- If you buy a bond at 100p and it pays you a coupon of 5p, the yield on the bond is 5% (5p/100p x 100).
- If you buy a share for £25 and it pays you a dividend of £1 the yield on this investment is 4% (£1/£25 x 100 = 4%).

You can see that in each case the income return from the investment has been expressed as a percentage of the cost of making the investment (the capital value).

The beauty of an investment with a good yield lies in the fact that it supplies an income stream without eating into your capital pot. In each of the three examples briefly given above – the savings account yielding 5%, the bond yielding 5% and the share yielding 4% – the original capital invested is not affected by the income payments.

Understanding yield and how different investments generate yield is important in grasping how income investing works. While it is a straightforward concept it can sometimes get confusing because an investor will be confronted with a variety of yield concepts and measures, depending on the nature of the underlying investment.

We will look at yield in more detail in Part B, for each of the asset classes that we discuss there.

THE SEARCH FOR HIGH YIELD

Yield can be used by income investors to find investments with regular and attractive payouts. Comparing yields enables investors to compare similar investments, for example comparing one share with another. Shares across different sectors and markets can also be compared against each other by looking at the average yield ratios. Yields also enable investors to compare investments across the different asset classes, for example an investment in a savings account with an investment in shares.

The risk of seeking high yield

While yield is a useful yardstick for comparisons based on an investment's actual cash payout, an investment strategy based on chasing high yields can be very risky. There are a number of issues of which one should be wary. For a start, high yield can be a very subjective concept. Some investors might regard a 4% to 5% return as high while others expect a much higher return of 8% to 10% from investments dubbed as high yield. Regardless of what you regard as high yield, it is important to remember that the higher the yield, the higher the investment risk.

The question every income investor should be asking themselves when confronted with a high yielding investment is: Why is this investment paying such a high yield? It may be the case that the investment is structured to pay out a large proportion of its profits – for example real estate investment trusts (REITs), which are required by law to pay out 90% of their profits back to investors as income. Or it may be an incentive to stop investors from selling the investment when profits are waning.

The biggest risk attached to a high yield investment is the simple danger that the yield will not be maintained. High yielding companies can often include those where the dividends are most vulnerable, as investors found out to their detriment during the financial crisis of 2007-2009 when banks and other companies cut their dividend payouts, pushing down yields.

LOOK FOR A PROGRESSIVE YIELD

A wiser income investing strategy, rather than chasing high yield, is to opt for an investment which offers a *progressive yield*, in other words, where the income payout has increased consistently for a number of years. As will be explained in Part B, making long-term capital growth part of your investment programme is important and this can only be done if your high yield investments are relatively secure and consistent.

* * *

Whatever the interest rate and yield of your investment, your investment returns will be impacted by inflation. It is therefore important that we look at inflation in some detail – this is the subject of the next chapter.

3

INFLATION

Understanding inflation

DEFINING INFLATION

Inflation is an increase in the general price of goods and services, and an associated fall in the purchasing power of money. It is expressed as a percentage. A high level of inflation can be the income investor's worst enemy because it erodes the purchasing power of income, making it detrimental to the spending power of future interest and dividends payments. As the preservation of capital is an important consideration when investing for income, it is worth noting that persistently high inflation also eats away at the worth of original investment capital.

While inflation is detrimental to the value of investments, it is important to realise that it is, as one writer put it, "a Jekyll and Hyde character"[10]. In times of inflation the value of money diminishes, which is bad news for investors and income seekers, but for borrowers an inflationary environment will mean their loans decrease (as the value of money falls, so too does the value of debt – money owed). For government, inflation reduces the burden of public debt.

Moderate inflation can also be indicative of a growing and buoyant economy and could signal a good time to be investing in the stock market, although, as stated, runaway inflation will be detrimental to investments.

Deflation, which is characterised by prices falling and the purchasing power of money increasing, might sound like a positive alternative to inflation but such an environment could be damaging to an economy and investments. Have a look at the note below on the different types of inflation for more detail on why a deflationary scenario is equally detrimental to economic growth.

Figure 3.1 shows historic rates of inflation in the UK. It is worth noting the severe inflation spike the UK suffered in the 1970s often referred to as the *great inflation of the 1970s*. At the time, incessant price increases wreaked havoc for businesses and individuals, showing just how devastating inflation can be to a country's economy. In 2008 we can see that inflation dropped to historic lows. This situation sparked concerns that the UK might be headed for a deflationary environment. The Bank of England responded by loosening monetary policy – lowering interest rates – to encourage consumers to spend.

---

[10] D. Paarlberg, *An Analysis and History Of Inflation* (Praeger Publishers, 1993).

Figure 3.1 – historic rates of inflation as measured by the Retail Prices Index (RPI)

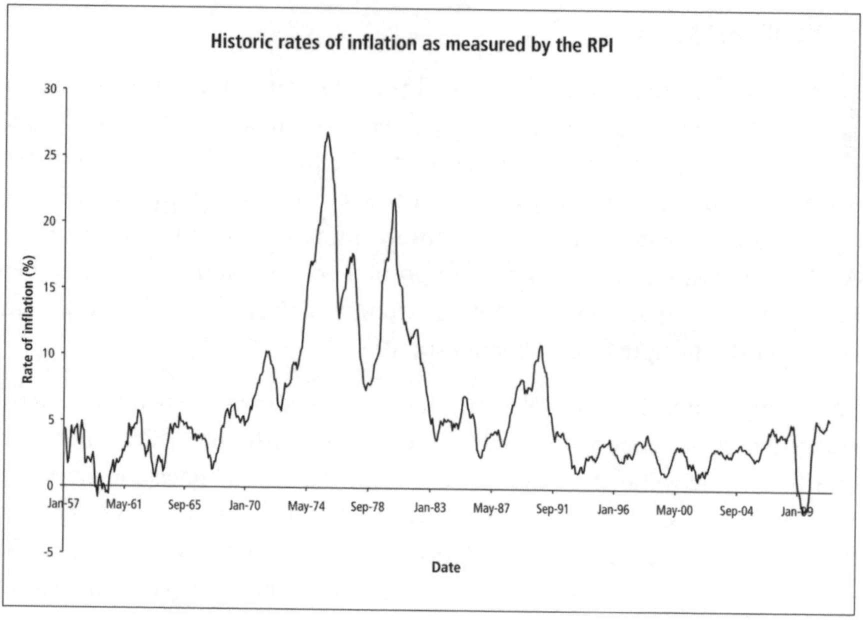

Source: Office of National Statistics

MEASURING INFLATION

The preferred way to measure inflation is with the *Consumer Price Index (CPI)* and the *Retail Prices Index (RPI)*. Each of these measures is best thought of as a shopping basket containing goods and services on which people typically spend their money. As the prices of the items in the baskets change over time, so does the total cost of the basket, reflecting either a rise or fall in the level of inflation.[11]

Generally the contents of the CPI and RPI baskets are very similar although the weights of items in the shopping basket will differ. The most important difference is that the RPI basket includes items representing housing costs, such as mortgage interest payments, which are excluded from the CPI. As a result the RPI in the UK tends to be higher than the CPI over the long term.

[11] Philip Gooding, *Consumer Prices Index and Retail Prices Index: The 2010 Basket of Good and Services* (Office for National Statistics, 2010), p. 1.

The difference between the RPI and CPI may sound academic but it is in fact very significant. Many people's pensions are linked directly to one of these measures – in June 2010 the UK government announced that from April 2011 onwards, public sector and state pensions would be increased each year in line with the CPI, instead of the RPI.

This could mean that pension increases are on average 1% lower each year. Over a lifetime, this will amount to a significant loss. The interest rates on investments such as inflation-linked bonds and NS&I index-linked savings certificates are also directly linked to one of these two measures. For example, the May 2011 issue of NS&I savings certificates was set up to pay index-linked returns over a five-year term as measured by the RPI, plus a fixed rate of interest of 0.5%.

YOUR PERSONAL RATE OF INFLATION

You can calculate your own personal rate of inflation based upon the goods and services you usually pay for. You could do this yourself using Excel or another spreadsheet if you have kept receipts for similar items you have bought over the years, or you could use an online calculator, such as the one provided by the BBC: **www.news.bbc.co.uk/1/hi/business/7669072.stm**

To determine how inflation will impact your future income you can use the *deflator.*

THE DEFLATOR: MEASURING THE IMPACT OF INFLATION ON INCOME

The deflator is a statistical factor designed to measure the effect of inflation – it helps you to work out how much your capital will be worth in the future taking into account inflation. To find the deflator, you need to subtract the rate of inflation from 100, then divide this figure by 100 to express it as a percentage. So:

```
(100 - rate of inflation)/100 = deflator
```

Let's assume inflation will average out to 4% a year. This means the deflator will be:

```
(100 - 4)/100 = 0.96
```

If you want to find out how much your money will be worth in 30 years time, you will need to multiply the amount of money you have now by the deflator to the power of the amount of years in question (in this case 30). The formula for this is:

$$\text{capital} \times \text{deflator}^{\text{time in years}}$$

Let's say you want to find out what £1000 will be worth in 30 years time with inflation constant at 4% for the 30-year period. Your calculation will be:

$$£1000 \times 0.96^{30}$$

$$= £293.86$$

This means £1000 will be equivalent to £293.86 in 30 years time if inflation averages at 4%.

Figure 3.2 shows how inflation averaging at 4% over a period of 30 years can erode the value of £1000. As you can see, at the end of 30 years the £1000 would be worth less than £300.

If the income return from investments is not level with or greater than the rate of inflation, you are losing money.

Figure 3.2 – erosion of £1000 over 30 years, with inflation at 4%

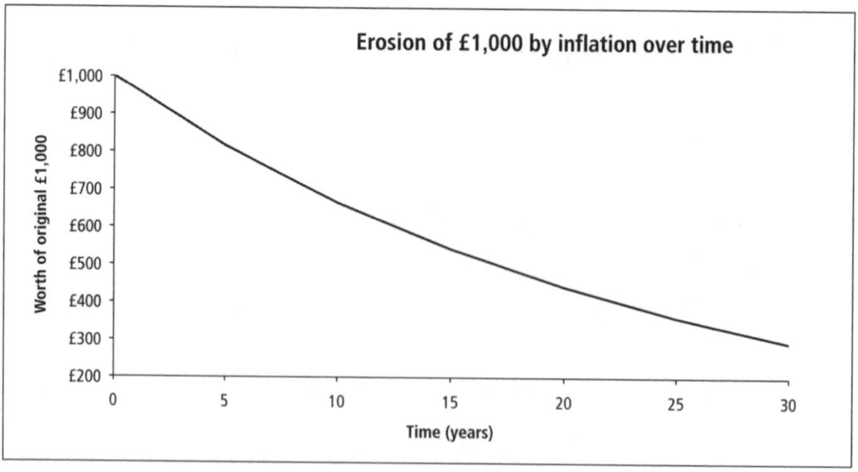

Different types of inflation

Inflation can come in many guises and it is important to know the difference between these. Here are some brief explanations of the different types:

- *Inflation*: A persistent increase in the general price level of goods and services.
- *Hyperinflation*: Very high inflation which often leads to the collapse of a country's monetary system. The threshold used to define hyperinflation is usually price increases exceeding 50% per month. The most recent example of hyperinflation – and the first occurrence of the 21st century was in Zimbabwe where inflation peaked at an astounding monthly rate of 79.6 billion % in November 2008 – with prices doubling every 25 hours. Once it reached this point, people refused to use the Zimbabwean dollar and the hyperinflation came to an abrupt halt. Zimbabwe's unfathomable high inflation rate was however not the highest ever seen. In Hungary in July 1946 it took just 15 hours for prices in the country to double.[12]
- *Stagflation*: A combination of high inflation and economic stagnation (high unemployment and low demand for goods and services). The 1970s in Britain is often labelled as a decade of stagflation. High inflation coupled with soaring unemployment rates culminated in the so-called *Winter of Discontent* from 1978 to 1979. At the time the government froze public sector wages to control inflation, giving way to widespread strikes by trade unions.
- *Deflation*: Occurs when prices are falling and the purchasing power of money is increasing. A deflationary environment is synonymous with high unemployment rates, low growth and reduced output by companies. Japan is an example of a country that has suffered from a deflationary spiral for more than two decades following the combined collapse of the Tokyo stock and real estate market in 1980. High employment and low income means people are reluctant to spend – this keeps prices low and the economy in limbo, reflecting the self-perpetuating risk of deflation.
- *Disinflation*: Not to be confused with deflation, disinflation is when the prices of goods and services are still rising, only at a slower rate. Disinflation is a drop in the inflation rate whereas deflation is characterised by persistent weakness in demand rather than by falling prices.

---

[12] Steve H. Hanke and Alex K. F. Kwok, 'On the Measurement of Zimababwe's Hyperinflation' *Cato Journal* 29:2 (Spring/Summer 2009). (**www.cato.org/pubs/journal/cj29n2/cj29n28.pdf**)

Quantitative easing and the risk of inflation

In most of the developed world, governments have managed to keep inflation under control by setting inflation targets – a rate at which they would like inflation to be maintained. At the time of writing the UK's inflation target stood at 2%. In many countries, inflation targeting has lead to an extended period of price stability. But concerns have been raised over the likelihood of maintaining inflation targets following the financial crisis of 2007-2009 and the deluge of monetary policies implemented by central banks to get economies back on the move.

The policy which raised most concerns was *quantitative easing* (QE), implemented by central banks such as the Federal Reserve, the European Central Bank and the Bank of England. These institutions define QE as injecting money into the economy by purchasing financial assets. Many economists, however, say QE is nothing other than printing more money to expand central banks' balance sheets.

A country's central bank implements QE by first crediting its own account with money it has created *ex nihilo* (out of nothing). It then uses this money to purchase financial assets such as government bonds and corporate bonds. The banks and financial institutions selling these assets will then have excess money in their accounts. In this way QE boosts the money in supply and hopefully gets an economy moving again.

If QE is more effective than it should be it can lead to inflation or, in the worst case, hyperinflation, stripping a country's currency of its value.

Investments that shield against inflation

Whether you leave your money in cash, buy a bond or opt for equities, if inflation is present it will inevitably have an impact on the income you receive from your investment. And should inflation remain persistently high over the long run it can significantly erode what your original investment capital is worth.

Considering the damaging impact inflation can have on income, it follows that any asset allocation decisions within your broader income portfolio should not only be led by your risk/reward preference but also by your view on inflation. However, as inflation expectations are continually shifting and because there is a wide divergence of inflationary views and outlooks, taking a view on inflation is rather tough for ordinary investors.

In recent years policies such as quantitative easing have left even expert economists divided over whether the developed world is headed for an inflationary environment, stagflation or a self-perpetuating deflationary cycle.

So, what are income investors to do about inflation? Helpfully, there are some investment vehicles that tend to offer stability in periods of high inflation. You can include exposure to these in your investment portfolio to help combat the effect of inflation – these are known as *real assets* or *physical assets*.

REAL ASSETS

Real assets have intrinsic worth, are finite in supply and identifiable in appearance, with the most common examples being land, property, agriculture and precious metals. These are the opposite of *financial assets* such as shares and bonds which are a paper claim on the wealth of a company or government. Financial assets are often also called *paper assets*.

Real assets are favoured during inflationary periods because of their ability to retain their intrinsic value and therefore maintain purchasing power.

Examples of real assets:

- **Gold** is a firm favourite for hedging (protecting) against the risk of inflation. Thanks to its ability to preserve its worth over time, the yellow metal has cultivated a status as a safe haven investment. During the uncertain times succeeding the economic downturn of 2007-2009 investors rushed to buy gold pushing up the gold price to record highs.
- **Property and land** are two other investments viewed as attractive inflation hedges. Both have intrinsic worth and, given that supply is limited, tend to benefit from a rise in demand which is characteristic of an inflationary environment.
- Similarly, **commodities** such as industrial metals and agricultural products tend to appreciate when inflation is rising, as the economy is expanding and with it consumer demand for raw materials.

REAL ASSETS AND INCOME SEEKERS

Assets finite in supply have an enticing investment case backing them during inflationary times but there is one big caveat for the income investor. All of the real assets mentioned here tend to be classified as *growth investments* (see page 7).

While growth assets have an important role to play in an investment portfolio's total return, none of these investments that help to combat inflation – with the notable exception of property – generate an income return or yield. Therefore, as an income investor you would not want to build your entire portfolio out of real assets, because if you do, you won't be earning a regular income.

Generating secure and consistent yields from a spread of investments in different asset classes is the foundation of a successful income portfolio and this is what we go on to look at in Part B.

PART B:

INCOME GENERATORS

Having read the first part of this book, you should now have a good grounding in the basic theory surrounding investment income. You should know how interest rates, inflation and yield work, and have an understanding of the influence of each of these on the search for income. In Part B this knowledge is applied by taking a closer look at a range of different investment vehicles and how these can be used to generate an income.

In this section the different income investments are divided up according to their risk level. As explained in chapter 1, risk in the investment context is a synonym for uncertainty. It refers to the likelihood that an investment's return will deviate from the expected outcome, and as result the investor may suffer a capital loss.

Investments rendering predictable, fixed income streams such as cash deposits and bonds make up the safer end of the risk spectrum. We will start this section by looking at these and then move on to the more risky investments, those typically relied on as sources of variable income such as equities, funds and property. In discussing each of these investments, the risks are clearly highlighted along with factors that will impact the reward. The reward we are interested in is the income return.

Part B concludes by highlighting some unconventional ways of securing an investment income via alternative investments such as structured products, infrastructure funds and timber.

LOW-RISK INCOME INVESTMENTS

Investors want their income to grow quickly but at the same time do not want to erode their base capital through losing money when investments turn against them. Unfortunately these two requirements are somewhat mutually exclusive: if you reduce the risk you take with your investments then your investment return will be reduced too. This is because low-risk income investments come with more muted returns. Likewise, investments that pay high returns present a greater risk.

All investors should have some allocation to low-risk investments as this helps to balance a portfolio by cushioning against the risk of the uncertainty of returns.

In this section on low risk investments we will look first at cash and then at bonds. These are both considered low-risk investments because their returns are not volatile and hence the risk of an unpredictable income, and of losing your initial capital investment, is lower.

4

CASH

Cash is the safest of all investments and should be the income investor's first consideration when setting up a portfolio. It is important that you see your cash holding as an investment and part of your income portfolio.

Cash holdings are usually deposit-based, with the investment return generated via the interest payments on the capital deposited. The original amount of capital deposited does not change and is reclaimed at the end of the deposit term. It is this unique characteristic of cash – to maintain the level of the original capital while producing income – which sees it classed as the safest investment route to income.

Cash is even sometimes referred to as an entirely risk-free investment, but this is inaccurate, as we will discuss.

Yield

Your yield on cash will be the interest rate offered by a bank or building society on a deposit. For example, if you deposit £1000 in a savings account and the interest rate is 5%, the yield of this investment is 5%.

The yield on a cash investment needs to be high enough to sustain a level of income that meets your income needs and keeps pace with inflation. If this is not the case, you may be forced to draw some of the capital from your deposit or else opt for a riskier investment offering a higher yield.

Depositing cash

Drawing an income from cash is typically done via a deposit-based investment with a financial institution such as a bank or building society. In return for having use of the money over the period of the deposit, the bank or building society will pay an income in the form of an interest return. Generally, the more restrictions you are willing to accept, the greater the interest rate the bank will offer and the greater the income return will be.

Deposit accounts can be split into *fixed* and *variable* accounts. The former pays a predetermined return which is fixed from the outset, while the latter will vary the interest rate depending on the prevailing bank rate or other conditions such as the inflation rate. With an inflation-linked variable account, for instance, the interest paid will vary depending on movements in the inflation rate.

Most financial institutions offer a range of different types of deposit accounts that pay either fixed or variable interest rates. These include:

1. Instant access accounts.
2. Restricted access accounts.
3. Tax advantageous accounts.
4. Inflation-linked accounts.

Below is a summary of these four types of accounts.

1. INSTANT ACCESS ACCOUNTS

- *Instant/easy access savings accounts.* As the name implies, these accounts will allow you immediate access to your cash.
- *Regular savings accounts.* These accounts tend to pay higher interest but come with limited functionality. Some regular savings accounts will limit the number of withdrawals you can make in a year, while others will only be accessible via a local branch or the internet. Interest rates can also be tiered meaning that the greater the amount of money invested, the greater the interest.
- *Bonus accounts.* A bonus account will pay you a bonus rate on top of the interest rate offered. Tread carefully with these accounts as bonuses are typically only added for limited periods, such as 12 months, after which your interest rate will revert to a lower level, often without any warning from the financial institution. Best-buy tables from savings comparison websites (these are discussed in greater detail later) also often include the bonus into the interest rate quoted, which can give a skewed picture of the actual interest rate over the long term.

2. RESTRICTED ACCESS ACCOUNTS

- *Notice accounts.* Notice accounts usually offer more attractive rates than an instant access account but require you to give a period of notice to the bank should you wish to make a withdrawal.
- *Fixed-term account.* Also referred to as term deposit accounts or fixed rate bonds, these accounts tend to offer higher interest provided you tie up your cash for an extended, predetermined period, for example three

or five years. The interest paid on these accounts is usually a predetermined amount fixed at the outset.

- *Money market accounts*. These accounts generate a return via a financial institution which lends your money to the money markets – these are investment markets in which large amounts of short-term funds are borrowed or loaned. These accounts often pay higher interest returns but may require higher minimum balances and could limit withdrawals.

3. TAX ADVANTAGEOUS ACCOUNTS

- *Cash ISAs*. Cash Individual Savings Accounts (ISAs) are savings accounts that allow you to earn an interest return free of tax. There are limits on how much you can deposit into a cash ISA each tax year – known as your annual allowance. If money is withdrawn from the ISA account it cannot be replaced unless you are still within the annual allowance.
- *Offshore accounts*. Offshore accounts allow you to deposit and withdraw money in currencies other than your home currency. Interest on offshore accounts is paid without tax being deducted, although a UK taxpayer must still declare any income derived from an offshore account on their annual self-assessment tax form. An advantage of these accounts is that the tax is not taken off your interest payments automatically, which means money that would otherwise be deducted stays in your account longer, earning more interest. Interest rates may be tiered depending on how much money you deposit in the account, and generally tend to be low.

4. INFLATION-LINKED ACCOUNTS

- *Inflation-linked savings accounts*. The returns from these accounts are linked to the inflation rate, as measured by either the RPI or CPI. The account will stipulate which measure of inflation your income return will be linked to. For example the Yorkshire Building Society Protected Capital Account introduced in February 2011 is a five-year savings account which pays a return linked to the RPI.
- *National Savings and Investments (NS&I) index-linked savings certificates*. NS&I is a financial institution set up by the government in 1861 to encourage ordinary wage earners to save "to provide for themselves

against adversity and ill health". NS&I index-linked savings certificates offer interest rates that move in line with inflation as measured by the RPI, with interest added on each anniversary of the investment. Advantages of these vehicles are that they are tax free and because NS&I is backed by HM Treasury, the money you invest is fully protected.

COMPARING DEPOSIT ACCOUNTS

Table 4.1 shows how interest rates available for different types of cash deposit accounts changed from May 2009 to May 2011. As you can see there is a marked different between the highest interest rate available on an instant access account in May 2011 (3.01%) and that offered on a five-year fixed-rate bond (5.05%). This is because the latter comes with much more restricted access. The table also shows how interest rates have changed over the two years from 2009 to 2011 owing to the low base-rate at 0.5%.

Table 4.1 – change in the average and highest savings rates since the bank base rate last changed

Savings account	Average gross AER (%) March 2009	Average gross AER (%) May 2011	Difference	Highest gross AER (%) March 2009	Highest gross AER (%) May 2011	Difference
Instant/easy access: £1000 balance	0.89%	0.96%	0.07%	3.26%	3.01%	-0.25%
One-year fixed rate bond: £5000 balance	2.73%	2.82%	0.09%	4.1%	3.5%	-0.6%
Five-year fixed rate bond: £5000 balance	3.07%	4.35%	1.28%	4.1%	5.05%	0.95%
Regular monthly savings account (if save £100 each month)	2.7%	2.82%	0.12%	10.00%	8%	-2%
Easy access cash ISA: max annual limit	1.74%	1.76%	0.02%	3.61%	3.35%	-0.26%
One-year fixed rate cash ISA: max annual limit	2.70%	2.86%	0.16%	3.2%	3.3%	0.1%
Five-year fixed rate cash ISA: max annual limit	3.04%	4.45%	1.41%	3.25%	5%	1.75%
Five-year fixed rate cash ISA: max. annual limit	3.04%	4.45%	1.41%	3.25%	5%	1.75%

Source: Defaqto, April 2011, www.defaqto.com

Using comparison websites

Comparison websites can be useful tools for comparing cash deposit accounts and the interest rates on offer. These are relatively simple to use: you select the options that best fit your requirements, such as the period for which you want to invest your cash or the type of deposit account you are looking for, and the website presents the options with the most attractive interest rates.

This is a quick and convenient way to trawl the current market offerings but there are drawbacks. The majority of these sites are advertiser-driven and hence only list the products and services of those institutions that pay to advertise with the site, rather than the entire spread of offers on the market. Most comparison sites fail to explain the commercial relationships they have with product providers.

Some of these sites also omit to mention whether the financial institution offering the deposit account is regulated and covered by a depositor protection scheme such as the Financial Services Compensation Scheme (FSCS) or the Irish deposit protection scheme. However, these are the exception rather than the rule – if for instance you use Moneyfacts (**www.moneyfacts.co.uk**) you will find it only lists companies that are regulated and also includes details of which depositor protection scheme they are covered under. Moneyfacts also highlights when companies are covered under one banking license.

Moneysupermarket.com is another example of a comparison website which highlights the issue of protection schemes. Early in 2011, for example, it highlighted that the just-issued John Lewis Partnership Bond was not protected by the FSCS. The importance of the FSCS in protecting your cash investment will be explained in greater detail later.

Money market funds

WHAT A MONEY MARKET FUND INVOLVES

Collective investment vehicles known as money market funds (or cash funds) are another way of investing in cash for an income return. These funds, usually offered by asset managers, life insurance companies and some banks, pool the monies of many investors and then invest across a spread of different investments. Money market funds invest in cash or cash equivalents such as bank deposits, certificates of deposit and short-term fixed-interest investments. In return for investing cash in the fund, investors are paid a share of its earnings in the form of dividends at set intervals.

Money market funds may deliver higher yields than deposit-based accounts, depending on the earnings of the underlying investments, but they are higher risk and more complex. Unlike a cash deposit, capital invested in such a fund is not guaranteed: if the assets of the fund decrease – meaning that it loses money from its investments rather than earning it – investors run the risk of getting back less than they invested.

The complexity comes from the broad variance in the underlying portfolio of investments these funds may hold. These are often not clearly understood by the investor or, in the worst case, unknown to the investor and incorrectly marketed as cash investments by the fund provider.

Money market funds are nonetheless one of the safer investment vehicles. Individuals nearing retirement, for example, often choose to transfer their pension fund into a money market fund to reduce risk to their investment portfolio and steer clear of stock market volatility.

Further, as investments in a money market fund are spread across a number of financial institutions it spreads the risk. A typical cash deposit account is usually only backed by the one financial institution holding the deposit and if this institution gets into financial difficulties there is a risk that some or all of the cash deposited could be lost.

WHAT TO FIND OUT ABOUT A MONEY MARKET FUND

It is important to make sure you know what the underlying investments of a money market fund are before investing. Information on the fund's underlying holdings will usually be published on its factsheet which is published monthly by the provider of the fund although the information here may be limited to the top ten largest investments. For a more detailed list of the fund's investments it is best to consult the quarterly report which will typically be published on the fund provider's website.

Also always compare a fund's charges – what it will cost you to invest in the fund – with that of its peers as high charges will eat away at a fund's income return. A fund's total expense ratio (TER), usually found on the fund's factsheet (available from the fund provider's website) or accessed via a fund data provider such as Morningstar (**www.morningstar.co.uk**) is the best measure of a fund's charges. Fund management charges and their impact on the income return of an investment are discussed in greater detail in chapter 7.

MONEY MARKET FUNDS AND THE 2007-2009 FINANCIAL CRISIS

A criticism of money market funds in recent years has been that the risks inherent with these funds and the details of their underlying holdings have not always been made clear to investors. During the 2007-2009 financial crisis many funds labelled as cash funds were invested in esoteric, high-risk investments. When the downturn hit their performance suffered, leaving those who had invested in these funds facing huge losses.

An example of a money market fund which disappointed was the Standard Life Pension Sterling Fund. It suffered significant losses in 2008, letting down investors who had transferred money into the fund believing it to be a low-risk investment (an estimated 98,000 investors had money in the fund when it suffered losses).

Later, the UK's financial regulator, the Financial Services Authority (FSA), fined Standard Life £2.45 million for incorrectly marketing the fund as being wholly invested in cash, when the majority of the fund was invested in higher risk, floating rate notes[13].

Subsequent investigations by the FSA into money market funds offered by other fund providers raised further concerns over the poor governance of these funds. The use of the term *cash* in the marketing material of many funds was described by the regulator as misleading as this implies little risk to capital.

Holding cash in reserve

You might choose to keep your money in cash between big financial transactions or while you are deciding which investment to make. A money market fund is one place where investors tend to hold cash in reserve but, as discussed, there are a number of risks involved. Individual Savings Accounts (ISAs) and Self-Invested Personal Pensions (SIPPs) have facilities where cash can be held while you decide where to invest, and can act as alternatives to money market funds.

---

[13] FSA 'FSA fines Standard Life £2.45m for serious systems and controls failures', press release (20 January 2010). Available at:
www.fsa.gov.uk/pages/Library/Communication/PR/2010/010.shtml
[Accessed 17 January 2010.]

ISA CASH RESERVE ACCOUNT

Investors uncertain of which investments to choose in a stocks and shares ISA (these are similar to a cash ISA but invest in shares and collective investment vehicles) and who do not want to lose out on their annual ISA allowance can make use of an ISA cash reserve account. This operates as a temporary shelter, giving you more time to decide where to invest the money you have put aside for your stocks and shares ISA. It is available for new money, or to switch existing investments. Any money invested into the ISA cash reserve account or disinvested from ISA holdings into the ISA cash reserve account remains tax exempt.

This can be a useful facility as cash is not an eligible investment within a stocks and shares ISA, while parking cash within a cash ISA with the intention of later transferring it into a stocks and shares ISA can be a cumbersome process.

Depending on the conditions of the cash ISA you may need to fill out a transfer form and the transfer itself can take time – anything up to 15 days – making it difficult for you to take immediate advantage of investment opportunities as and when they arise within a stocks and shares ISA. These problems do not arise with an ISA cash reserve account.

But there are drawbacks to an ISA cash reserve account. Interest rates offered on cash parks tend to be low – often below the bank rate – and any interest earned is subject to a tax charge of 20% by HM Revenue & Customs (HMRC). The cash cannot be left in the account indefinitely and revenue legislation stipulates that it must be held with the purpose of investment. Usually the provider of the ISA cash reserve account will send you a letter reminding you of when you should invest the cash.

Also note that when you switch out of the cash reserve account into your chosen investments there may be a charge levied. ISA providers that offer these accounts include Hargreaves Lansdown and Fidelity.

SIPP CASH ACCOUNT

A Self-Invested Personal Pension (SIPP) is a private pension scheme which allows you to manage your own investments. You are allowed to hold cash in your SIPP account, which is not permitted with a stocks and shares ISA – SIPPs have a default cash account into which cash holdings can be deposited to balance portfolio risk when income from other investments becomes uncertain, for the purposes of future investment or from which an income can be drawn. While some SIPPs only permit cash holdings to be held within their specified default cash account, others allow external cash accounts to be used.

The interest rates offered by these accounts can vary widely and it is important to look for the best returns on your SIPP cash holdings rather than to accept the default rates, which are often low.

The interest rates tend to be tiered according to the size of your cash balance. Securing a higher rate will usually mean committing to a minimum balance and tying up your money for a fixed period. For example, a three month tie-in will offer a lower rate than a 12 month tie-in.

Investment Sense (**www.investmentsense.co.uk/free-services/best-buy-savings-accounts/accounts-for-pensions**) is a comparison site that provides best-buy tables for SIPP cash accounts.

The risk of the deposit taker defaulting

Cash-based deposits are one of the safest routes to an income; they are not, for example, subject to the fluctuations of the stock market. But this does not mean that cash is without risk.

One risk is that the institution holding deposited cash will get into financial difficulties, which could mean that the total capital deposited, along with any interest accrued, will not be returned. Past events, most notably the Great Depression of the 1930s when around 9000 banks collapsed, and more recently the global financial crisis of 2007-2009, are testament to the fact that even the largest and most established financial organisations can fail.

Fortunately, the risk of losing a cash deposit in this way is minimised by the presence in many countries of financial regulators who keep an eye on the books and business dealings of financial institutions such as banks and building societies.

Many countries have also established compensation funds to provide some form of reparation should these institutions collapse. In the UK the Financial Services Compensation Scheme was setup for these purposes. Below is more detail on how this body works and the steps you can take to ensure the safety of your cash deposit.

THE FINANCIAL SERVICES COMPENSATION SCHEME (FSCS)

Banks and building societies are generally regarded as the safest places to leave cash but these institutions can fail. In the UK, if a financial firm becomes insolvent or ceases trading, the Financial Services Compensation Scheme (FSCS) may be able to pay compensation to that firm's customers. Of course, if all or a number of financial firms were to fail in unison there is the risk that the FSCS could run out of funds. Some other important factors to bear in mind are:

- The FSCS covers business conducted by firms authorised by the UK's financial regulator. If you leave your money in an unregulated deposit investment, you cannot expect compensation from the FSCS. You can find out whether a firm is authorised by using the FSA's Firm Check Service on its consumer website at **www.fsa.gov.uk/register/firmSearchForm.do**. You can also find out about the status of a firm by telephoning the FSA's Consumer Helpline on 0845 606 1234.
- There is a limit to how much compensation the FSCS will pay. At the time of writing, the maximum compensation limit for cash deposits stood at £85,000 per person, per authorised firm. For investments the amount is £50,000 per person per firm. Make sure you do not deposit more than these limits with any one firm to avoid the risk of not having your entire deposit or investment covered.
- Compensation will be paid based on amounts held in cash accounts regardless of the amounts you may owe the bank. But this does not mean that you will not have to repay amounts owed such as loans, mortgages or credit card debts. Any outstanding amounts owed to the firm in administration will be collected by the liquidator.
- Protection is offered per banking institution and not per account. This can get complicated as a number of banks in the UK share a banking license and therefore might share the compensation limit between them. This is case with Halifax, Bank of Scotland and Birmingham Midshires, all part of the HBOS group. Accounts with any of these banks are only covered up to £85,000 combined. This

is not a blanket rule though, for example, should you deposit cash with the Royal Bank of Scotland, NatWest and Ulster, all part of the RBS group, you will get separate £85,000 protection for each bank. To make sure you don't get caught out by this, make sure you know whether a bank shares its FSCS compensation limit with a sister bank or within a larger conglomerate. You can find this out in of the following ways:

- Visit the FSA's website :

  (**www.fsa.gov.uk/Pages/consumerinformation/uk_groups**), which shows which banking groups currently operate shared authorisation.
- Compare your deposit account providers' FSA registration numbers to check if any are the same – if they are the same, they share authorisation.
- Ask your deposit taker whether they share a banking authorisation with any other firm.

Factors to consider when investing in cash for income

As mentioned, the more restrictions you are willing to accept on a cash deposit, the higher the income return you can expect to generate from the investment. Cash deposited over a longer term or with specific notice periods and restrictions attached to withdrawals will typically attract higher interest rates than those offered by accounts that allow instant access. If you refer back to Table 4.1 you can see that an instant access account pays less interest than accounts that tie up your funds for fixed periods.

As an investor, you need to determine how long you are willing to tie up your money for and the interest return you are willing to sacrifice for this.

Other factors which determine the actual or net return you receive from cash include:

1. Frequency of interest payments.
2. Currency movements.
3. Interest rates.
4. Inflation.

Let's look at each of these in turn.

1. FREQUENCY OF INTEREST PAYMENTS

The interest rate quoted on deposit accounts will typically be the nominal rate. This is the headline interest rate paid per year.

The actual or effective interest, however, is known as the Annual Equivalent Rate (AER). This figure takes into account the frequency of payment, whether this is half yearly, quarterly or monthly, and considers the impact this has on compounding. It is usually higher than the nominal rate, and while not always quoted by banks and other financial institutions, it is a more accurate reflection of the actual interest rate (or income) received.

The difference between the nominal rate and the Annual Equivalent Rate is best explained by use of an example.

Let's assume you want to deposit £10,000 into an account which pays 10% interest annually (the nominal rate). This means at the end of the year you will have earned: £10,000 x 10% = £1000. This will grow your £10,000 deposit to £11,000.

But what if it was stated that the deposit account would pay interest half yearly? Then the actual rate paid will be 5% for the first six months and 5% for the next six months. If we apply this to the £10,000 deposit, after the first six months the account will pay you £10,000 x 5% = £500, growing your deposit to £10,500. When the second payment of 5% is calculated it will be based on £10,500, so: £10,500 x 5% = £11,025.

The compounding effect of half yearly interest payments means you would have effectively earned £1025 on your £10,000 deposit, which represents an increase of 10.25%. So, 10.25% is the AER (more than the nominal interest rate quoted of 10%).

Now let's say the same account pays interest on a quarterly basis. On a deposit of £10,000, interest payments would be as shown in Table 4.2.

Table 4.2 – the effect of frequent interest payments on the AER

Period	Interest rate at 2.5% applied to capital	Interest earned
First quarter	£10,000 x 2.5% (10% divided by four quarters)	£250
Second quarter	£10,250 (£10,000 + £250) x 2.5%	£256
Third quarter	£10,506 (£10,250 + £256) x 2.5%	£263
Fourth quarter	£10,769 (£10,506 + £263) x 2.5%	£269
		Total = £1038

If you add up these four payments the compounding effect of receiving quarterly interest means you would have effectively earned £1038 on your £10,000 deposit, meaning your capital is now £11,038. This represents an AER of 10.38%.

Thus we can see that the more often interest is paid, the more income will be received if the rate is compounded. The AER is therefore a more accurate interest rate figure than the nominal interest rate.

In the UK financial institutions have discarded the use of nominal rates altogether and the amount of interest received on cash deposit accounts is just listed in AER form. If you wish to calculate the AER, the formula for this is:

$$AER = (1 + r/n)^n - 1$$

n = amount of times a year interest is paid

r = interest rate

Using this formula to calculate the AER for the last example (where the nominal rate was 10% and interest was paid quarterly) gives:

$$AER = (1 + 0.1/4)^4 - 1 = 0.1038 = 10.38\%$$

2. CURRENCY MOVEMENTS

For those who hold cash in a different currency to their home currency, for example UK investors who hold US dollars or Euros in an offshore account, there is the danger of currency risk. Movements in the exchange rate – the rate at which one currency can be converted to another – can have a negative effect on an investment and its income return. If the currency of the cash deposited weakens relative to the investor's home currency, i.e. if the dollar depreciates against the pound your dollar holdings will be worth less in pounds.

The opposite also applies: if the exchange rate moves in your favour and the currency in which your cash is held strengthens relative to your home currency, the effect will boost your investment's return and increase the size of your capital pot.

It should be noted that playing currency and exchange rate movements is a very high risk, speculative investment strategy, and definitely not a safe way of generating an income. However for those who hold cash in currencies other than their home currency it is important to be aware of the influence movements in the exchange rate can have on your cash deposit.

3. INTEREST RATES

The attractiveness of a cash-based investment will move in line with the prevailing interest rate. So an environment of low interest rates will mean a low income return on cash-based deposits, making cash a less attractive investment option. If interest rates are at competitive levels relative to the income that can be generated from other types of investment, holding cash will have greater appeal.

Say you are receiving an interest rate return of 2% from your investments (in shares for example) while bank interest rates are at 5% – you would logically question whether it is worth investing your money at a return of 2% when you could be receiving a higher return of 5% by depositing the money with a bank. A cash deposit is after all regarded as the safest of all investments.

When interest rates fall

If interest rates fall and remain low for an extended period, deposit rates will fall too meaning that the income you receive on a cash investment is reduced.

A good way to judge whether interest rates are low would be to take a look at the Bank of England's average bank rate. This data can be obtained from the statistics page on the Bank of England's website (**www.bankofengland.co.uk**).

Figure 4.1 – the average bank rate from 2000 to 2011

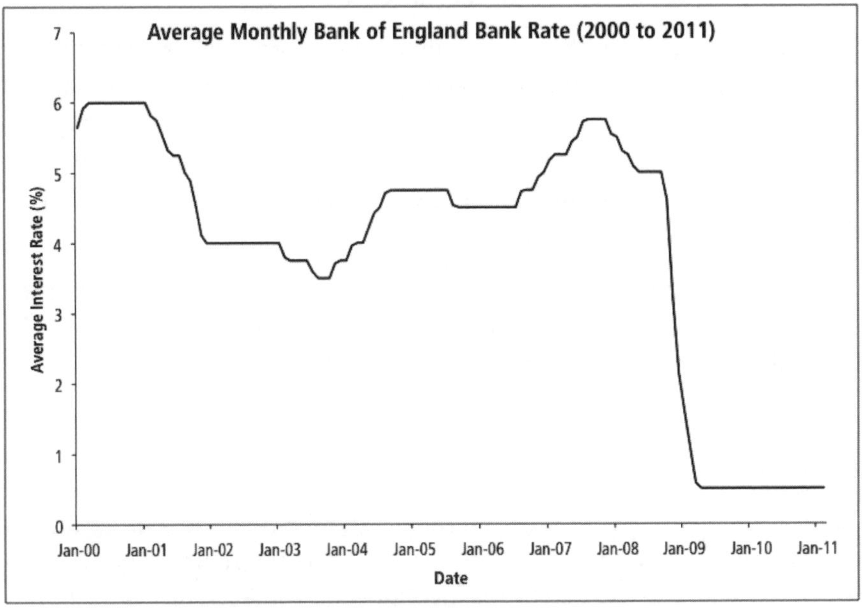

Source: Bank of England

Figure 4.1 shows the average bank rate from 2000 to 2011. In the wake of the 2007-2009 financial crisis, the Bank of England cut its bank rate to an all-time low of 0.5%, while high street banks and building societies reduced the rate on deposit accounts to as little as 0.1%. This drastically reduced the attractiveness of a cash-based investment relative to other asset classes.

It also meant that not being able to draw an adequate income from their cash investments, many people were forced to dip into their cash holdings to fill the gap left by reduced income.

Research published by UK-based asset manager Schroders in August 2010 found that in the preceding 12 months almost a third of UK adults had drawn on savings and investments to supplement their incomes.[14] Collectively these adults used an estimated £60bn to cover living expenses. Dipping into your capital to supplement an income shortfall is dangerous as it depletes the investment pot and potentially reduces income for years to come. For individuals nearing retirement the risks are amplified as they have less opportunity to replenish lost income and rebuild savings.

Tying up your cash for an extended period

Another risk related to interest rates may come when you have tied up your cash for an extended period at a fixed interest rate. For example, let's say you have tied up your cash for five years at an interest rate of 5%. If during this time the market interest rate moves up, say to 7.5%, your return on the cash investment will be lower than what it may have been if it was not tied up in the fixed-interest account.

Of course, the flipside is also true: if interest rates fall and you have fixed the return you are receiving on cash at a higher rate, your return will be favourable relative to the prevailing market interest rate.

4. INFLATION

To measure the impact of inflation on a cash investment it is important to distinguish between the *nominal return* and the *real return*. The *nominal return* is the interest received by the investor while the *real return* is the return on an investment after inflation has been accounted for. The *real return* is calculated by deducting the rate of inflation from the *nominal return* (the quoted rate of interest).

```
real return = nominal return - inflation
```

[14] Schroders, 'Capital erosion: Britons spend 360 billion of savings to recover income shortfall', press release (23 August 2010). Available at: **http://bit.ly/druDZb** [Accessed 17 January 2010.] Note: Research was conducted by ICM who interviewed a random sample of 2011 adults aged 18+ via online omnibus between 11 and 13 June 2010. Surveys were conducted across the country and the results have been weighted to the profile of all adults. ICM is a member of the British Polling Council and abides by its rules. Further information is available at **www.icmresearch.com**.

If you are leaving cash in a deposit account offering a fixed rate of interest, the rate on offer will need to exceed the current rate of inflation for you to receive a positive real rate of return. So if inflation is 2.5% and the interest rate offered by the deposit account is fixed at 4%, then your real return is 1.5%, calculated as follows:

```
4% - 2.5% = 1.5%
```

In this example the real return is positive but should the inflation rate exceed the interest rate on offer you will end up receiving a negative real return on your investment. This means the income you receive will not be sufficient to keep pace with price increases.

Erosion of capital by inflation

In addition to impacting income, inflation which is present over the lifetime of an investment and which continually exceeds the interest rate will erode the real value of the capital you invested. Such a situation means there is little incentive for you to leave your money in a cash deposit as its worth will be declining rather than increasing.

Assume you deposited £10,000 into a savings account when the deposit rate offered on the account was 5% and the rate of inflation in the UK was 3%. If these rates remained constant, at the end of the first year you would have received £500 income on the deposit (5% x £10,000). However, over this period the value of your capital (£10,000) has been eroded by inflation to the tune of £300 (3% x £10,000). So, while you gained £500 in income your original capital is worth £300 less. This means you have made a net gain of £200 (which is just 2% of your starting capital).

Now, take the same case but where the deposit rate was 2% and inflation was 6%. This time, by the end of the first year, you would have received £200 in income (2% x £10,000) but the value of your capital would have been eroded by £600 (6% x £10,000) to £9400. Your £10,000 would still be sitting there in the account, but its spending power has been reduced by £600. Your net position in the year would therefore be a loss of £400 (£200 - £600). This represents a return of -4% on your starting capital of £10,000.

It is therefore important to focus on the real return – and not the nominal return – generated by an investment. It is, for example, preferable to earn interest at a rate of 2% when inflation is 1% (making your real return 1%)

than it is to earn interest at a rate of 5% when inflation is 6%, as in this case the real return from your investment is -1%.

Beat inflation as an investor

A situation of rising inflation and stagnant interest rates in the UK meant that in February 2011, with CPI inflation at 4%, RPI inflation at 5.1% and the bank rate at 0.5%, higher rate tax payers in the 40% tax band needed to find a bank account paying at least 6.67% to beat inflation while basic rate tax payers in the 20% tax band needed an account paying 5% a year. According to comparison website Moneyfacts.co.uk, at the time there were only 21 accounts available to higher rate taxpayers which met this criteria, all of which were ISAs. No accounts were available for any taxpayer that beat RPI.

One way of mitigating the impact of inflation is to opt for a cash investment which pays a variable interest rate linked to the rate of inflation. If inflation goes up, the interest paid goes up in line with this, and vice versa. Examples of such accounts include five-year NS&I index-linked savings certificates which for an investment of between £100 and £15,000 guarantees a return of 0.5% above RPI over the account's period. Table 4.3 shows the return investors in different tax bands will make investing in NS&I savings certificates with RPI inflation at various levels. Note that the vehicles are withdrawn from the market when they are oversubscribed (this happened in the latter part of 2011).

Table 4.3 – return from NS&I index-linked Savings Certificates

RPI	5%	4%	3%	2%	1%
Basic rate (20%) taxpayer	6.88%	5.63%	4.38%	3.13%	1.88%
Higher rate (40%) taxpayer	9.16%	7.50%	5.83%	4.16%	2.50%
Top rate (50%) taxpayer	11%	9%	7%	5%	3%

Source: *Investors Chronicle*, May 2011

Inflation-linked cash ISAs are another way of protecting your cash investment from inflation. At the time of writing five-year inflation-linked cash ISAs paying RPI plus 0.1% were available from Barnsley Building Society, Chelsea Building Society and the Yorkshire Building Society for a minimum investment of £3000. Note though that these three building societies count as one institution under the FSCS.

An advantage of inflation-linked ISAs is that the income returns won't be taxed as an ISA is a tax exempt vehicle. The drawbacks are that accounts with longer terms, such as five years, often do not permit early withdrawal or closure and if they do, you may incur penalty fees. It may also be the case that the inflation-linked return is calculated over five years rather than yearly, meaning savers will lose out if there is a period of deflation.

DEFLATION

We should also consider the impact of deflation on a cash investment. Theoretically deflation should increase the buying power of cash as prices are falling. In practice, however, things pan out quite differently. A deflationary environment is characterised by low, near zero, interest rates which means your cash deposits will deliver little, if any, income.

You could argue that this won't matter as deflation means falling prices, which should mean the purchasing power of your money will automatically be rising. In reality, however, it will take extreme deflation – as opposed to just a low or moderate level of deflation – to make cash a profitable investment.

Extreme deflation can lead to the collapse of a country's banking system which, needless to say, is not good news if you have left your money on deposit in the bank.

Once again then, you need to take account of interest rates *and* inflation (i.e. calculate the real return) when weighing up an investment.

5

GILTS AND CORPORATE BONDS

The basics of bonds

Lending money to the government or large corporations may at face value seem an unlikely way of generating an investment income, but this is essentially what a bond investment is: a loan to a company, government or other official body, set up for a fixed term. Bonds issued by the UK government are known as *gilts* while bonds issued by companies are generally referred to as *corporate bonds*. Collectively these vehicles are referred to as *fixed-interest* investments.

In return for loaning money – in practice buying a bond – the investor earns a regular income from interest payments (known as the coupon) at a pre-determined amount and at fixed, regular intervals, until the term of the bond expires (on its redemption date) and the loan is repaid.

The coupon is set when the bond is issued, at which point the level of the coupon depends on the prevailing interest rates, the credit rating of the bond issuer and other factors such as the bond's length of maturity. Both the coupon a bond pays and the price at which it is redeemed are fixed at issuance.

Typically a bond will be launched at a price of, or close to, par (100p in the pound). The attractiveness of the bond lies in the promise of fixed return and the guarantee that an investor buying the bond will have their capital redeemed at par when the bond reaches its maturity date – whatever market price fluctuations.

This means that if you buy a bond for £1000 you will pay £1000 for it when it launched (this is the par price of the bond) and will be paid £1000 for it on the redemption date of the bond. This is provided that the *issuer* – the company or government to which the loan was made – does not default on this promise.

Yield

With bonds there are three types of yield to consider:

1. The coupon rate.
2. Running yield.
3. Redemption yield.

Let's look at each of these concepts in more detail.

1. COUPON RATE

The *coupon rate* is the fixed rate of interest paid on the bond. This applies for both undated bonds – bonds that run into perpetuity – and dated bonds with a set expiry date. The coupon is usually given in the name of the bond, for example the **Treasury 5.25% Treasury Gilt 12**. This is a government bond (gilt) which pays a coupon rate of 5.25% and has its redemption date in 2012. If you buy the bond at issue, you will get 5.25% of the bond's value at issuance paid annually for the life of bond.

The coupon rate is not of much use to investors because most will usually not buy bonds when they are issued, but rather buy them on the secondary market. For this reason, the running yield of the bond is of more interest.

2. RUNNING YIELD

Running yield – also known as the interest yield, flat yield, current yield or straight yield – expresses the annual interest on a bond (the coupon) as a percentage of the market price of the bond.

Once a bond is issued it is freely traded on the secondary market and its price will fluctuate according to supply and demand. As the bond's price changes so does its running yield.

To calculate running yield, the coupon is divided by the bond's current price and the result is multiplied by 100 to express the bond's current yield as a percentage return.

```
running yield = (coupon/bond price) x 100
```

The calculation shows that the relationship between the price of a bond and its yield is an inverse one: if a bond's price rises, the yield falls, and vice versa. This is also illustrated in Figure 5.1.

Figure 5.1 – the inverse relationship between bond prices and bond yields

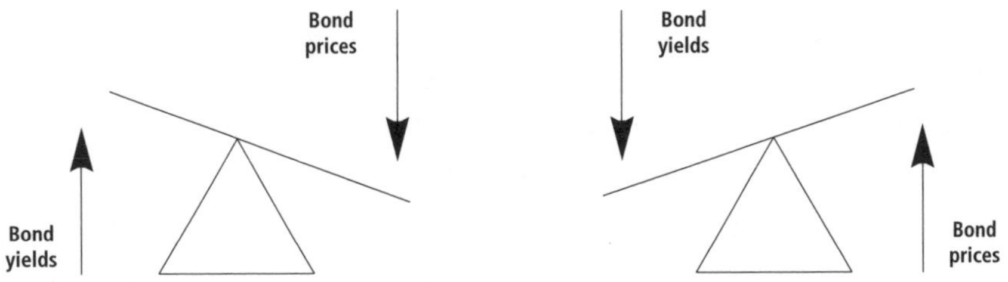

Source: Esme Faerber, *All About Bonds, Bond Mutual Funds, and Bond ETFs*[15]

Let's say a bond is issued at 100p and pays a 5p coupon, the running yield of the bond is:

```
(5p/100p) x 100 = 5%
```

The yield on this bond is currently 5%. This means the income return on the bond is 5% of the current price of the bond.

Now say the bond's price falls to 90p. As a bond's coupon is fixed for life, it remains at 5p, but the yield on the bond for the investor will rise to 5.56%. This is calculated as follows:

```
5p/90p x 100 = 5.56%
```

Investors buying on the secondary market after a price has fallen will therefore receive a higher yield than those who bought the bond when it was issued, while those buying bonds in the secondary market after the price has risen will receive a lower yield.

3. REDEMPTION YIELD

The *redemption yield* on a bond, also referred to as the real yield or the yield to maturity, shows what the total income return on a bond will be if it is held to maturity – i.e. its redemption date. It takes into account the interest payments a bondholder will receive and the capital gain/loss they will make

[15] Drawing sourced from: Esme Faerber, *All About Bonds, Bond Mutual Funds, and Bond ETFs* (McGraw-Hill Professional, 2009), p. 32.

on the bond when it matures. This type of yield does not apply to undated bonds, since these have no pre-determined maturity date.

Bond investors who buy in the secondary market receive the bond's price at par when the bond matures rather than the price they actually paid. Therefore, depending on whether they bought a bond at less than par or more than par, they will either make a capital gain or loss.

The redemption yield spreads any such gains or losses over the bond's lifespan to give an estimate of your total income return. While an important measure, calculating the redemption yield involves complex maths and the longer the bond has to run, the harder the sum.

Unless you particularly enjoy number crunching, you be will better off using an online calculator to work out the redemption yield of a bond. There is one available at: **www.moneychimp.com/calculator/bond_yield_calculator.htm**

Note that although this calculator takes inputs of the bond's par value and current price in dollars, other investors can still use it as a guideline to find out the current yield and redemption yield of a bond issued in the UK.

THE YIELD ON BOND FUNDS

Investing directly in bonds can be tricky and may require expert knowledge of the bonds market. Many investors may prefer to invest in this asset class via bond funds. We will look at bond funds in detail in chapter 7, but for now we are concerned with the yield these funds pay. Bond funds typically quote two yields:

1. Distribution yield.
2. Underlying yield.

The *distribution yield* takes into account the bond price and the ongoing yield, making it a good indication of what the returns on the bond will be over the next 12 months. It does not, however, account for the bond's capital value at maturity.

As such, the *underlying yield* is regarded as a more comprehensive measure of the income return as it looks at the bond fund's returns after expenses, including the interest payments, and also takes account of any capital gain or loss made when the bond matures. These figures will usually be quoted on the fund's monthly factsheet.

Generating higher yield

There are two main ways to generate higher yields and increase the income from bond investments:

1. Buy lower grade bonds

The price and the level of yield depends on the class of bond. The lower the quality of the bond, the lower its price and thus the higher its yield. The greater the quality of the bond, the higher its price and the lower the yield.

To increase the income generated by your bond investments you can buy lower grade bonds or non-investment grade bonds, often referred to as *junk bonds*. These are higher risk investments which offer higher returns to compensate the investor for the increased risk.

2. Buy longer dated bonds

The other way to increase the income from bond investments is to invest in bonds with longer maturity dates – bonds with longer terms. Remember, though, that the longer the term of a bond, the more vulnerable it will be to rising interest rates and inflation, which are harder to predict over the long term. This is in fact why yields on bonds with longer maturity dates are higher – because the income returns are more unpredictable.

The yield curve is a useful tool to use when choosing which maturities of bonds to buy. Figure 5.2 shows the yield on UK bonds with different maturities as at 30 May 2011. As you can see, as the term to maturity of bonds increases, as does the yield they provide.

Figure 5.2 – yields on UK bonds with different terms to run until maturity

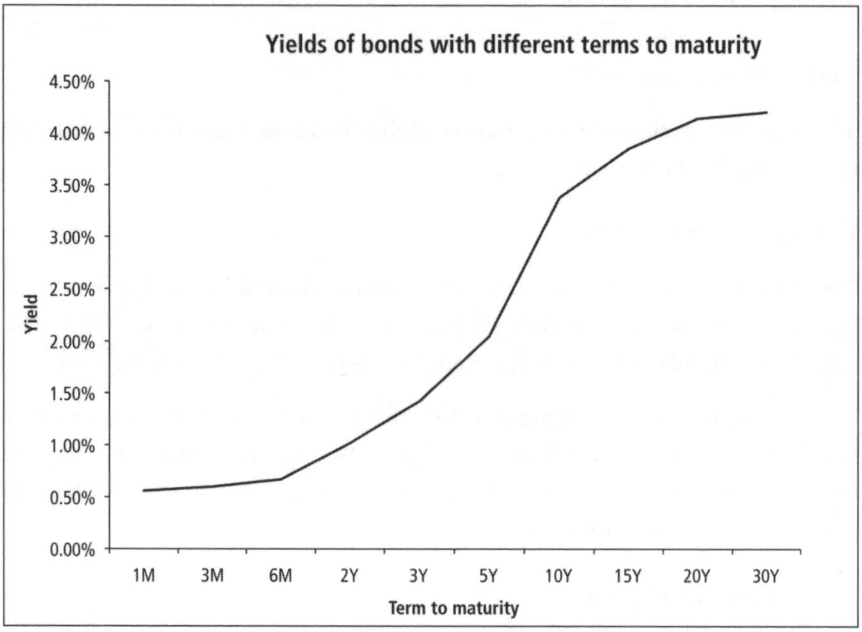

It is possible to draw up your own yield curve for bonds, as explained below.

The yield curve

Conducting an analysis of yield before you invest can make a significant difference to your eventual income return. When it comes to bonds, the yield curve will help you with this analysis.

The yield curve is a line graph that tracks the yields of similar quality bonds (usually gilts) against their various times to maturity.

Typically, bonds with longer maturities will pay more income to compensate investors for the increased risk of locking up their cash for longer. Such a situation – where long-term yields are higher than short-term yields – is considered a normal yield curve.

A normal yield curve will be gently upward-sloping, indicating that the longer the maturity of the bond, the greater the interest return. Changes in the yield curve will generally be reflected by shifts of the curve up and down over time. Figure 5.3 shows the normal yield curve.

Figure 5.3 – normal yield curve

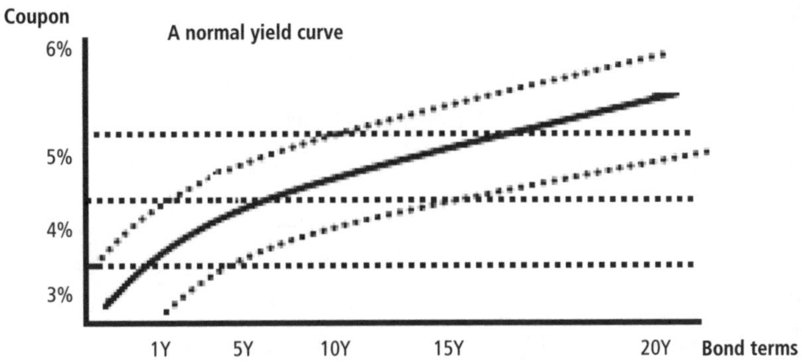

Changing expectations for the economy and inflation can cause the yield curve to take on different shapes.

A flat yield curve (as shown in Figure 5.4) indicates that long and short-term yields are almost equal and indicates that the economy is changing. It could be indicative of an economic slowdown, although this is not always the case.

Figure 5.4 – flat yield curve

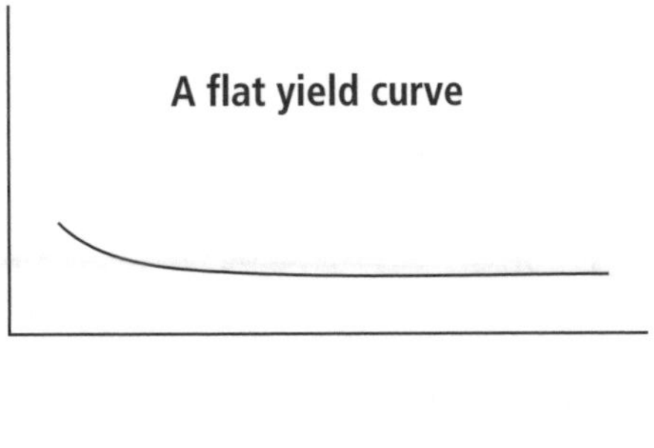

A steep yield curve (Figure 5.5), on the other hand, is an early sign of a rising economy. This will fuel expectations for inflation and interest rate rises in the future and investors will be reluctant to tie themselves into lower-yielding bonds. Demand for longer-term bonds will thus fall, pushing down bond prices and increasing yields.

Figure 5.5 – steep yield curve

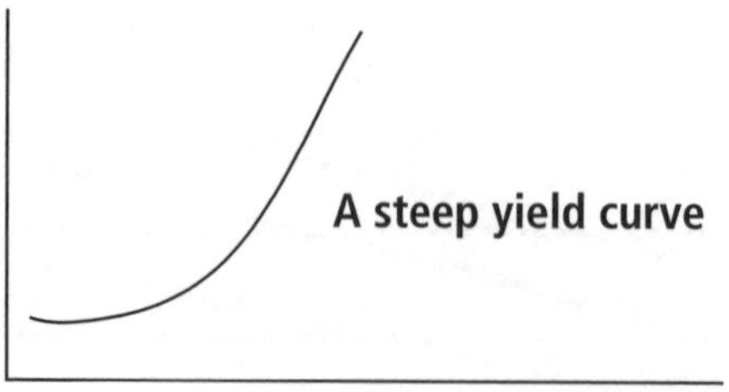

An inverted yield curve (Figure 5.6), where the curve has a downward slope, means short-term yields exceed long-term yields. This is unusual and indicative of a recession. The threat of inflation may now be lower, but falling inflation may lead investors to believe that long-term bond yields will be lower in the future and they are therefore better off buying bonds now and locking in a better rate. An increased demand for long-term bonds drives prices higher and yields lower, further flattening higher short-term rates, and causing an inverted curve.

Figure 5.6 – inverted yield curve

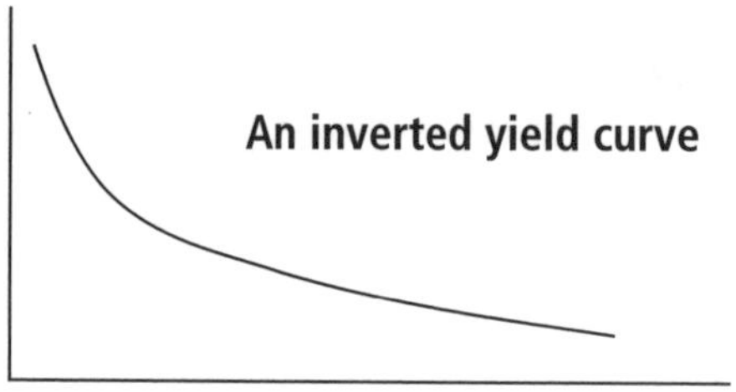

Constructing a yield curve

The yield curve can be a useful way of forecasting the yields and prices of bonds as well as the direction and state of the economy, and it can be used to position your income portfolio accordingly. You can use the internet to obtain the yields of different bond maturities and then use Microsoft Excel to construct a yield curve – the shape will help you to decide whether it is best to invest in long-term or short-term maturity bonds. Here's how to go about it:

- First you need the yield data – this can be obtained from the London Stock Exchange's website (**www.londonstockexchange.com**).
- Now open a blank worksheet in Excel. Type in the relevant yield information, which should include the different bond maturities (for example one month, two years etc.) and the yield for each into two adjacent columns. You can also import a yield table into the spreadsheet. To do this click on 'Data' and then 'From web'/'From Text'/'From Access' depending on where you are importing the table from. Once you have located the data from the relevant source, click 'Import'.
- Make sure the data is correctly formatted – the maturity dates should be in the first column, followed by the yield data. Now use Excel's chart wizard to create your yield curve: highlight the relevant cells by holding down your mouse, click 'Insert', then 'Chart' and choose the 'Scatter' option.

Bond trading on the secondary market

Once a bond has been issued, it trades on the secondary market, where most investors tend to buy bonds. A bond's price on the secondary market will be directly affected by changes in interest rates. The effect of higher interest rates on bonds is to lower their prices. Conversely, lower interest rates raise bond prices. As a bond's price changes, so does the yield it delivers.

Let's say a new bond, Bond A, is issued with a higher coupon than is available from an existing bond, Bond B. Let's also assume that Bond A and Bond B are both trading at par. This means that when Bond A trades on the secondary market it offers a higher yield to investors than Bond B.

In response to the higher yield offered by Bond A, investors will sell Bond B, which will push its price down due to the fall in demand, and they will buy Bond A, pushing its price up due to the rise in demand.

As more investors buy into Bond A its yield will fall – its price has risen and its coupon has remained the same – while at the same time the yield of Bond B will rise because its price has fallen and its coupon has remained the same.

As you can see the coupon is largely irrelevant to investors buying on the secondary market, rather it is the yield – the income return of the bond based upon the price at which they bought it in the secondary market – that is important to them. Figure 5.7 shows the relationship between interest rates, a bond's price and its yield.

Figure 5.7 – the relationship between bond prices, yields and interest rates

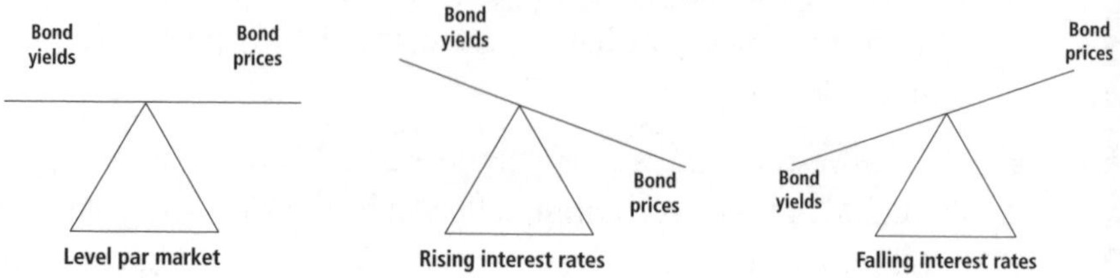

The role of bonds in a portfolio

As one of the three main asset classes alongside cash and equities, fixed interest is an essential tool in the asset allocation process. Over the short term, bond investments can be used to preserve capital, for example protecting your pension or keeping your investment assets out of the stock market when returns from equities are uncertain. Over the medium to longer term, bonds play an important role in meeting the income needs of those who are less risk tolerant.

Consequently, virtually every income portfolio will need to have an allocation in bonds. The amount of exposure your portfolio holds in the asset class will of course vary depending on your risk appetite and specific income goals.

Main types of bonds

The bond market is huge and varied. Bonds are defined and distinguished based on a number of factors, such as the type of issuer, the bond's date to maturity and its credit rating. Bonds also differ in the method by which they pay interest. In the main, however, bonds tend to be defined based on the institution that issued them, whether a government, corporation, or foreign body.

The main types of bond investments are:

1. Government bonds (gilts)
2. Corporate bonds
3. Foreign bonds
4. Index-linked bonds
5. Zero-coupon bonds
6. Permanent Interest Bearing Shares (Pibs)
7. Floating-rate bonds

Figure 5.8 provides an illustration of the risk of different types of fixed-interest investments.

Figure 5.8 – fixed-interest investments and their levels of risk

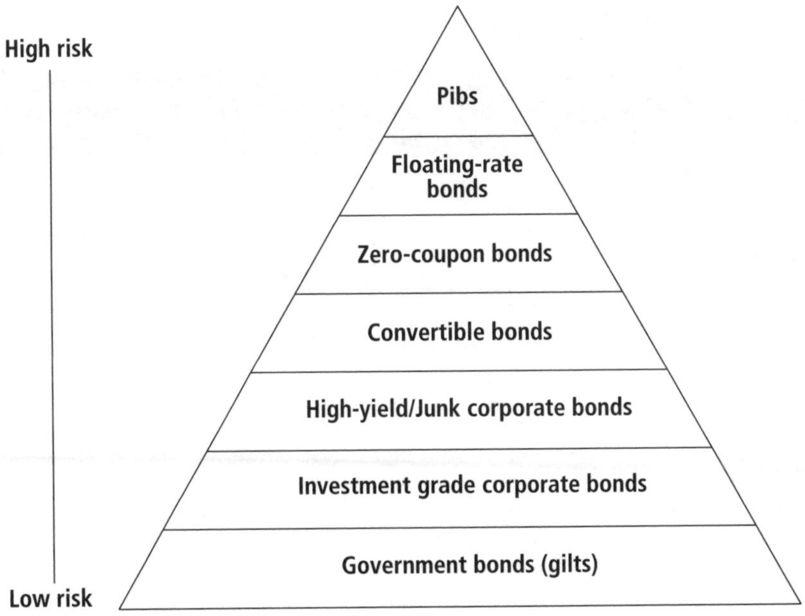

Let's look at each of these types of bonds in turn.

1. GOVERNMENT BONDS

Bonds issued by the UK government are called gilts. The term dates back to the debt securities issued by the Bank of England which had a gilt (gold) edge.

Gilts can be classified by the number of years to run to maturity: short-dated gilts (shorts) typically have 0 to seven years to run; medium-dated gilts (mediums) have 7 to 15 years; and long-dated gilts (longs) have over 15 years until expiry. These time frames can differ though.

Undated gilts have no fixed repayment date, while some gilts will repay within a date range, for example 2012 to 2016, which means the government can choose to repay at any time from 2012 but must repay by 2016 at the latest. Table 5.1 provides some examples of gilts. As you can see short-dated gilts, for example UK Gilt Treasury Stk 3.25% offer lower yields and coupons than those with longer time frames such as the UK Gilt Exchequer 12% and UK Gilt Exchequer 8%.

Table 5.1 – a selection of gilts

Issuer	Coupon (%)	Date of maturity	Price	Running yield (%)	Redemption yield (%)
UK Gilt Exchequer 12%	12	12/12/2017	135.13	8.88	1.55
UK Gilt Treasury Stk 2%	2	22/01/2016	98.885	2.02	2.25
UK Gilt Treasury Stk 3.25%	3.25	07/12/2011	101.53	3.20	0.47
UK Gilt Treasury Stk 8%	8	07/06/2021	139.465	5.74	3.34
UK Gilt War Loan Stk	3.5	Undated.	74.3	4.71	4.71

Source: Fixed Interest Investor, as at 19 May 2011

Gilts can be bought directly by investors at issue – the UK's debt management office has a list of the gilts market latest prices and yields at **www.dmo.gov.uk/index.aspx?page=Gilts/Daily_Prices.**

After issuance, gilts can be bought in the secondary market via a stockbroker or bank.

When gilts beat equities

Gilts are dubbed the safest type of fixed-interest investment and therefore have the reputation of providing low income returns, but past figures tell a different story. The Barclays Capital Equity Gilt Study (2010) which analysed the real returns of the major asset classes in the UK found that income from gilts over 10 and 20-year holding periods up to 2009 outperformed that of shares (see Table 5.2).

Table 5.2 – real investment returns by asset class (% per annum)

Asset class	2009	Over 10 years	Over 20 years	Over 50 years	Over 110 years
Equities	25.9	-1.2	4.6	5.2	5
Gilts	-3.3	2.6	5.4	2.3	1.2
Corporate Bonds	15.8	2.9	n/a	n/a	n/a
Index-linked	3.1	1.9	3.8	n/a	n/a
Cash	-1.7	1.8	3.1	1.9	1

Source: Barclays Capital Equity Gilt Study 2010

It is however very rare for bonds to outperform equities over long holding periods, given that shares are generally regarded as offering better returns over the long term. As you can also see in Table 5.2, over holding periods of 50 and 110 years equities did outperform all other asset classes.

One of the reasons for the outperformance of equities by gilts for the 10 and 20-year holding periods shown in Table 5.2 was due to the low to moderate inflation which dominated over this period; when inflation is low real returns from bond investments are better.

It is not possible to be sure whether gilts will display the same outperformance of equities over the next two decades. The massive quantitative easing programmes launched by central banks in the wake of the 2007-2009 financial crisis could potentially lead to either inflation or deflation. Both scenarios will be detrimental to bond returns over the long term.

2. CORPORATE BONDS

The main difference between a corporate bond and a gilt is risk. While governments are seen as unlikely to default on a loan – albeit following the 2007-2009 financial crisis some countries are much less financially stable than others – the same cannot be said of companies. As a result these vehicles are seen as carrying a higher risk of default and typically offer a higher interest rate (coupon) to compensate.

Table 5.3 provides a sample of some corporate bonds and their coupon, price, maturity, and yield at the time of writing. As you can see some are trading above par (100p in the pound) – for example BP, Scottish Power and Total, while others are below par – Aviva and BAA. The bonds trading below par are those with longer maturity dates. As we would expect, the yields on bonds with longer maturity dates are higher – the income returns are more unpredictable over the long term and these bonds are therefore viewed as higher risk.

Table 5.3 – a selection of corporate bonds

Issuer	Coupon (%)	Date of maturity	Price (% of par value)	Running yield (%)
Aviva Plc	6.125	16/11/2026	95.755	6.40
BAA Plc	5.75	10/12/2031	96.15	5.98
BP	4	29/12/2014	104.155	3.84
Cable & Wireless Plc	8.75	06/08/2012	104.9	8.34
Carlsberg	7	26/02/2013	107.45	6.51
GKN Plc	7	14/05/2012	104.425	6.70
Halifax Plc	9.375	15/05/2021	116.525	8.05
Scottish Power	8.375	20/02/2017	122.715	6.82
Total	4.25	08/12/2017	106	4.01
Unilever	4	19/12/2014	105.9	3.78

Source: Fixed Income Investor, as at 19 May 2011

For a full list of corporate bonds and their current gross redemption yields, have a look at the Fixed Income Investor website:
www.fixedincomeinvestor.co.uk/x/bondtable.html?groupid=4

Convertible bonds

Convertible bonds are a variety of corporate bond. They are often thought of as a hybrid between a corporate bond and a share because a convertible may start life as bond with specified yield and maturity, but then can be exchanged at a predetermined time in the future for a specific number of shares in the company. Proponents of convertible bonds claim they offer the best of both worlds, however these are higher risk investments and will not fit the risk profile of most investors.

3. FOREIGN BONDS

A foreign or international bond is issued in a local market by a foreign entity. This can be in the local market's currency, known in the UK as bulldog bonds, or raised in currencies other than that of the local market, for example Eurobonds.

Emerging market bonds are another form of foreign bonds – these are issued by developing countries, usually in dollars or the developing country's own currency. Investing in foreign bonds can be a good way of diversifying your investment portfolio with overseas exposure but it will mean you have taken on exposure to currency movements.

4. INDEX-LINKED BONDS

Index-linked bonds are those in which both the coupon and the capital redemption are linked to the rate of inflation as measured by the Retail Prices Index (RPI). Most index-linked investments are issued by the government as gilts and Table 5.4 provides examples of some of these.

It is worth noting that the yields on index-linked bonds will often appear to be lower than the yields of conventional gilts because index-linked yields are the values received with inflation taken into account, whereas inflation is not included in the yield figures for conventional gilts.

For example, an index-linked gilt offering a yield of 2% is equivalent to a conventional gilt offering a yield of 5% when inflation is 3%. Or otherwise put: a conventional gilt with a yield of 5%, at a time when inflation is 3%, is actually delivering a yield of 2%.

Table 5.4 – a selection of index-linked gilts

Gilt	Coupon	Date of maturity	Price (% of par value)	Running yield (%)
UK Gilt Index-linked STK 1.25%	1.25	22/11/2017	110.29	1.13
UK Gilt Index-linked STK 1.25%	1.25	22/11/2027	108.045	1.16
UK Gilt Index-linked STK 2.5%	2.5	26/08/2011	307.95	0.81
UK Gilt Index-linked STK 2.5%	2.5	16/08/2013	285.345	0.88
UK Gilt Index-linked STK 2.5%	2.5	26/07/2016	325.825	0.77

Source: Fixed Income Investor, as at 19 May 2011

Table 5.4 shows a selection of index-linked gilts. Are these attractive investments? Let's consider the UK Gilt index-linked paying an interest (coupon) of 1.25%.

If we add this to the rate of inflation as at May 2011 (RPI = 5.3%), the gilt will pay a return of 6.55%. While this might sound attractive it is worth noting that the bond only matures in 2017 so you will be tying your money down for more than five years. In this time inflation may rise or fall. In comparison an investment in a five-year NS&I index-linked certificate in May 2011, based on RPI of 5.3%, will deliver a return of 9.67% for a 40% taxpayer.

Note that this is a very simple way of assessing the return from an index-linked gilt; a more accurate way is by looking at the real yield between the bond's purchase date and its maturity, which is dependent on the current market price of the bond. This will be explained in greater detail later.

Index-linked corporate bonds

A few index-linked bonds are not issued by the government as gilts but are issued by other financial institutions, mostly utility companies. These are becoming an increasingly popular investment.

To see what other kinds of index-linked bonds are available it is instructive to look at the holdings of an example fund, such as the M&G index-linked bond fund, which invests in a basket of different index-linked bonds. The fund holds exposure to gilts such as the Treasury 2.5% Index-linked 2016 but is also exposed to index-linked corporate bonds issued by UK supermarket chain Tesco and railway operator Network Rail. Table 5.5 provides a summary of the fund's main investments as at July 2011.

Table 5.5 – holdings of the M&G index-linked bond fund as at July 2011

Issuer	Proportion of fund
UK index-linked	85.8%
US Treasury index-linked	5%
Sweden	2.7%
BAA	0.9%
European Investment Bank	0.8%
Tesco	0.7%
Germany	0.6%
Network Rail	0.6%
National Grid	0.6%
Toyota Motor	0.6%

Source: www.mandg.co.uk

5. ZERO-COUPON BONDS

Zero-coupon bonds pay no interest. Instead, these are sold at a deep discount. The return to the investor is determined by the difference between the redemption price of the bond on maturity and the price at which it was purchased. These vehicles are also often referred to as non-interest bearing bonds.

As these bonds pay no interest they are not of much interest to income investors.

6. PERMANENT INTEREST BEARING SHARES

Permanent interest bearing shares (Pibs) are building society shares listed on the London Stock Exchange (LSE). These investments have characteristics that are closer to bonds than shares and therefore are regarded as a form of fixed-interest investment. Pibs typically pay interest twice yearly.

As with bonds, Pibs have a fixed coupon but unlike most bonds they do not have a fixed period to maturity – instead they have 'call dates' when the issuing society has the option to redeem or extend the shares. Other differences between bonds and Pibs are that interest payments on Pibs can be missed in exceptional circumstances and if missed they do not necessarily need to be made up at a later stage. Pibs are also not protected by any compensation schemes.

These characteristics make Pibs higher risk than other forms of fixed interest but this also means that they can produce higher yields. For investors willing to do their homework Pibs can provide a reliable income stream and provide welcome diversification to an income portfolio. But remember that while Pibs can be an attractive income-generating investment in an environment of low interest rates, if interest rates rise the market value of Pibs will fall.

Previously, many Pibs were issued by building societies. When these building societies then demutualised (converted to public limited companies) their Pibs became perpetual subordinated bonds (PSBs).

Table 5.6 shows a selection of Pibs that are available to UK investors. If you look at the name of the pib, the number, for example, Halifax Plc. **13.625** refers to the interest (coupon) paid by the investment. As Pibs are also issued at 100p a price below this will indicate the investment is trading below par, while a price of 122p, as is the case with the Halifax offering, shows a premium to par.

Table 5.6 – a sample of Pibs

Issuer	Price
Bradford & Bingley PLC 13 Pibs	61.5
Halifax Plc.13.625 Pibs	122
Manchester Building Society 6.75 Pibs	84.75
Nottingham Building Society 7.875 Pibs	87
West Bromwich Building Society 6.15 Pibs	17.75

Source: The Fixed Income Investor, www.fixedincomeinvestor.co.uk

The Fixed Income Investor website provides a full list of Pibs and their prices (**www.fixedincomeinvestor.co.uk/x/bondtable.html?groupid=11**).

7. FLOATING-RATE BONDS

Unlike ordinary bonds – which pay out a fixed amount each period – a floating-rate bond pays out interest according to changes in market interest rates. These investments therefore provide a way for investors to take advantage of an uncertain interest rate environment. If interest rates rise, the rate payable on a floating-rate bond will too.

RBS offers a floating-rate bond (maturity date 1 November 2022) with a minimum fixed return of 3.9% per year (gross), or the three-month Libor rate, whichever is higher. The floating-rate bond is listed on the London Stock Exchange which means that investors can buy or sell the bond at any time during trading.

A floating-rate bond can be held as a direct investment or in a SIPP. It can also be held in a stocks and shares ISA, provided the remaining life of the bond is greater than five years at the time of purchase.

The biggest caveat with floating-rate bonds is that the capital invested is not covered by the Financial Services Compensation Scheme (FSCS). So if the bond issuer goes into default, your money could disappear with it. As such these should be considered high-risk investments.

Now that you have a good idea of the different types of bonds, we will move on to look at how you can go about investing in bonds.

Buying fixed-interest investments

The two varieties of bonds that income investors are most interested in and most likely to invest in are gilts and corporate bonds.

As we will see, there are two main options – bonds can be bought either directly or indirectly – although the situation is more complex with corporate bonds than it is with gilts.

BUYING GILTS

Investors have a choice between purchasing gilts directly, or indirectly via funds.

Direct purchase

- Gilts can be purchased at issue from the Debt Management Office, a government department which issues gilts on behalf of HM Treasury. More information is available on the department's website (**www.dmo.gov.uk**). The advantage of purchasing at issue means there are no additional costs such as commission involved with the purchases.
- Gilts can also be purchased on the London Stock Exchange through a stockbroker or through the Post Office.

Buying gilt funds

- You can invest in gilts indirectly via an actively-managed gilt fund which will contain a pooled collection of gilts with varying dates and structures, or via an index-tracking fund such as an exchange-traded fund (ETF) which tracks an equity or bond index. These will be explained in greater detail in chapter 7.

BUYING CORPORATE BONDS

While it has always been possible to buy gilts directly at issue or via a stockbroker, the same has not applied to corporate bonds. The sheer size of the corporate bond market and the varying complexity of different issues depending on the bond's maturity, structure and risk of default mean that researching bonds with the view to investing can be challenging and time consuming.

Aside from the complexity and various influences on bond prices, such as inflation and interest rate movements, a barrier to entry for private investors was formerly the high investment amounts involved – in the past a direct investment in bonds would require a minimum investment of around £50,000 or more, making this the preserve of institutional investors and the very wealthy. For ordinary investors, the preferred way to invest in corporate bonds was via collective investment funds which offer the advantages of instant diversification, smaller investment amounts and professional management.

However, in 2010 the London Stock Exchange (LSE) launched a retail bond market, known as ORB (order book for retail bonds) making it easier for private investors to trade bonds directly. In May 2011 there were almost 150 bonds listed, which investors can buy in denominations of £1000; similar to the minimum amount required to invest in bond funds. Investors also now benefit from reasonable charges and online access.

There are advantages and disadvantages to buying corporate bonds directly.

Advantages of buying bonds directly

The advantages of buying bonds directly include:

- The potential of a higher income return, as you are cutting out the commission and total expense ratios involved when buying via a fund.
- Certainty of income and redemption dates. Most gilts pay income half-yearly, and so do many corporate bonds. The payment date is often the same day each year as the bond's final maturity date.
- Knowing exactly when each bond matures and the amounts to be paid out (subject of course to none of them defaulting). This can enable you to construct your own monthly or quarterly income schedule, which can be useful within a broader income portfolio. The maturity value across the bonds can be used to meet financial needs such as school or university fee payments. This matching of bond payments and your personal income needs is not possible with an investment in a bond fund as the income will be subject to fluctuations – this can happen when the manager at the helm of the fund decides to change the fund's investment process or makes changes to the fund's underlying investments.
- Ability to hold the bond until maturity and reclaim the full principal (unless the issuer defaults). With funds there is the risk that the principal may not be fully recovered if the share price of the fund is below the purchase price when you sell your shares in the fund.

Disadvantages of buying bonds directly

A strong case can be made for accessing bonds directly, but there are caveats. These are:

- The research which needs to go into adequately evaluating the security of a bond can be complicated. Credit agency ratings can help but judging the risk of default of an individual corporate bond is not straightforward. There is a wide variance in the types of corporate bonds issued and bonds' claims to the underlying assets of the company that issues them can differ greatly, impacting the security of the bonds. Many investors may not have the time, skills or necessary tools to conduct the research and analysis needed to accurately assess a corporate bond. When you invest in a corporate bond fund this analysis is left to the professionals – the fund manager and their team of analysts. Bond fund managers do not necessarily hold bonds to maturity but actively trade them, with the intention of increasing the assets of the fund.

- Investing directly into bonds can also mean a lack of choice and can cause issues with diversification. While the LSE is constantly adding more corporate bonds for private investors, the choice is still not as wide as those available to bond fund managers who have more capital to invest.
- When purchasing a single corporate bond, you are exposed to a single company, which means your investment risk is concentrated. With a corporate bond fund, the fund manager spreads the investment across a portfolio of different corporate bonds – diversification is thus taken care of for you. Often holdings in corporate bond funds are easier to sell than individual bond issues.
- Bonds can only be held in a stocks and shares Individual Savings Account (ISA) if they are not convertible and have a maturity of more than five years. Provided they are UK-domiciled, any bond fund can be held within a stocks and shares ISA.

Summary

Buying bonds directly can be a useful investment strategy for those that want to draw up an income plan to meet specific financial needs. For the inexperienced investor though, the bond market can be a high risk.

If you do opt to invest directly into bonds as opposed to buying a fund, you need to do your homework. Mitigate the investment risks involved by holding a diversified selection of bonds with different performance characteristics, credit ratings and maturity rates. The London Stock Exchange has information on this on its website:

www.londonstockexchange.com/exchange/prices-and-markets/retail-bonds/retail-bonds-search.html

Table 5.7 provides a summary of the important differences between buying an individual corporate bond and investing via a corporate bond fund.

Table 5.7 – comparing the features of corporate bonds and corporate bond funds

Feature	Individual corporate bonds	Corporate bond funds
Income stream	Fixed	Varies from month to month.
Management fees	None	Varies between 1% and 1.5% depending on the fund.
Returns	Not diminished by fees.	Return reduced by fund's total expense ratio (TER).
Safety of principal	If it is a high quality bond held to its maturity date, the principal is received.	A chance that principal may not be fully recovered if share price of fund is below the purchase price when shares are sold.
Holdings	Known	Not disclosed until end of the month/quarter.
Diversification	Need a large amount of money to build a diversified portfolio.	Small investment buys a holding in a diversified portfolio.

Factors to consider when investing in bonds for income

Despite the fixed nature of bond income, there are a number of factors that can influence the real income return generated by these vehicles, including:

1. Interest rates
2. Bond maturity
3. Security of issuer
4. Inflation

Let's look at these four factors in turn.

1. INTEREST RATES

One of the main risks when investing in a bond is that interest rates could change after it is bought – this is known as *interest rate risk.*

When you buy a bond, you should be aware of the following:

- Bond prices are more sensitive to a reduction in interest rates than to an increase in interest rates.
- Bonds paying a low coupon are more sensitive to interest rate changes than high coupon bonds. The smaller the coupon rate of the bond, the greater the possible fluctuation in its price subject to interest rate changes.
- Some bonds are more sensitive to change in interest rates than others because of their different maturities. The longer the term to maturity of a bond, the greater the risk that interest rate changes will impact the market price of the bond.
- Duration measures a bond's sensitivity to interest-rate movements. A bond with a duration of 5% will decrease in value by 5% if interest rates rise 1% and increase in value by 5% if interest rates fall by 1%.

So how can bond investors protect against uncertainty in interest rate movements? A floating-rate bond could be an option. If interest rates go up, the rate payable on a floating-rate bond will follow suit, which means the real income delivered does not suffer in the same way in which that of an ordinary bond does when interest rates and inflation rise.

In an environment of low interest rates, such as has been the case from late 2008, a floating-rate bond would still be worth considering. The RBS floating-rate bond, for example, which promises 3.9% annual interest is attractive if bank savings rates are at or close to zero. Given that this bond matures in November 2022, this also means that you are accounting for the possibility that interest rates might rise in the future.

2. BOND MATURITY

You can increase the income return from a bond investment by buying bonds with longer maturity dates. However, if interest rates are expected to rise in the future, it would be a mistake to consider bonds beyond the short and medium ranges as you risk locking into an investment paying a low interest rate. If faced with this situation and you decide not to hold the bond to redemption, in other words you cash it in early, you face the risk of a capital loss.

It is important to look at the yield curve of a bond. Check that the curve indicates that long-term rates will remain higher than short and medium-term rates. If so, buying a bond with a longer maturity rate will make sense. But remember that the longer the bond's maturity the more susceptible it will be to inflation and price volatility.

3. SECURITY OF ISSUER

A fixed-interest investment is only as safe as the institution that borrows the money from the investor and its ability to repay the loan. One of the biggest risks is that the bond issuer cannot pay the interest due – meaning it defaults on the coupon payment – or it cannot pay back the capital at the end of the term.

Investors can partially gauge the risk of a bond issuer defaulting by looking at a bond's price and its yield. The higher the yield of a bond, the higher the likelihood of it defaulting, and vice versa. Gilts usually have lower yields because the government is always expected to be able to pay investors back in full. In other words, there is a low risk that investors in gilts will fail to receive their interest payments and their capital back at the end of the term.

This is not to say that gilts are a totally risk-free investment. With every bond, there is a chance that the issuer may default on their payments. The more risky a bond, the greater the income return required by the investor to compensate for the greater chance of non-payment.

Let's take an example. As at July 2011, the yield to maturity for a Vodafone corporate bond maturing in five years is 2.662%, compared to the yield to maturity of 1.716% for the generic UK five-year government bond index. The 0.95% (95 basis points) difference is the *credit spread.*

Investors must ask themselves if the additional 0.95% yield that can be earned from the Vodafone bond is adequate compensation for the risk that Vodafone might default.

Investors can make this decision by referring to the bond's credit rating.

Credit rating

The risk of a bond issuer defaulting is reflected in the bond's credit rating. This measure is comparable to the credit rating financial institutions assign to individuals who have credit obligations, such as credit cards or a mortgage.

In the case of bonds, this indicator is assigned by a credit rating agency – such as Moody's or Standard & Poor's – which assesses the credit worthiness of an issuer and the quality of the bond, i.e. how likely the issuer is to meet interest payments and repay the loan. A company with a high credit rating is regarded as a safer bond issuer than a company with a low credit rating.

Credit ratings are typically expressed as letter designations such as AAA, B or CC. Bonds with the highest credit ratings (AAA) will typically be investment-grade bonds, while those rated lower (below Baa/BBB) are usually high-yield or junk bonds. Table 5.8 provides more detail on Moody's and Standard & Poor's bond ratings.

Table 5.8 – interpreting Moody's and Standard & Poor's bond ratings

Moody's	Standard & Poor's (S&P)	Interpretations of Ratings	
Aaa	AAA	Highest-quality obligations	Investment grade ↓
Aa	AA	High grade	
A	A	Upper medium graded	
Baa	BBB	Medium-grade quality	
Ba	BB	Non-investment grade, speculative	High yield 'junk' bonds ↓
B	B		
Caa	CCC	Extremely speculative, high risk	
Ca	CC	In default with little prospect for recovery	
	C		
C	D	In default	

For the investor in bonds, it is important to understand how likely bonds of various credit ratings are to default.

According to a Moody's report on Corporate Default and Recovery Rates 1920-2010, the average default rate for a Baa-rated issuer over a five-year period is around 3% (based on global issuers over the period 1920-2010). A Baa-rated issuer is on the cusp of investment-grade status. Those issuers rated above Baa can be expected to default at a much lower frequency. The highest-rated Aaa issuers hardly ever default. Below Baa, those bonds known as high-yield debt or speculative grade default with greater frequency. The speculative grade default rate over the same period is 18% for a five-year investment horizon.

These data can be used by investors to work out the expected default rate of a bond.[16] In the case of the Vodafone bond mentioned above, which pays an income of 6%, if the bond was rated at Baa you might reason that it is worth investing in the corporate bond rather than a gilt generating a yield of 4.5% because the risk of the Vodafone bond defaulting in the next five years is just 3%.

To fully understand bond defaults, you need to know what the repercussions are when a bond issuer default occurs.

The consequences when a bond issuer defaults

What happens when a bond issuer defaults on an interest payment?

Do you lose all your money or just a bit of it? Bond fund manager Ian Spreadbury of asset manager Fidelity, says that typically investors do not lose all of their money in the event of default. Investors are usually able to negotiate a *recovery value*. This is an amount that satisfies their claim on the companies' assets after the claims of investors higher in the companies' capital structure have been satisfied.

The recovery value depends on the security of the bond. Bonds can be split into secured and unsecured vehicles. Secured bonds are backed by some form of collateral, for example real estate owned by the company, while unsecured bonds are not backed by equipment, revenue, or mortgages on real estate. These bonds only have the issuer's promise that they will be repaid.

An investor holding secured bonds should expect most of their investment back, since the collateral securing the bond can be sold and the proceeds specifically used to repay the debt. An investor holding an unsecured bond will have to wait until all secured creditors are paid before staking a claim on the companies' assets. Consequently their recovery value may be lower. The recovery value is usually expressed as a percentage of par value.

[16] Moody's Investor Service, 'Corporate Default and Recovery Rates, 1920-2010' (28 February 2011).

CORPORATE BONDS DURING THE CREDIT CRUNCH

Comparing the credit spreads of corporate bonds to historic default rates or the probability of downgrade indicates how cheap or expensive they are. However, the market may not always offer a credit spread that is fully reflective of the issuer's ability to make all of the payments on their bonds. Sometimes spreads can over or under compensate investors for the level of credit risk.

During the financial downturn of 2007-2009 ratings agencies were worried that certain companies were getting into financial difficulty and as a result downgraded these companies' credit ratings. The ratings of all bonds, even those at the highest level, fell dramatically as the risk of default was perceived to have increased significantly and in response credit spreads widened sharply. The vast majority of bonds offered a credit spread that over-compensated investors for the historical level of default. For example, the credit spread demanded by investors to compensate them for the additional risk of holding BBB-rated company bonds over gilts reached 9.4%[17], its highest level ever.

During this time bond prices fell so far that they suggested the recession would be far worse than the Great Depression of the 1930s – the worst period in the history of fixed-interest assets.

The fall in bond prices meant that their potential income returns (yield) substantially increased. Those bonds at the least credit worthy end of the range – i.e. below investment grade, ccc, cc and c – as expected rose the most. At the peak of the crisis US high yield defaults peaked at about 13% per annum. By May 2011 they were right down to around 4%.

Investors twigged that bonds were cheap and, provided the company issuing the bond did not default, getting into these vehicles presented a good level of income and capital gain on the low prices. This is exactly what happened. Later, as the fear of default subsided, the security of the bonds increased once again and credit spreads narrowed. Investors who had recognised the opportunity and invested when the fear factor was at its peak and bond prices were at historical lows secured handsome income and profits from investing in corporate bonds.

[17] Bloomberg, 'BofA ML Sterling Corporate BBB Index' (8 July 2011).

4. INFLATION

The *fixed* income returns of fixed interest assets make these unattractive investments in an inflationary environment because inflation will mean two things:

1. The income from the bond's coupon (the interest return) which is fixed from the outset will be eroded by rising inflation.
2. The real value of the capital repayment when the bond reaches maturity will be less. The longer the term of the bond, the more vulnerable the investment is to inflation. For example, the impact of inflation at 3% on a £100 bond over periods of one year, five years, ten years and 20 years are shown in Table 5.9.

Table 5.9 – the impact of 3% inflation on a £100 bond maturity repayment over varying time frames

Years	Worth of capital (£)
1	97
5	86
10	74
20	54

As you can see from the table, inflation at 3% over 20 years would reduce the spending power of £100 by almost 50%. This means that if a £100 bond matures after 20 years of 3% inflation the £100 you invested in the bond will only be worth half what it was when you originally bought the bond.

Inflation expectations and the price of fixed-interest investments

Inflation expectations also have a direct impact on the prices of bonds. If inflation is expected to increase, the attractiveness of bonds as an income-generating investment will diminish (as the real value of the interest return will fall) and, in response, bond prices will fall.

If inflation rates are expected to fall, the fixed returns from bonds will become relatively more attractive and prices will increase.

Mitigating the risk of inflation with an index-linked purchase

Investing in index-linked gilts, where the interest payments adjust in line with the Retail Prices Index (RPI), is one way of mitigating the risk of inflation. An index-linked bond will ensure your income is over and above inflation.

When deciding the merits of buying an index-linked gilt you will have to balance the merit of an index-linked bond paying, say, 2% over inflation, with the yield offered by a normal bond investment. The important measure here is the real yield, which is the return over and above RPI inflation between the bond's purchase date and its maturity, and which is dependent on the current market price of the bond.

The *Financial Times* publishes daily tables for bonds which provide a quick way to compare the returns offered by index-linked gilts and those of conventional bonds, saving you the need to make a complex calculation. In the table entitled 'Bonds – index-linked', the column 'Break even inflation' provides the inflation rate required for the index-linked gilt to break even with conventional gilts.

Table 5.10 provides a sample of one of the *FT*'s bond tables showing the break even inflation column. If you expect inflation to exceed this level over the life of the bond, it would make more sense to buy conventional gilts.

Table 5.10 – sample index-linked bond table

Bond	Price March 17	Yield March 17	Yield March 16	Month return	Break even inflation
UK 2.5% '16	318.37	-0.32	-0.37	0.56	2.93
UK 2.5% '24	284.05	0.69	0.67	0.48	3.25
US 2% '35	166.42	0.72	0.71	0.54	3.59
US 3% '12	107.41	-2.45	-2.38	0.82	2.81
US 3.625% '28	130.95	1.55	1.56	2.76	2.54

Source: *Financial Times*

Index-linked gilts should be avoided when deflation is a possibility as the inflation adjustment factor can work both ways, which means deflation will reduce interest payments on the gilt.

Inflation-linked bond funds

An inflation-linked bond fund which invests in a spread of different inflation-linked corporate bonds is another bond investment choice which can help shield your portfolio against the risk of inflation. Bear in mind though that the yield on a bond fund is not predetermined and will fluctuate depending on changes to the fund's holdings and investment process. Fund charges can also have a significant impact on the income return (see chapter 7).

Deflation and fixed-interest investments

The impact of a deflationary environment on bonds is slightly more complicated. In the case of government bonds (gilts), deflation can be a positive for a number of reasons.

First, the prospect of falling prices means that the fixed nominal income offered by gilts becomes more attractive. Second, deflation is associated with a recessionary environment, under which conditions investors might move from higher-risk assets to lower-risk assets, meaning a switch from shares to gilts, and so an increase in gilt prices.

Finally, central banks tend to fight deflation by printing money (see the note on *quantitative easing* on page 44 for more detail on this) which is typically facilitated by central banks buying government bonds, which raises their price. There is, however, one important caveat to this. By raising the price of its bonds, it becomes harder for the government to repay its future debts. This would be detrimental for gilts if it leads to concerns that the government might default on its debt obligations.

For corporate bonds, deflation is bad news. When prices fall, company revenues usually follow suit, making it harder for companies to repay their debts. Markets might therefore fear default, causing bond prices to fall.

HIGHER-RISK INCOME INVESTMENTS

It has been said that no one ever became a millionaire by leaving their money in a savings account. The same could probably be said for fixed-interest investments such as bonds or gilts, unless of course you have a lot of capital to start off with.

Savings accounts and bonds might be a good way of securing a consistent, low-risk income stream, but generally the income from these investments will be moderate. Remember the risk versus reward trade-off: the less risky an asset class, the smaller the income reward it is likely to generate.

In these chapters we will look at adding risk to your investment portfolio by investing in equities, funds and property. These assets sit at the riskier end of the risk versus reward spectrum – so while you will be adding risk to your income portfolio, you will also magnify your chance of higher income returns. We will start with equities, an asset class which over the last 100 years has outperformed every cash and fixed-interest investment.[18]

[18] Sreekala Kochugovindan, 'UK asset returns since 1899', Barclays Equity Gilt Study (2010), pp. 36-40.

6

EQUITIES

Income from equities

An equity investment represents ownership of part of a company in the form of company shares. The investment return from share ownership is twofold: it comes from income, in the form of dividends, and capital growth, in the form of an increase in your original capital investment caused by movements in the company's share price. Our concern is mainly with the income part of a share's return, thus the dividends equities pay to shareholders.

There is always a gap between the selling price and the buying price of shares. The former is known as the bid price and is always lower than the latter, known as the offer price. The difference between them is known as the bid-offer spread. Market makers – stock brokers that buy and sell shares in specific companies – make their profit from this spread, buying shares at the bid price and selling them at the offer price.

From an investor's point of view the spread should be viewed as an extra cost and the tighter the spread (i.e. the smaller the difference between the bid and offer price) the more profitable the investment. Spreads are generally only important to those who actively trade shares and want to make profits on the stock market within hours or days – they are of less concern to the long-term income investor.

Dividends

The main aim of any company is to make a profit and any profits made after costs and tax belong to the company's shareholders. Of course, the company also needs to invest some of its profits back into the business to further growth and expansion and so a balance has to be struck between paying dividends and reinvesting profits.

As a general rule, large, established companies known as blue chip companies and their shares, blue chips, tend to pay dividends to shareholders. Smaller companies usually choose to reinvest profits to maintain and expand their business.

Companies which pay dividends tend to do so twice yearly while a few pay quarterly dividends, but this does vary from one company to the next. Dividends are normally declared as part of a company's half-yearly and annual performance results, which tell you the dividend that will be paid per share owned and the date on which it will be paid. By way of example, Table 6.1 lists some companies and dividends they paid in 2011.

Table 6.1 – a selection of companies and their dividends paid

Company	Frequency of dividend payments	Latest dividend paid per share (p)	Date paid
Vodafone	Twice a year	6.05	05/08/2011
Diageo	Twice a year	15.5	06/04/2011
Marks & Spencer	Twice a year	10.8	15/07/2011
GlaxoSmithKline	Quarterly	16	07/07/2011
BAT	Twice a year	81	05/05/2011

Source: Respective company websites & accounts

As you can see from Table 6.1, some companies pay a higher dividend than others. The dividend in isolation however does not tell us much about the income delivered by a company. Rather the income investor should look at the yield the share provides.

Yield

In terms of equities, we need to consider three important measures, all of which are indicative of the income generated by this asset class. These three are:

1. Dividend yield.
2. Dividend payout ratio.
3. Dividend cover.

1. DIVIDEND YIELD

The individuals or institutions that have invested capital in a company in return for shares – the company's shareholders – receive a share of that company's profits in the form of dividend payments at certain intervals throughout the trading year.

The measure of how much income investors receive for every pound they have invested in a company share is called the dividend yield. It is expressed as a percentage and the higher the dividend yield, the better the income return from the equity investment.

Dividend yield is calculated by taking the dividend per share a company pays and dividing it by the price the shares are trading at. This figure is then multiplied by 100 to convert the decimal to a percentage.

```
dividend yield = (dividend per share/price per share) x 100
```

If the dividend is £1 and the share trades at £25 per share, then the dividend yield calculation will be:

```
(£1.00/£25 x 100) = 4%
```

So, the dividend yield in this situation is 4%. This means the investor is getting 4p in dividends for every pound they have invested in the company.

How dividend yield is used

Dividend yield is widely used both by the financial press and within the investment community, largely due to the relative ease of calculation. It should be used with care though as it is only one component of equity returns. It can be useful as a yardstick to compare the income returns from shares across sectors and different markets, and with investments in other asset classes, but it does not necessarily give any indication of the income a company will pay to shareholders in the future.

Further, while some dividend yield calculations are based on the latest annual dividend paid (historic dividend yield), others are based on the dividend which is expected to be paid in the current year (prospective dividend yield). Since dividends can vary from one year to the next, a calculation based on the latest dividend paid may vary from a yield calculation based on the expected dividend in the future.

It is therefore important to make sure you know which basis has been used to calculate the dividend yield figures – especially if you are planning to compare companies based on their dividend yield.

Finally, remember that high dividend yields are not the be-all and end-all. It can be the case that companies with very high dividend yields are doing so not because the dividend increased but rather because the share price has collapsed. This could mean the company is likely to be facing financial problems and may in the near future be unable to afford to pay any dividend. Dividends are paid out of cash from the company's earnings so make sure you have a good idea of a company's capital and capital growth so that you can determine whether the current dividend yield is sustainable. Dividends and capital growth are not mutually exclusive – the two go hand in hand and sustainable capital growth will be the engine of a company's future dividend payments.

2. DIVIDEND PAYOUT RATIO

The *dividend payout ratio* measures what proportion of a company's earnings have been distributed by way of dividends. This is calculated by dividing the dividends paid by the company's net income in the period, and then multiplying this by 100 to convert this to a percentage:

```
dividend payout ratio = (dividends/net income) x 100
```

So if a company paid out £10m in annual dividends and had £30m net income, the dividend payout ratio will be:

```
(£10m/£30m) x 100 = 33%
```

This means one-third of the company's net income has been paid out as dividends.

At its simplest the dividend payout ratio shows how many times bigger a company's earnings are than its dividend commitments. The higher the dividend payout ratio, the less profits are invested back into the company to create future growth, and the greater the percentage profits paid to shareholders.

It is difficult to assess whether a dividend payout ratio is good or bad by looking at this measure in isolation. The dividend payout ratio needs to be viewed in context of the size and type of company as well as the industry or sector in which the company operates. Small companies will retain more of their profits to fund growth and will therefore pay lower dividends while bigger, more mature companies with little further room to grow tend to pay higher dividends.

The most important thing to assess is whether the dividend payout is sustainable – there's no point investing in a company with a high payout ratio if the company goes bust soon after because it did not reinvest enough of its profits or did not have sufficient earnings to pay the dividend. To help you make this assessment you can use the *dividend cover*.

3. DIVIDEND COVER

The *dividend cover* measures how many times the dividend paid by a company is covered by the earnings of the company and it therefore tells you how sustainable a company's dividend is. Dividend cover is calculated by taking the earnings per share (EPS) and dividing this by the dividend per share.

Earnings per share indicates how much profit a company has made for each of its shares. It is calculated by dividing the net income by the number of shares held by investors, as follows:

```
earnings per share = net income/number of shares outstanding
```

Dividend cover is then calculated as follows:

```
dividend cover = earnings per share/dividend per share
```

If, for example, the company has a net income of £100m, 10m shares in issue and pays a dividend of £5 per share, its earnings per share is £10 (100/10) and the dividend cover will be:

```
10/5 = 2
```

This dividend cover of 2 means the dividend could have been paid twice over out of the company's earnings.

Generally, dividend cover of 2 or higher is regarded as reasonably safe in the sense that the company can well afford to pay the dividend, while cover of 1.5 or below means the company requires closer scrutiny.

A company should never be paying out more than 100% of its earnings as dividends. If the dividend cover is below 1, alarm bells should start ringing. This means the company does not have enough profits to pay its dividends and so it is borrowing money to pay shareholders a dividend – such a situation is obviously not sustainable over the long term.

The higher the dividend cover, the better the company's ability to maintain dividends should profits fall in the future. A good track record of a high dividend cover means the company will have retained earnings over time to maintain or expand its business – it can potentially pay dividends from these retained profits in years when profits are low, maintaining its dividend payout level.

Cash flow

While the dividend cover is an important measure, it is worth remembering that companies tend to pay dividends out of their cash flow rather than their earnings. So a company's cash flow – its income less expenditures – can at times be a more accurate reflection of its ability to pay a dividend. The simplest test will be to establish whether a company will cover its dividend payments with the flows of cash through the business. High quality companies that are industry leaders, boast high profitability, conservative financials and management leadership tend to be those companies with the most robust cash flows.

HOW TO USE DIVIDEND YIELD AND DIVIDEND COVER TOGETHER

Using dividend yield and dividend cover together is important for the income investor because you are looking for companies that offer a good and sustainable dividend yield. By using dividend yield and dividend cover together you can make an assessment about whether a company would make a good income investment.

For example, if you are weighing up the shares of two companies, BT with a dividend yield of 3.5% and Barclays with a dividend yield of 2%, you may at first be attracted to BT as it is paying a higher income for each pound you have invested. However, further scrutiny of the figures in Table 6.2 is needed.

Table 6.2 – earnings per share, dividend and dividend yield for two companies

Company	Earnings per share	Dividend	Dividend yield
BT	13.3	5.5	3.5
Barclays	30.4	6.9	2

Source: Respective company websites & accounts

Using the companies' earnings per share figures we can calculate that BT has a dividend cover of 2.42 (13.3/5.5) and Barclays has a dividend cover of 4.4 (30.4/6.9); this means Barclays may provide a more sustainable return for the long term. This is a situation you would have to monitor regularly once you have invested in a company's shares.

HIGH-YIELDING SHARES

Shares are often classified by the level of dividend yield they deliver. Those which generate a high dividend yield, typically 4% plus, are described as income shares, while those with smaller yields of less than 2%, and where a larger proportion of the company's profits are usually reinvested to help future growth, are known as growth shares.

Income shares and growth shares can both be used to produce income but, as a general rule, for the income investor, high-yielding companies are sought and shares will typically be picked for their dividend yield.[19]

There are a number of income-related advantages to dividend-yielding shares. When your income comes from dividends this is money that can be used right away to pay bills, invest in other instruments or increase your shareholding by reinvesting the income to buy more shares.

Also, an income investor does not necessarily have to be alarmed if the share price of an income-yielding company falls. The fact that your income is drawn from dividends rather than expected capital growth means you can keep drawing your income as a company's share price fluctuates, as long as the company maintains its dividend payments over the long term.

This point about the long term is significant: if you're looking for a decent income return from equities, the asset class is best viewed as an investment to hold across a long time frame. We will look at the importance of this in more detail next.

[19] Jordan Goodman, *Fast Profits in Hard Times* (Business Plus, 2008).

Invest for the long term

No risk, no return is probably the phrase which best describes the stock markets. For speculative investors the temperamental nature of equities is one of the asset class's attractions as it can mean lucrative gains, provided you get your timing right. But for those looking for consistent, secure income returns, the volatility of shares can be a huge frustration. Unlike cash or fixed-interest investments, equities come with no assurance of a consistent level of income. This volatility and uncertainty of income means equities are best suited to investors who can stomach the risk and are investing for the long run.

Over a long time horizon, the ups and downs in a company's share price can be evened out and usually the return from equities will outstrip that of cash or fixed-interest investments.

The Barclays Capital Equity Gilt Study of 2011 supports this view. Looking at the real returns of asset classes over various time horizons, it shows equities to be the worst performing asset over the decade running to 2010, producing a meagre inflation-adjusted return of just 0.6 %, compared to 2.4% for gilts.

But examining returns over various holding periods, the study found the variance of equity returns to fall significantly in relation to other asset classes as the holding period is extended. When equities are held for as long as 20 years the minimum return is greater than for either gilts or cash.

Tables 6.3 and 6.4 show respectively the performance of equities against cash and gilts for different holding periods. The first column of Table 6.3 shows that over a holding period of two years, equities outperformed cash in 73 out of 110 years – thus the probability of equity outperformance is 66%. If the holding period is extended to ten years this rises to 90%.

Table 6.3 – the relative performance of cash and equities with investments held over various numbers of years

Number of consecutive years	2	3	4	5	10	18
Outperform cash in x years	73	75	78	80	92	93
Underperform cash in x years	37	34	30	27	10	1
Total number of years	110	109	108	107	102	94
Probability of equity outperformance	66%	69%	72%	75%	90%	99%

Source: Barclays Equity Gilt Study 2011

Similarly, Table 6.4 shows that equities have been found to outperform gilts the longer the investment is held.

Table 6.4 – the relative performance of gilts and equities with investments held over various numbers of years

Number of consecutive years	2	3	4	5	10	18
Outperform gilts in x years	76	81	82	80	81	84
Underperform gilts in x years	34	28	26	27	21	10
Total number of years	110	109	108	107	102	94
Probability of equity outperformance	69%	74%	76%	75%	79%	89%

Source: Barclays Equity Gilt Study 2011

Beyond having a long-term investing horizon, the key to unlocking the long-term income potential of equities lies in reinvesting income returns.

REINVESTING INCOME FROM SHARES

When investing in asset classes such as equities or fixed interest, the equivalent of compound interest (see pages 29 to 32) is reinvesting the dividends earned on share holdings or the income payments from bonds back into your original investment.

In a similar fashion to compound interest, reinvested dividends can significantly grow your original capital investment, making a difference to your investment's total return over the long term. If the asset class you are reinvesting in performs well, increasing its return over time, the effect of reinvested income is magnified even more.

The annual Barclays Capital Equity Gilt Study looks at the effects of reinvested dividends and has consistently found the reinvestment of dividend income to be the biggest contributor to an investor's return over the long term. The 2011 study found that £100 invested in UK equities in 1945 would have been worth £7932 in 2011 in nominal terms, while the same amount invested into gilts would have been worth £53. Table 6.5 shows the results of the study. Nominal refers to the return received without taking account of inflation.

The real return is the return on an investment after inflation has been accounted for.[20]

Table 6.5 – worth in 2011 of £100 invested in 1945

Asset	Nominal terms	Real terms
Equities	£7932	£255
Gilts	£53	£2

Source: Barclays Equity Gilt Study 2011

However, had the dividends earned been reinvested, that same £100 invested in equities in 1945 would have grown to £136,107 by 2011. An investment in gilts with income reinvested would have come to £5565, while the same investment in cash, with interest reinvested, would be £6163. Table 6.6 shows these results.

Table 6.6 – worth in 2011 of £100 invested in 1945, with income reinvested

Asset	Nominal terms	Real terms
Equities	£136,107	£4370
Gilts	£5565	£179
Cash	£6163	£198

Source: Barclays Equity Gilt Study 2011

Ploughing back your income, whether by compounding interest or reinvesting dividends, is a powerful investment strategy and utilising this can have a significant impact on your income over the long term.

Further evidence of this is provided by figures from Fidelity which show that an investor who had invested £10,000 in the FTSE All-Share index at the end of 1985 and left it there until February 2011 would have seen their initial

[20] Kochugovindan, 'UK asset returns since 1899', pp. 36-40.

investment grow by almost £68,000 more if they reinvested income than if they did not reinvest income. Figure 6.1 provides an illustration of this situation.

Figure 6.1 – the difference reinvesting your income payments can make to performance

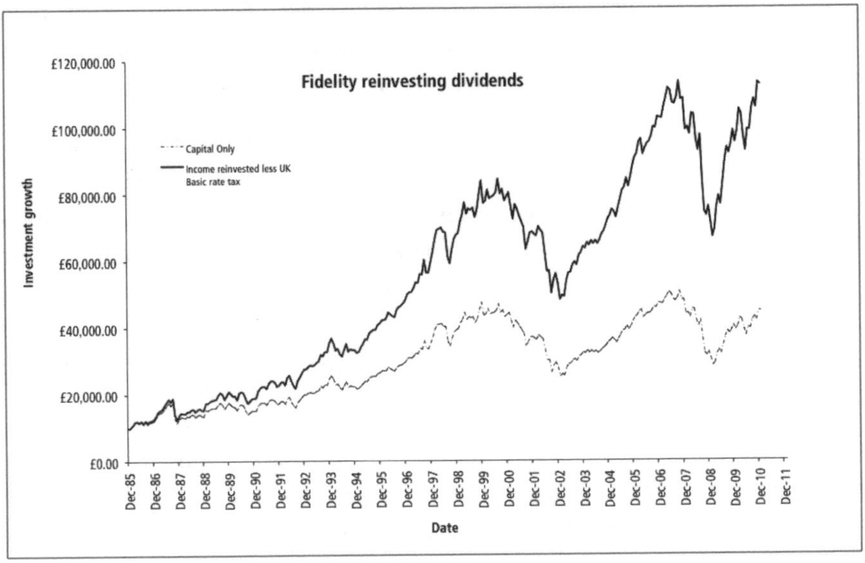

Source: Fidelity using Morningstar figures from 1/01/1986 to 01/02/2011

The most common way for investors to reinvest income from shares is through a *dividend reinvestment plan.*

Dividend reinvestment plans

Dividend reinvestment plans (DRIPS) are offered by companies directly to shareholders or can be accessed via most stockbrokers, who may levy a charge for administering the reinvestment. DRIPS allow you to use share dividends to buy more shares, thereby growing your initial investment.

Let's take an example: Jack Frost owns 1000 shares of Vodafone. The share currently trades at £20 per share and the annual dividend is 0.40p per share. The twice-yearly dividend has just been paid (40p divided by two payments a year is equal to a 20p per share twice yearly dividend).

Before he enrolled in Vodafone's dividend reinvestment plan, Jack would have received a cash deposit of £200 (1000 shares x 20p) in his brokerage account twice a year. However, as he has enrolled in the DRIP he will log into his account online and find that he now has 1010 shares of Vodafone. The £200 dividend that was owed to him was reinvested in whole in more shares of the company at £20 per share.

The next time the dividend is paid, Jack will be owed £202 (1010 shares held x 20p per share dividend) in dividends. This is a small increase in dividends for the year, but over time this will become significant.

A DRIP enables you to invest small amounts of money over time, which can be a more affordable strategy than buying all at once for a lump sum. It also allows you to benefit from *pound cost averaging*, a strategy through which stock market fluctuations are mitigated by regularly investing similar amounts, rather than a one-off large sum, thus minimising the risk of investing at the wrong time such as just before a market downturn (when share prices will fall). Most DRIPS only require a small initial investment amount and charge reasonable fees.

With DRIPS, your dividends are directly reinvested in the underlying equity, which means you benefit from capital appreciation without having to pay unnecessary brokerage fees. Remember, though, that ploughing your dividends back into shares won't exempt you from paying tax on the income reinvested (unless your investment is held within a tax exempt wrapper).

* * *

In summary: income investors are looking for (1) high-yielding shares that are likely to (2) maintain their dividend payments over the long term, and should ideally be looking to (3) reinvest income from these shares.

One problem income investors are faced with is that the number of companies in the UK that pay dividends has become increasingly concentrated. A situation that only became worse following the dividend cuts of 2009 and 2010.

Let's look at the issues of dividend cuts and dividend concentration in more detail.

DIVIDEND CUTS

A company under financial pressure may be forced to cut its dividend in order to save cash. This will reduce the income investors receive from equity investments. The story of how companies did just this in the wake of the 2007-2009 global recession is provided below.

Generally though a company will do everything in its power not cut its dividend[21] – as author Rodney Hobson points out: "cutting the dividend carries a certain degree of opprobrium for directors, carrying as it does an unspoken implication that they have not done their job properly."[22]

Even so, sometimes a cut is inevitable. The most telltale sign of a possible dividend cut is when a share's yield reaches a level far outside anything in the company's history. If a share offer yields far in excess of the market yield this could also be indicative that the company is likely either to cut its dividend or grow it at a slower rate than its peers.[23] Other reasons why a company may decide to cut its dividend include the inability of earnings to support the dividend rate over the long term or the need to service new debt from profits rather than paying out profits to shareholders.[24]

The banks, BP and the slashing of dividends

In the aftermath of the 2007-2009 global financial crisis, cutting bank interest rates was seen as mandatory in order to get economies back on the move and help mend bank's broken balance sheets. But it wasn't only interest rates that got cut. Many companies saw their profits plummet and as a result were forced to suspend their dividend payments to shareholders. Banks, not surprisingly, were the worst hit.

Given the reluctance of companies to cut dividends, the majority of dividend reductions only fed through in 2009. According to the Capita Registrar UK Dividend Monitor, which analyses data on every dividend paid in the British market, UK companies slashed dividends by £8.7bn in 2009, paying out 13%

---

[21] Rodney Hobson, *How to Build a Share Portfolio* (Harriman House, 2011), p. 99.

[22] Hobson, *Share Portfolio*, p .111.

[23] A. Spare and P. Ciotti, *Relative Dividend Yield* (John Wiley & Sons, 1999).

[24] According to authors Anthony Spare and Paul Ciotti.

less to shareholders than they did in 2008. A staggering 202 companies cut payouts.

The majority of cuts came from the banking sector, which halved its share of UK dividends, accounting for more than £6bn of the total fall in dividends witnessed in 2009. Prior to these dividend cuts, banks had been regarded as the bedrock of dividends in the UK and the large-scale cutting of dividends left many income investors with severely deflated payouts.

Investing in equities is high risk and in 2010 BP shares proved this truth. A much publicised oil spill in the Gulf of Mexico saw the oil giant's profits fall dramatically and subsequently BP cancelled £5.4bn in dividends.

This cancellation of dividends by BP was a hard blow for income investors. After the large scale dividend cuts by banks, BP had become the biggest dividend payer in the UK market, accounting for approximately £1 in every £6 of dividends paid in 2009. Had BP not cut its dividend in 2010, dividends in the UK would have risen by 7.5% rather than falling another 3.3% in 2010. Figure 6.2 illustrates the fall in UK dividends between 2008 and 2010.

Figure 6.2 – the fall in UK dividends from 2008 to 2010

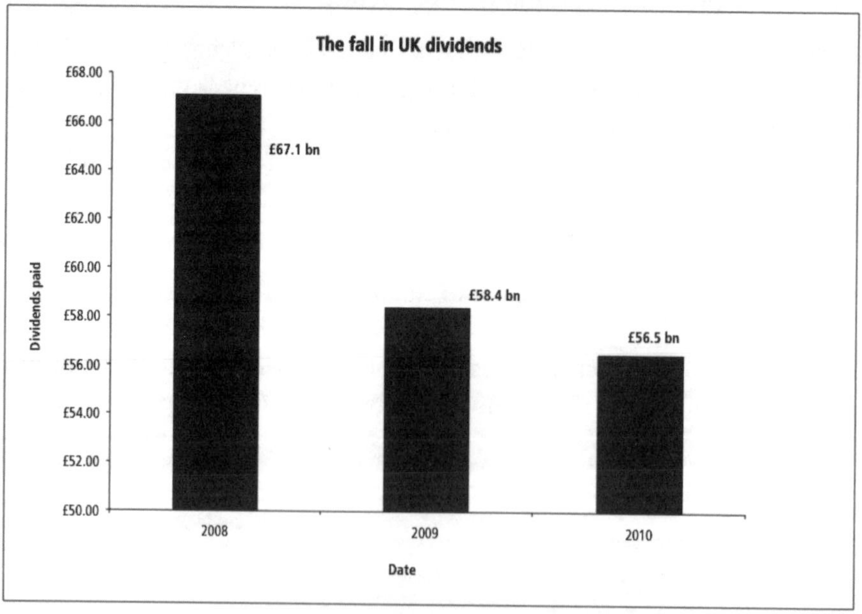

Source: Capita Registrars Dividend Monitor 2009 & 2010

DIVIDEND CONCENTRATION

The dividend cuts of 2008 and 2009 has not helped the problem of dividend concentration in the UK – many UK income investors are investing in the same companies that dominate the dividend scene. This concentration of dividend-paying companies arises because the FTSE 100 index – the index of the 100 largest UK companies listed on the London Stock Exchange – produces around 90% of the UK's total dividends.

Within the FTSE 100 there are only a few companies which contribute the bulk of UK dividends. According to figures from Capita Registrars, five companies – BP, Royal Dutch Shell, HSBC, Vodafone and GlaxoSmithKline – contributed almost half (46%) of all dividends in the UK market in 2009. At a sector level, oil and gas companies made up almost one-third of the total dividends paid in 2009 – most of this coming from just two companies: BP and Shell.

This concentration of dividend payers makes it increasingly difficult for investors to adequately diversify their income portfolio across a number of dividend-paying companies. Table 6.7 shows how the UK's largest companies make up a large proportion of all dividends paid – companies are ranked according to the company that paid the highest proportion of the total UK dividends.

Table 6.7 – the increasingly concentrated nature of UK dividends

Rank	2007	2008	2009	2010
1	HSBC Holdings	HSBC Holdings	BP	Royal Dutch Shell
2	Royal Dutch Shell	BP	Royal Dutch Shell	Vodafone
3	BP	Royal Dutch Shell	HSBC Holdings	HSBC Holdings
4	Vodafone	Vodafone	Vodafone	GlaxoSmithKline
5	GlaxoSmithKline	GlaxoSmithKline	GlaxoSmithKline	AstraZeneca
Total paid by top five companies	**£21.8bn**	**£25.0bn**	**£26.9bn**	**£21.7bn**
Proportion of total dividends (%)	**35%**	**37%**	**46%**	**38%**
6	Barclays	Barclays	AstraZeneca	British American Tobacco
7	Lloyds Banking Group	Lloyds Banking Group	British American Tobacco	BP
8	HBOS	British American Tobacco	BHP Billiton	BHP Billiton
9	AstraZeneca	AstraZeneca	Tesco	Tesco
10	BT Group	BT Group	Diageo	National Grid
11	British American Tobacco	Reed Elsevier	National Grid	Standard Chartered
12	Aviva	Aviva	Unilever	Diageo
13	Diageo	Tesco	Standard Chartered	Unilever
14	Tesco	Anglo American	Aviva	Imperial Tobacco Group
15	Royal Bank of Scotland Group	Diageo	Imperial Tobacco Group	Reckitt Benckiser Group
Total paid by top 15 companies	**£35.7bn**	**£39.4bn**	**£39.0bn**	**£34.4bn**
Proportion of total dividends (%)	**57%**	**58%**	**66%**	**61%**

Source: Capita Registrars

As you can see, in 2010 the top five dividend paying companies paid more than one-third of the total UK dividends. It would be difficult for an income investor to avoid investing in these companies if they are realistically looking to draw an income from UK-listed investments.

The problem of dividend concentration also affects managers of collective investment funds who are increasingly investing in the same shares. This issue, referred to as *dividend clustering*, is discussed in chapter 7.

SHARES IN SMALL COMPANIES

The shares of small companies, referred to as small-caps, are generally regarded as growth or value investments – investors buy these shares in the hope that their share price will grow enabling them to eventually be sold at a profit or capital gain.

However, with many large cap companies disappointing on dividend payouts following the 2007-2009 financial crisis, investors have looked for income from other sources, with small and mid-size companies that are committed to progressive dividend payments being one option. As with large company shares, not all of these small companies are guaranteed to maintain dividend payouts and the majority may not pay a dividend at all given their focus on capital growth.

If you're looking to invest in small companies the places to look include the FTSE 250 index, the FTSE Small Cap index, the FTSE Fledgling index and the Alternative Investment Market (AIM), which lists the shares of small companies that either cannot afford, or do not qualify, to list on the London Stock Exchange's Main Market.

The risks of small company shares

The risk of problems preventing dividend payouts tends to be higher with small companies, as these are less diversified and therefore have a greater chance of experiencing financial hardship if economic conditions deteriorate. A small company tends to be focused on one sector, and may have fewer clients and customers. If a client goes under or cancels a contract with the company, it can seriously damage profits and thwart dividend payouts.

Low liquidity is also a major risk with small company shares. These shares are less traded than shares in companies on the Main Market and this can mean that you won't always be able to buy or sell small-cap shares when you want to. Of course if you are planning to hold on to the shares for the long term, as an income investor should, then this will be less of an issue.

What to look for in small company shares

The same rules apply when evaluating the income paying credentials of a smaller company as for a large company: look for companies with strong and consistent earnings growth, solid cash flows and low debts on their balance sheets, a good level of cover on their dividend payments and a history of growing dividend payments. Also, make sure you diversify your holdings – a small-cap investment fund with an experienced manager at the helm is a good way of spreading the risk.

Renowned small cap fund manager, Gervais Williams who joined the fund management group, MAM Funds at the start of 2011, has long since been advocating an income-orientated approach within the small cap space. The group's Diverse Income Fund specifically targets small companies with decent dividend yields and those that have the ability to grow their dividend payouts.

Another option is the closed-ended Acorn Income Fund, which uses a conservative, low risk approach to identify small companies that have an attractive dividend.

Factors to consider when investing in equities for income

Equities are volatile, high-risk investments with the reality that swings in the stock market can wipe out savings in the blink of an eye. However, as already mentioned, over the long term investing in income-paying equities, and reinvesting income, has proven to be the most reliable way to grow returns. Other factors likely to influence the capability of a given equity investment to deliver and maintain income include:

1. Dividend yield
2. Dividend growth
3. Balance sheets and debt
4. The price paid for the share
5. Interest rates
6. Inflation

1. DIVIDEND YIELD

As the dividend yield of a share is an historic figure, evaluating a company's likelihood of paying an income in the future involves more than just looking at the figure for the last year. There are a number of factors to consider and the checklist below will provide a good starting point in assessing the income paying capabilities of a company:

- Does the company have a progressive dividend policy? In other words, does it intend to maintain or grow dividends in future?
- Are the company fundamentals, such as its cash flow and balance sheets, secure?
- Do earnings in the current year cover the dividend payout (this can be calculated using the dividend cover)?

The best place to look for this type of information is in the company's annual reporting accounts. These will be available on the company's website or from Companies House, the official UK government register of UK companies (**www.companieshouse.gov.uk**). Make sure you look at the company's five-year record in order to make a proper assessment of the above factors.

It is important to examine whether dividends have been maintained over a period of years. For example, say Company A's share price is 100p and it pays a dividend of 3p in year 1 (so its dividend yield is 3p/100p = 3%). Then in year 5 its share price is 200p and it pays a dividend of 6p (again dividend yield is 3%). In this case the company is maintaining the dividend yield at 3%. If the share price has risen to 500p in year 10 and the company pays a dividend of 12p this might look good at first glance as the dividend paid is higher than in previous years but in fact the dividend yield has dropped to 2.4% (500p/12p) so the share is offering a less significant return for investors.

Check the ex-dividend date

When evaluating the income paying capabilities of a company it is also important to take note of the company's ex-dividend date. This is the date on or after which the shareholder would not be entitled to receive a recently declared dividend. In other words, once the shares go ex-dividend they are traded minus the right to collect a dividend.

If you buy company shares on/after the ex-dividend date, you will receive a lower income for that quarter or half year and will have to wait until the next dividend is paid to receive an income. This loss of dividend may be somewhat mitigated by the fact that shares trading after the ex-dividend date tend to be cheaper by the amount of dividend lost.

One way of checking a company's ex-dividend date is via the share service pages in the *Financial Times*, although not all companies are included in this list.

2. DIVIDEND GROWTH

Over the long term, a company that grows its dividend consistently can provide more income than a company that delivers a high yield that grows slowly. This is illustrated by Table 6.8 which shows how a company that has a relatively low but fast-growing dividend can outstrip a company with a high initial dividend that only grows slowly.

In Table 6.8, Company A increases dividends at 30% a year, while company B starts with a high yield but grows it more slowly, at 5%. Over ten years company A has delivered a higher yield by consistently growing its dividend than company B which started with a high yield.

Table 6.8 – comparing the yield delivered by a companies that grow dividends at different rates

Year	Company A consistently growing its dividends (p)	Company B delivering a high initial yield (p)
1	3	6
2	3.9	6.3
3	5.1	6.6
4	6.6	6.9
5	8.6	7.3
6	11.1	7.7
7	14.5	8
8	18.8	8.4
9	24.5	8.9
10	31.8	9.3
Total	**127.9**	**75.5**

Source: Nick Louth, *Investors Chronicle*, 3-9 September 2010, Volume 173/2206, pp. 19.

Further, a company with a track record of continually growing its dividends will be more focused on maintaining this record and its payout. Hence a history of progressive dividend growth can be a good indication of a company's income paying capabilities and intentions. Companies usually publish a dividend record table on their investor relations website or in their annual reports.

3. BALANCE SHEETS AND DEBT

The company books are an important factor in assessing the likelihood of a dividend payment being made and maintained over the long run. Companies that boast strong financials and sound balance sheets are generally in a better position to deliver a progressive dividend payout. Strong cash flows, the lifeblood of any business, can help cover dividend payments in the leaner years.

Companies that have high, unmanageable levels of debt should be approached very carefully. Also remember that an indebted firm which goes bust is first obliged to repay banks and bond holders before it can commit to delivering a dividend payment.

The balance sheets of a company are also important if you're concerned about inflation impacting your income return. In an inflationary environment, it is wise to avoid investing in a heavily indebted firm with poor cash flows. Companies better positioned to survive an inflation spike are those with a strong business franchise and brand.

4. THE PRICE PAID FOR THE SHARE

When investing in shares it is important to separate yourself from what's happening in the broader economy and focus on how much you are willing to pay for a given share.

The ten years from 2000 to 2010 are often described as the lost decade for equities, due to the paltry returns generated by this asset class in the period. A good reference to this is the Barclays Capital Equity Gilt Study (2011) which found that the real return from equities stood at a dismal 0.6% for the period 2000 to 2010, compared to a return of 2.4% for gilts (refer back to chapter 5, page 87 for the note on when gilts beat equities).

Many are left puzzled as to why equities performed so poorly over a time frame when the UK was enjoying relatively strong macroeconomic growth and strong corporate profit growth, as shown in Table 6.9.

Table 6.9 – UK macroeconomic growth and corporate profit growth, 2000 to 2010

	2000	2001	2002	2003	2004	2005	2006	2007	2008	2009	2010
GDP growth (%)*	3.9	2.5	2.1	2.8	3	2.2	2.8	2.7	-0.1	-4.9	1.9
Corporate profit growth (%)**		3.4	-18.6	12	21.6	29.8	27.7	12.7	-10	-35.3	5

Source: UBS, 31 August 2010

*As at December each year.

**As at August each year.

The reason for this anomaly could lie in how much investors paid for equities between 2000 and 2010, as reflected in the price-to-earnings (P/E) ratio of the shares purchased. The P/E ratio is used to value a share – a higher P/E ratio means investors are willing to pay more for each unit of income earned by the company per share. It means the shares are more expensive compared to a company on a lower P/E multiple. The P/E ratio is calculated by taking the price of a share and dividing this by its earnings.

price-to-earnings ratio = share price/earnings per share

Thus, if a share is trading at £40 and has earnings per share of £20, the P/E ratio will be 2 (40/20). Here's a simple way to think of the P/E ratio: if a company was to buy all its shares back, the P/E ratio will be the number of years worth of earnings it would take. So for a company on a P/E ratio of 2, it will take two years to pay for itself, while a company on a P/E ratio of 20 will take 20 years to buy its shares back. In other words, the lower the P/E ratio the cheaper the investment.

Generally, companies on a low P/E ratio tend to be those out of favour and not at the top of investor's buying lists while high P/E ratios mean investors are expecting superior earnings growth from the company in the future. Of course, this does not mean a company will necessarily deliver the higher growth promised by its P/E ratio. When assessing companies, it is important to compare a company's P/E ratio to that of other companies in the sector as well as to the broader market to make sure you are not paying too much for your equity investment.

The starting P/E multiple of a share, rather than its predicted profit growth, can be one of the best determinants of a share's future returns. Investing in out of favour sectors – those with a low P/E multiple – can lead to strong income returns. To find such investments, you need to compare a company's current P/E ratio to its historical P/E multiples and also have a look at the broader market's multiples. This method of investing is known as value investing – finding shares that are trading for less than their intrinsic value – and has been advocated by some of the world's most famous investors such as Warren Buffet and the late Benjamin Graham.

5. INTEREST RATES

The attractiveness of equity investments is inversely related to the interest rate set by a central bank. In an environment of low interest rates, investing in shares become a more attractive option than saving because if, for example, bank interest rates are at 1% an investor may feel that they can beat this return by investing in equities.

Conversely, in a high-interest rate environment – let's say interest rates are at 6% – investors may prefer the relative safety of putting their money into a savings account and securing this 6% return as opposed to taking the risk of investing on the stock market.

In addition, stock markets tend to rise in periods of low interest rates. This is because companies benefit from low interest rates as their borrowing costs become lower while increased spending by consumers (due to saving not being attractive) drives up the demand for goods and services. This increase in demand will boost company profits, which can result in higher share prices and higher dividend payments for investors.

6. INFLATION

There are conflicting views about the impact of inflation on shares. Traditional economic theory suggests that inflation is bad for companies as it devalues future earnings, the major driver of share prices. Inflation also leads to higher interest rates, increased borrowing costs and slower consumer demand – which are all bad news for a company's growth and share price performance.

On the other hand, slightly higher inflation usually implies heightened economic activity, which could see some companies enjoying higher profits leading to higher returns on shares.

The impact of inflation will depend largely on the type of company. At times of high inflation, heavily indebted companies tend to struggle, while those with stable balance sheets and robust business models will be in a stronger position. As a company's input costs will be rising under inflation, it will need to raise its prices in order to preserve profits. *Pricing power* – the ability to compel customers to pay higher prices – is therefore of the utmost importance. Companies with unique products and branding power are usually in a better position to pass on higher costs to customers and are therefore likely to have better pricing power. Nestlé is an example of a company with significant pricing power. It has created a collection of brands that consumers like (KitKat, Shredded Wheat, Nescafé, etc) and because it is the world's largest food manufacturer, benefits from significant scale advantages. This coupled with its ability to innovate and find more efficient production techniques, means that Nestlé is a low cost producer, with good pricing power and a capability to continue growing earnings in times of inflation.

Companies which generate stable earnings despite economic conditions, are labelled as defensive companies, and usually have a better chance of surviving inflationary bouts than cyclical companies, or those reliant on long-term, fixed-price contracts. Defensive companies include pharmaceutical and tobacco companies which enjoy a relatively stable demand – people don't just stop smoking or taking medication if the economic situation deteriorates.

Deflation and equities

The impact of deflation on equities will also depend on the type of company and how indebted its balance sheet is. Deflation raises the real value of company debt which should make investors cautious about investing in heavily indebted companies in deflationary periods.

EQUITIES, RETIREMENT AND THE INCOME IRONY

The demand for income is expected to grow as the baby boomer generation – those born during the post-World War II baby boom era – begin to retire and seek ways to draw an income from their accumulated wealth.

Traditionally those investors in or near retirement might have looked to shift their investment portfolio holdings towards fixed-interest assets as these are lower risk investments that come with the guarantee of a fixed income stream. However, increasing longevity means the average retiree could very well have another 20 to 30 years ahead of them left to live. This has significant ramifications for the income which retirees will need to live off.

For a start, retirees are going to need greater levels of income because they are living longer. The problem with bonds is that they typically only pay a fixed, level income, and over a long retirement even moderate inflation will destroy the purchasing power of a level income. Even moderate inflation of 3% per annum will reduce the real value of your income by almost half over 20 years (see page 103). There is an argument that given a longer life expectancy, retirees can afford to take more investment risk.

So do equities hold the answer to income in retirement? Independent financial adviser, Brian Dennehy, of Dennehy Weller & Co thinks so. He uses the analogy of the human heart to describe the way equities generate income: while a heart changes shape, it continues to consistently pump blood – similarly the price of equities may change shape over time, but most will continue to pump out a dividend. It is true that dividend payouts of equities have tended to be less volatile than share prices over time. Even if profits are volatile, companies will rarely cut dividends and will do everything in their power to avoid a dividend cut.

This situation changed during the 2007-2009 financial downturn but it is important to remember that these were exceptional times. The financial crisis was so severe that many companies decided it was better to hoard cash to ensure their survival than to pay shareholders dividends. The positive flipside of this is that companies' balance sheets have emerged from the crisis in a robust state. At the end of 2010, the Bank of England estimated that two-thirds of companies were holding above normal cash levels.

It could be that the very companies which cut dividends during the financial crisis are the ones most likely to again be paying dividends in coming years. This has been referred to by some investors as the 'income irony of our time': the fact that the most attractive sectors for income in future years might be the very ones which paid no income post-credit crunch.

7

FUNDS

Besides investing in company shares and bonds directly and on your own behalf you can access these investments and tap into the income they provide by investing in collective investments such as funds. Funds are pooled investments that bring together the money of a number of investors; this money is then invested by a skilled manager in a basket of different bonds, shares or other securities, depending on the type of fund. Each investor owns an equity position in the fund and, in effect, its underlying holdings.

As with individual equities, funds can be split into income funds and growth funds. The difference between income funds and other funds is the payment of regular income distributions to fund shareholders. These distributions are considered dividends rather than interest and can be paid monthly, quarterly or twice yearly. In this section we will discuss what types of funds exist, how funds deliver an income for investors and how to go about investing in funds to access this income.

Let's begin by looking at what varieties of funds are available.

The funds universe

There are a large variety of funds, which invest in a range of assets and make use of different investment techniques. As a first point of reference, Figure 7.1 provides a summary illustration of the funds universe.

Figure 7.1 – the funds universe

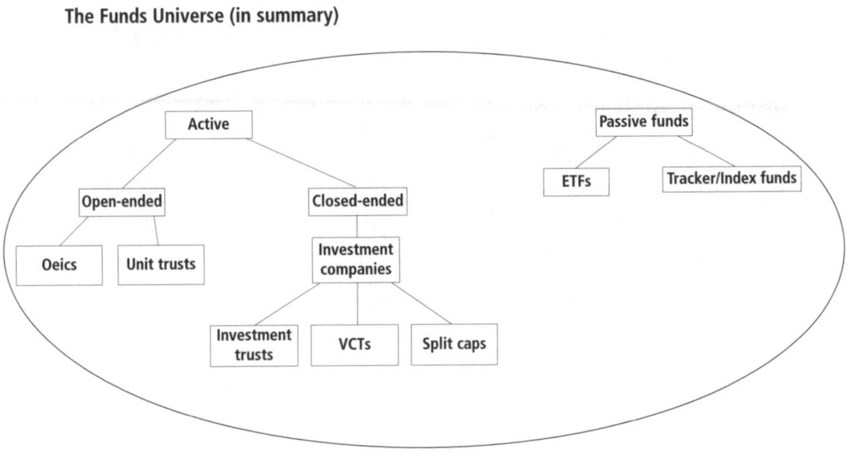

As you can see in Figure 7.1, the first important distinction to make is between passive and active funds.

PASSIVE FUNDS

Passive funds have no manager at the helm making investment decisions. These vehicles simply track the performance of a given market or index using a portfolio of securities selected according to an established criteria. Passive funds are generally competitive in terms of charges compared to active funds because the assets of the fund require less management, which means there is less justification for the fund provider to charge management fees. There is also strong competition among providers of these funds, which helps to keep fees down.

The two main types of passive funds available to private investors are *index funds and exchange-traded funds (ETFs)*:

1. *Index funds*, also known as trackers, have been around for more than 30 years. These funds are designed to track a specific financial market index such as the FTSE 100 or the S&P 500 with the aim of mirroring the performance of that market as closely as possible. If the index rises, so will the tracker, and vice versa. Companies such as Legal & General (L&G) and HSBC are providers of index funds in the UK and boast a broad choice of funds. The entry of US-based asset manager, Vanguard to the UK in early 2009 further increased competition in this space. Vanguard, set-up by famed passive fund investor John Bogle, is renowned for its low fees.
2. *ETFs* are a relatively new development, having only been around since the early 1990s. Similar to index funds, these vehicles track an index, a commodity such as oil or gold, or a basket of assets. The main difference between tracker funds and ETFs is that shares in the latter are traded in a similar way to shares on a stock exchange. The main providers of ETFs in the UK are iShares (part of BlackRock asset management), db X-trackers (Deutsche Bank's ETF platform), Lyxor and HSBC although new players are constantly entering this market.

ACTIVE FUNDS

An *active fund* will have investment decisions actively made by a fund manager or team of managers who base their buy and sell selections on quantitative and qualitative research, meetings with company management and analyst recommendations, among other factors. Actively-managed funds can be split into two groups:

1. Closed-ended funds
2. Open-ended funds

1. Closed-ended funds

A closed-ended fund (also referred to as an investment company or investment trust) issues a set number of shares in an initial public offering (IPO) and these shares trade on a stock exchange like shares in companies. These vehicles are regarded as the original collective investment fund having first been introduced in the UK in 1868 with the launch of the Foreign & Colonial Government Trust, which still exists today as the Foreign & Colonial Investment Trust.

Closed-ended funds were established to help small investors have the same advantage as the large investors, providing them with easy, low-cost access to shares.

A limited pool of shares

Closed-ended funds only issue a limited number of shares that are traded on the open market, as such a fund's share price is affected by supply and demand for the shares in the market as well as the fluctuating value of the fund's underlying investments. As listed vehicles closed-ended funds can suffer volatility similar to shares however because the number of shares are fixed, these funds will not suffer huge redemptions or outflows if demand wanes. This structure enables the fund manager to take a longer-term view of the market as they will not be forced to sell holdings to raise funds to pay for cash outflows when demand falls, which can be the case with open-ended funds where the number of units or shares in issue depend on demand.

Smoothing dividends

Closed-ended funds have another advantage over open-ended funds in that they can retain up to 15% of the income they receive and use this to build up a revenue reserve. It means that there will be extra money built up within the closed-ended fund from which to pay an income in difficult years, such as when the trust's underlying holdings are cutting their dividends. (This structural benefit – known as smoothing dividends – is unique to investment trusts.)

For example, when BP suspended its dividends in mid-2010, many open-ended funds invested in the oil company suffered a substantial cut in income. In contrast, many of the investment trusts holding BP were able to dip into their revenue reserves to maintain income payouts.

The reserve is not a pot of money separated from the fund, but rather it is just an accounting treatment. The reserve is and remains money invested in the assets of the fund. Given that the reserve remains invested, returns are compounded. This ability to roll-up income can provide income investors with a higher and more sustainable income than other funds might do.

It is worth noting that not all closed-ended funds have a reserve from which to make income payments. The ability of an investment trust to build up revenues will depend on the fund, its mandate, expenses and the level of dividends it was looking to pay out. It will also depend on how long the fund has been around and what has been happening in the stock market. As long as the fund is not over distributing, and markets are strong, it is likely that the fund will be able to put money aside into the revenue reserve.

Checking whether a fund has a revenue reserve

If you want to check whether a fund has build up a revenue reserve the best place to look for this information is in the fund's literature. The most up-to-date figure should be in the fund's income statement contained within the fund's year end results. The interim management statement and fund prospectus may also contain information on the revenue reserve. All of these documents are usually published on the fund's website. An example of a fund which dipped into its revenue reserve to maintain income payments in 2009 and 2010, following the spate of dividend cuts suffered in the UK in the preceding years, is The Merchants Trust (part of RCM). Below is an extract from its final results for the year ended 31 January 2011:

> **Dividends**
> The Board is recommending a final ordinary dividend of 5.7p per share, payable on 13 May 2011 to Shareholders on the register on 15 April 2011. This payment would give a total of 22.8p for the year, an increase of 1.3% over the total for the previous year. In order to meet the payment it has been necessary to transfer £1,632,522 (1.6p per share) from our reserves, compared to a transfer of £3,724,961 (3.6p per share) last year. As at 31 January 2011 and after providing for this transfer, the Trust's reserves amounted to £12,775,572 (12.3p per share). This will be our twenty-ninth year of rising dividends. The Board and the Manager continue to remain focused on providing long-term steady income growth.

Unbroken dividend growth

As The Merchants Trust example illustrates, many investment trusts have a proud history of unbroken dividend growth and will go to great lengths to maintain this record. In 2011 there were 15 funds which boasted over 25 years of year-on-year dividend increases. These companies are listed in Table 7.1.

At the top of the list is the City of London Investment Trust, the origins of which can be traced back to 1860. The fund has managed to increase its dividend every single year since 1966. Had you invested £100 in the trust in 1965, and reinvested any dividends earned, your investment would have been worth £29,691 in absolute terms by 2010. This is another testament to the impact dividend reinvesting can have on an investment's total return.

Table 7.1 – investment companies with the longest record of year-on-year dividend increases

Investment company	AIC sector	Number of consecutive years dividend increased
City of London Investment Trust	UK Growth & Income	43
Alliance Trust	Global Growth	42
Bankers Investment Trust	Global Growth	42
Caledonia Investments	Global Growth	42
Albany Investment Trust	UK Growth	40
F&C Global Smaller Companies	Global Growth	39
Foreign & Colonial Investment Trust	Global Growth	39
Brunner Investment Trust	Global Growth	38
JPMorgan Claverhouse Investment Trust	UK Growth	37
Witan Investment Trust	Global Growth	34
Scottish Mortgage Investment Trust	Global Growth	34
Merchants Investment Trust	UK Growth & Income	27
Murray Income	UK Growth & Income	26
Scottish Investment Trust	Global Growth	26
Temple Bar	UK Growth & Income	26

Source: Association of Investment Companies (AIC) as at February 2011

Gearing of closed-ended funds

Closed-ended funds can borrow money to invest, which means they have extra cash available beyond the pool of capital paid into the fund by investors. This process is known as gearing.

Gearing works if the investments of the fund earn a high enough return to allow the loan and any costs associated with it to be repaid, and then for a profit to be made on top of that. If a company gears up and the returns from investments in the portfolio outstrip the costs of the borrowing, the return to the shareholder will be greater than it would have been if the trust has just invested the money paid into the fund by investors.

But there is a flipside to gearing. If the performance of the assets in the portfolio is poor, then losses suffered by the investor will be magnified due to the extra borrowing costs taken on by the fund. Closed-ended funds therefore tend to borrow when interest rates are low or at times when there is an attractive investment case to be made. Gearing can mean that exceptional gains are made during market rebounds, when the prices of stocks are rising very quickly and it is often difficult to move quickly enough to get invested.

The gearing ratio is the ratio of a fund's borrowings to its net assets. A fund with £100m in equity and £20m in debt is 20% geared. Investors should check the gearing of a fund before they invest. This information is usually published on the fund's factsheet, available online or can be accessed via fund data providers such as Morningstar or Trustnet.

A long-term investment

Closed-ended funds, in a similar way to equities, are better suited for those investors with a long investment horizon which will allow for the ups and downs of the stock market to be smoothed out. This gives the fund manager time to ride out bear and bull markets (downward and upward trends in the market) and allows time for the investment process of the fund to come into its own and deliver outperformance of the market or index the fund is benchmarked or measured against.

A longer time frame will also give the fund the opportunity to build up a revenue reserve that it can draw on in the years when its investment returns would not otherwise allow it to maintain its dividend payments.

THE DIFFERENCE BETWEEN AN INVESTMENT TRUST AND AN INVESTMENT COMPANY

The terms *investment trust* and *investment company* are often used interchangeably, though investment trust is more common. While both refer to closed-end funds with a fixed number of shares issued, there is a difference.

An investment trust is just one kind of investment company. Under the requirements of Section 842 of the Income and Corporation Taxes Act 1988, an investment trust must meet certain specific requirements, such as the fact that it cannot invest more than 15% of its total assets in one single company; the fund must be resident in the UK; it cannot be controlled by fewer than five people; and its ordinary shares must be quoted on the London Stock Exchange.

An investment company, on the other hand, is a term used to describe any closed-ended investment vehicle, of which an investment trust is just one. Investment companies invest in a wide range of different sectors and assets, including the shares and securities of other companies that trade on the stock markets around the world.

Investment companies include: investment trusts, offshore investment companies, Venture Capital Trusts (VCTs) and split capital companies.

2. Open-ended funds

Open-ended funds are collective investment vehicles which are not listed on the stock market. These vehicles therefore have no limit on the number of shares or units issued – shares are issued to investors by the fund without restriction to the amount. The fund will buy back shares from investors when they decide to sell. The capital value of the fund will therefore vary according to fluctuations in investor demand. Open-ended funds came into existence on 22 April 1931 when M&G Investments launched the First British Fixed Trust. In 2011, the two main types of open-ended funds are unit trusts and open-ended investment companies (OEICs). These two fund types are very similar – they both invest in cash, bonds or equities – but their structure is slightly different. In a unit trust, investors buy units, whereas an OEIC issues shares. The value of units and shares rises or falls according to the performance of the investments the fund holds.

Another difference between a unit trust and an OEIC is in the way their prices are calculated. This is done once a day. Unit trusts have two prices, the buy (bid) price and sell (offer) price. Purchases are made at the offer price, while sales are made at the bid price. OEICs have only one price.

Share classes with open-ended funds

Certain open-ended funds (usually OEICs) may have different share classes for different types of investor. You need to make sure you are investing in the share class meant for retail investors, as opposed to the share class meant for institutional investors (large organisations and pension funds). This is typically denoted by an 'R' at the end of the fund's name (meaning retail share class) or an 'A'. An 'I' or 'B' at the end of a fund's name tends to denote an institutional share class.

However, this naming structure can differ widely from one fund provider to another, for example the Artemis Income 'R' Fund has a minimum investment amount of £1000 and is aimed at retail investors. The Artemis Income 'I' Fund denotes the institutional share class of the fund and requires an initial minimum investment of £10,000,000. The latter is quite clearly beyond the reach of private investors and aimed at institutional investors such as pension funds. Meanwhile, Investec's Balanced Managed 'A' Fund, requires a minimum investment of £1000 while its institutional share class, the Investec Balanced Managed 'B' Fund requires a minimum investment of £10,000,000.

In most cases it is easier to look at the minimum investment amount required by the fund to deduce whether it is a suitable investment for you. Fund share classes aimed at retail investors typically have a minimum investment amount of around £1000 while institutional funds require much larger investments in the vicinity of £100,000 or more.

Income from open-ended funds

Another important distinction to make with regards to the share class is whether the fund is referenced as 'Inc' or 'Acc' at the end of its name. These stand for income and accumulation units, respectively. For example, you will find the Artemis Income 'Acc' fund and the Artemis Income 'Inc' Fund. For investors wishing to benefit from regular income payments from their fund investment, income units (denoted as 'Inc' at the end of the fund name) are the option to choose, as these pay out a dividend per unit.

Accumulation units ('Acc'), on the other hand, automatically reinvest profits back into the fund pot, increasing the fund's capital growth.

Most fund managers do allow investors in the income units of a fund the option to reinvest or roll-up dividends thereby growing their capital invested, with the option to start withdrawing the income when required.

SECTOR CLASSIFICATION OF FUNDS

When choosing a fund for income, whether closed-ended or open-ended, an important consideration is the investment objective of the fund and where it is investing its assets. In the actively managed funds space there is a wide range of fixed interest and equity-based funds with exposure to many different industries, companies and regions.

To make it easier to compare funds with a similar investment remit, funds are classified according to various sectors. These sectors are defined by trade associations such as the Investment Management Association (IMA) which looks at open-ended funds; and the Association of Investment Companies (AIC) which sets out sector definitions for closed-ended investment companies. Sector definitions tend to be based on assets, such as equities and fixed income, and may also have a geographic or industry focus.

The advantage of defining funds in this way is that it enables the investor to compare funds in one or more sectors, for instance by looking at performance and fund charges before looking in detail at individual funds. As new funds with varying investment remits and focus are continually being launched, trade bodies such as the AIC and IMA are continually monitoring their sector classification system, making the necessary amendments and introducing new sectors where required. Information on the different sectors and the funds listed under these can be found on these two organisations' websites: the IMA at **www.investmentfunds.org.uk/fund-sectors/fund-search** and the AIC at **www.theaic.co.uk/Search-for-an-investment-company**.

How funds deliver income

While sector classifications can be a useful way to search and compare actively managed funds, our concern in this book is specifically with those funds that deliver income.

Funds with an income objective will generate a return for investors in two main ways:

1. Increased net asset value
2. Payment of dividends

1. INCREASED NET ASSET VALUE

The net asset value (NAV) is the market value of a fund's share; this is what the shares of a fund are worth at present. NAV is calculated by dividing the total of all the cash and assets in a fund's portfolio, less any liabilities and fees, by the number of shares outstanding (shares sold and in the hands of shareholders).

```
net asset value = (total assets - liabilities and
costs)/shares outstanding
```

Therefore, if the total assets of Fund A are £20m and it has 10m shares in issue, its net asset value is £2.

If the market value of a fund's underlying portfolio increases, then the net asset value (NAV) of the fund increases, reflecting a higher value for your investment. Thus, if the assets of Fund A increase to £25m, the NAV would increase to £2.50 (£25m/10m shares). The opposite could also occur of course – if the investments made by a fund fall in price the net asset value of the fund will decrease.

It is important to recognise that a fund's shares will not always be bought and sold at the net asset value of the fund – they won't trade at what they are worth. In fact, they may trade at a price higher or lower than the net asset value figure. This situation is respectively called a premium or discount to NAV.

Premiums and discounts to NAV

The shares of funds that are listed on a stock exchange can trade at a premium or discount to net asset value. If the NAV of a fund is £2, but the shares are trading on the stock market at a higher price than this, say £2.30, the fund is trading at a premium to NAV. If a closed-ended fund is trading at a premium to NAV, it means that the underlying shares are worth less than the NAV of the fund and an investor will be paying more for the shares than what they are worth.

If the fund is trading at a discount to NAV, the underlying shares are worth more than the NAV and the investor will be paying less for the shares than what they are worth.

Buying shares in a closed-ended fund when they are trading at a discount to the fund's NAV can be a useful way to get added value when the discount narrows or moves to a premium.

How does this situation occur?

When a fund has a fixed number of shares, such as a closed-ended fund, and demand for these shares is high (perhaps because the fund has boasted good returns in the last year) the price of the shares will naturally increase. The reverse is true – a discount to NAV occurs when demand for a fund's shares is low and the share price falls as a reflection of this.

This is relevant to investors because if shares in the fund are sold when it is trading at a discount to NAV then you may get back less per share than you paid for them, resulting in a capital loss. If the shares are at a premium to NAV when they are sold, you may get back more than you paid per share.

Such a situation occurred in 2008. At the time the financial crisis meant investors wanted to sell assets, possibly at any price, and so were insensitive to what valuations they were given – they just wanted to exit their positions. In this situation there were more sellers than buyers and so NAV discounts widened.

Figure 7.2 provides an example of this. It shows investment trust company BH Macro over the last few years – the think line represents the share price, the dashed line the NAV. Looking at 2008 we can see that the NAV kept rising at first but as investors started selling holdings the trust's share price ran to a massive discount. As markets improved in 2009 the discount provided a buying opportunity and as investors took this opportunity the NAV discount started to close.

Figure 7.2 – BH Macro's widening discount

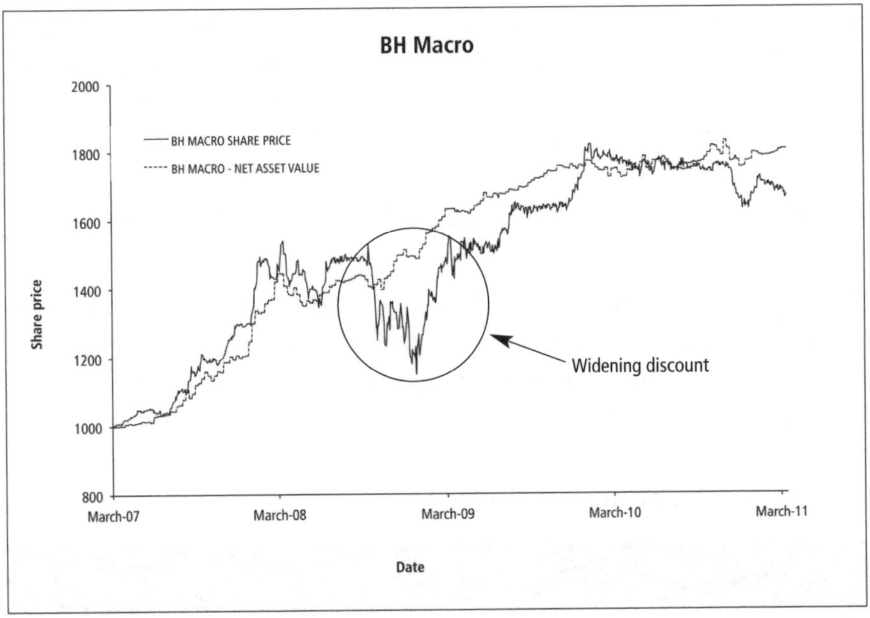

Source: AIC using Morningstar data

2. DIVIDENDS

As with shares, funds can generate an income via the dividends paid by the underlying holdings in the fund's portfolio. These are then redistributed by the fund to its shareholders. Dividends are paid by funds with an income objective – for example equity income funds or bond funds – but there is no uniform divided situation across funds. While funds will usually pay dividends quarterly or twice yearly, this will depend on the structure of the fund.

Like other assets, the return earned by an investor in a fund investment is measured using a yield calculation.

Yield

The yield of a fund is a measure of the dividend income, after expenses, paid to shareholders as a percentage of the price paid for the fund. This will usually be an annualised figure, making it is easy to track the returns of a fund in a given year and compare this to other funds' yields. Fund yields can be obtained with relative ease from the websites of data providers such as Morningstar, Trustnet and the *Investors Chronicle*, or from a given fund's monthly factsheet.

Table 7.2 below shows the yield of open-ended funds in the different Investment Management Association (IMA) sectors for the year to April 2011. As you can see the highest yielding sectors tend to be equity funds and the different bond fund sectors.

Table 7.2 – yields on open-ended funds

IMA sector	Average gross yield (%)	Highest gross yield (%)
Money market	0.4	1.2
Property	2.9	6.9
UK Gilts	2.9	4.3
Global Bonds	3.2	7
UK Equity & Bond Income	3.8	5.4
UK Equity Income	4.2	7.3
£ Corporate Bonds	4.6	6.8
£ Strategic Bond	4.6	7.4
£ High Yield	6.8	9.5

Source: Defaqto, April 2011, www.defaqto.com

Table 7.3 shows the annual yield of the AIC's highest yielding sectors. For more up to date yields use the AIC's website (**www.aicstats.co.uk/conventional**).

Table 7.3 – AIC's highest yielding sectors

Sector	Dividend yield (%)
Property Direct UK	6.5
UK High Income	6
Infrastructure	5.4
Global High Income	5.2
UK Growth & Income	4.2
Global Growth & Income	4
Property Securities	3
UK Growth	2.7

Source: AIC, as at May 2011

A good fund manager should be able to boost a fund's yield and its total return by seeking out the right investments at the right time and by keeping the fund's expenses low. The manager of an equity income fund, for example, will apply specialist expertise in choosing companies most likely to increase or maintain their dividends and then use these to compile a diversified portfolio of the best dividend-paying shares available.

But do not be enticed into a fund investment just because the fund offers high headline yield because there is no guarantee that the dividend payment will be maintained. Rather, examine whether the fund has progressively grown its dividend from one year to the next and find out if the yield in past years was due to any particular stock selection decisions and the amount of risk that this involved.

A useful service to keep track of dividend payments on open-ended funds is *Dividend Watch*. This is a research initiative by investment adviser Dennehy Weller which analyses the dividend payments by IMA equity income sector funds each month, highlighting changes in payouts, funds to buy and funds to avoid. It can be accessed online at:
retail.income.bnymellonam.co.uk/secondary/dividend_watch/dividend_watch.html

Now that we know how funds can generate income, let's look at the different types of funds typically used by the income investor.

Equity income funds

Equity income funds are a sensible place to start for investors looking for income-yielding funds. These tend to fall within the IMA's UK equity income sector or, in the case of closed-ended funds, within the AIC's 'UK High Income Funds' and 'UK Income and Growth' sector classifications.

These are funds which invest a significant proportion of their funds into UK equities focusing in particular on high-yielding shares with the aim of producing dividend growth for investors in the fund. Many, as we have seen with closed-ended funds, have an impressive track record of growing dividend payments year-on-year.

HOW TO MANAGE THE RISK OF EQUITY FUND INVESTMENTS

Funds by their very definition spread investment risk across a number of holdings, but if you're investing in equity income funds you will still be exposed to the ups and downs of the stock market, making this a higher risk investment.

There are a number of factors and investment strategies to consider when investing in equity income funds to ensure you are properly managing the risk that comes with these funds. These include:

1. Diversification
2. Compounding
3. Pound/cost averaging

Let's look at each of these in turn.

1. Diversification

An investor holding an equity income fund or selection of these funds in their portfolio should be looking to gain diversification from each of their holdings. Therefore, it is important to have a look at the underlying investments of an equity fund to find out what companies it is invested in.

As discussed in the section on equities (page 107), after a spate of dividend cuts in 2008 and 2009, the number of dividend-paying companies in the UK has become increasingly concentrated. More than half (54%) of income in the UK market comes from just ten companies. Consequently, many UK equity income fund managers are investing in the same dividend-paying companies. This means that holding a number of equity-based funds or investing in an equity-based fund in addition to your own direct equity investments may not give you the diversification you are looking for.

Have a look at the top ten holdings of most equity income funds and chances are you will see the same company names repeating – this overlap between funds' underlying holding is referred to as *dividend clustering*. Research conducted by Ignis Asset Management found that if an investor were to pick at random one of the top ten most popular UK equity income shares then, on average, eight out of ten income fund managers in the IMA's UK equity income sector would own that stock.

Table 7.4 shows the extent to which investments by funds in the UK equity income sector are concentrated in the same companies. In the table, *peer group ownership* refers to the percentage of the UK equity income sector holding the share in question and *peer group weighting* refers to what proportion of funds' assets are held in the share on average.[25] As can be seen, on average 81% of equity funds hold shares in the ten companies in the table. Also, on average, equity funds hold 5% of their shares in each of Vodafone, GlaxoSmithKline and Royal Dutch Shell.

Table 7.4 – UK equity income peer group concentration

	Peer group ownership (%)	Peer group weighting (%)
Vodafone	93	5
GlaxoSmithKline	93	5
Royal Dutch Shell	84	5
AstraZeneca	93	4
BP	85	4
HSBC	75	4
British American Tobacco	80	3
National Grid	77	2
Imperial Tobacco	72	2
BG Group	61	2
Average	81	4

Source: Ignis Asset Management (based on Lipper figures, January 2011)

[25] Ignis, 'UK equity income peer group too concentrated' (3 February 2011). Available at: **www.ignisasset.com/corporate/press-centre/press-releases/uk-equity-income.aspx**

If the equity income funds in your income portfolio share a high overlap of holdings it defeats the diversification object of holding a spread of funds. While it can at times be unavoidable to have some form of overlap, it is important to be aware of any duplication of holdings and make sure this only makes up a small proportion of your portfolio.

Circumventing the problem of dividend concentration

Given the concentration of dividend payments among a small number of large UK companies many fund managers now look for small companies with high dividend yields. The Ignis UK Equity Income Fund, for example, reports finding a broader spread of opportunities for decent dividends in medium (mid) and small-sized companies than among large companies. Less research coverage of companies by stockbrokers means that there is more potential for fund managers to add value for investors with their own analysis of small companies.

The Ignis fund's portfolio looks very different to that of its competitors, as Table 7.5 shows.[26] Whereas the equity income funds on average hold 32% of their assets in mid and small-cap shares, the Ignis UK Equity Income fund has 60% of its assets invested in these shares.

This shows that investing in an equity fund need not involve an over-concentration in the shares of a few large companies.

Table 7.5 – composition of the Ignis UK equity income fund compared to that of other equity funds

	Mega cap (%)	Large cap (%)	Mid cap (%)	Small cap (%)
Ignis UK Equity Income holdings	16	17	36	24
UK equity income peer group average	44	20	23	9

Source: Ignis (based on Lipper figures as at January 2011)

[26] Ignis, 'UK equity income peer group too concentrated'.

Global income funds

A number of global income funds have also been launched in recent years as fund management companies seek to diversify their investment focus by finding dividend paying companies from around the world.

This investment focus has even moved to the world's emerging markets, an area traditionally thought of as a growth investment. Table 7.6 shows the dividend growth achieved by a number of companies outside the UK over a period of five years.

Table 7.6 – dividend growth achieved by a number of global companies over a period of five years

Stock	Yield (%)	Historical five-year dividend growth (%)	Country
Zurich Financial Services	6.3	34	Switzerland
QBE	7.5	12	Australia
Takeda Pharmaceutical	4.6	13	Japan
Kimberly Clark de Mexico	4.1	9	Mexico
Taiwan Semiconductor	4.4	10	Taiwan
Telus	4.2	16	Canada
E.ON	7.1	14	Germany
Singapore Telecom	4.6	13	Singapore
Souza Cruz	4.6	14	Brazil
Novartis	4.4	14	Switzerland

Source: Aberdeen Asset Management based on figures from Bloomberg, March 2011

2. Compounding

If you can afford to reinvest your income payments from equity income funds, compounding means that your investment is likely to produce a significantly higher total return over the long term than if you had drawn income out from the fund.

Over 20 years to December 2010, reinvesting dividends in the average closed-ended fund would have boosted returns by some 58% on a £1000 investment, producing a total return of £6757, compared to £4271 without dividends reinvested. Table 7.7 shows the difference reinvesting dividends in the average closed-ended fund can make.

Table 7.7 – growth of a £1000 investment in closed-ended funds with and without dividends reinvested

Performance time period	31 December 2009 to 31 December 2010 (1 year)	31 December 2000 to 31 December 2010 (10 years)	31 December 1995 to 31 December 2010 (15 years)	31 December 1990 to 31 December 2010 (20 years)
With dividends reinvested	£1171	£1818	£3332	£6757
Without dividends reinvested	£1146	£1466	£2485	£4271

Source: AIC, using Morningstar figures

Notes: Performance figures are mid-market share price. Figures are based on the performance of AIC members only.

3. Pound/cost averaging

Investing a portion of your capital regularly into funds rather than investing a lump sum initially can be a good way to smooth the volatility of the market and help you to build up a holding of more shares in the fund, which in turn will mean a higher overall dividend payment.

Pound/cost averaging involves regular investment in a fund. When prices dip and are lower one month than they were before, a regular investment will buy more shares in the month when prices are lower (of course the reverse is also true). Over time, investors may end up paying a lower average cost per share and could end up with a bigger investment at the end of the year than a lump sum investor.

Figures from F&C Investments support this idea. They show that over the ten years to April 2011, a regular investor who put £100 a month into Foreign & Colonial Investment Trust or the FTSE All-Share Index each month from the start of one April to the next would, on average, be better off than a lump sum investor who put in £1200 at the start of the period.

Table 7.8 shows the effect: a lump-sum investment of £1200 in January when the fund's shares are priced at 100p would buy 1200 shares. But if you put in

£100 each month, you would finish the year with 1220 shares bought at an average price of 98.3p.

So the investor who puts in the lump sum of £1200 in January (buying 1200 shares) has a stake worth 10% more of the principle, or £1320, at the year-end. The regular investor also invests £1200 but because of share price fluctuation, buys 1220 shares, which at the year end are worth £1342 (110p x 1220), or 12% more than the initial investment. While the average price of the shares over the year is the same (100p) for both investors, the average cost to the regular investor is 98.3p.

Table 7.8 – the effect of pound/cost averaging

Month	Share price	Number of shares for £100	Cumulative number of shares
January	100p	100	100
February	110p	91	191
March	120p	83	274
April	120p	83	357
May	100p	100	457
June	100p	100	557
July	90p	111	668
August	80p	125	793
September	80p	125	918
October	90p	111	1029
November	100p	100	1129
December	110p	91	1220

Source: F&C Investments

In favour of regular investing

The idea of small regular investing rather than making a lump sum investment also seems sensible when you think about the difficulty involved in timing investments. There is always the risk of getting your timing wrong and buying high and selling low, if you make a lump sum investment you may risk doing so just at a time when prices are at their highest.

By investing small amounts of money into a fund consistently every month, you are likely to overpay at times when the market is high, for example during the tech bubble of the late 1990s, but you will also pay a fair price at other times, and sometimes you will underpay for your investments (or get more for your money) when the market is depressed, such as in late 2008. Over time these overpayments and underpayments should net out to a fair average. In volatile markets an investment made at regular intervals tends to outperform an investment made in the form of a lump sum.

Pound/cost averaging logic can work on the sell side, too. If you are ready to exit a fund and you slowly draw down your investment rather than taking out your capital all at once you avoid the risk of selling everything at a time when prices are low.

In favour of lump sum investing

An argument can also be made against pound/cost averaging and in favour of lump sum investing.

In a situation where a fund's share price increases steadily during a period when an investor makes a series of regular investments, an investor making a lump sum investment at the start of the period would be better off because their money will have been invested at the lowest possible average price – that is, the price of the fund's units or shares on the day they invested.

Another drawback to making regular, smaller investments is that if there is dividend income associated with the investment, you will get less if dividends are paid early in the year, when you own fewer units.

Historical data from the AIC shown in Table 7.9 suggests that the longer the time frame, the more lump sum investments tend to outperform regular investments. As you can see, if you invested £12,600 over 21 years from 1990 to 2011 it would be worth more at the end of the period if it was invested as a lump sum rather than as regular investments of £50.

Table 7.9 – comparing investment trust returns from regular investments with returns from a lump-sum investment

Performance from	30/06/2010	30/06/2006	30/06/2001	30/06/1993	30/06/1990
Duration (years)	1	5	10	18	21
£50 regular savings					
Sum invested (£)	600	3000	6000	10,800	12,600
Average investment company less 3.5% fees (£)	632	3727	10,057	23,645	34,071
Lump sum equivalent of regular savings					
Sum invested (£)	600	3000	6000	10,800	12,600
Average investment company less 3.5% fees (£)	710	3853	11,855	46,656	73,853

Source: AIC, August 2011

Whether you decide to invest regular small sums or put down an initial lump sum will depend on your individual circumstances and income goals. Many investors choose to combine the two approaches by investing a lump sum at the beginning and then undertaking to make regular investments in addition.

Bond funds

Bond funds are collective investment vehicles where investor capital is pooled together and then invested and managed by managers specialising in the field of bond investing.

Bonds have the advantage of offering a predictable, fixed income but navigating the risks – such as the potential for payment defaults, poor liquidity and wide credit spreads – requires investing skill. It is not surprising then that many investors choose to invest in fixed-interest assets via a fund structure. Most bond funds tend to be open-ended.

THE RANGE OF BOND FUNDS

Given the broad spread of bonds available, there is a wide range of different types of bond funds. Below is a brief summary, using the Investment Management Association (IMA) sector definitions as a guideline.[27]

Corporate bond funds

Corporate bond funds have the majority of their assets invested in sterling-denominated (or hedged back to sterling) corporate bonds with a credit rating of BBB minus or above. Corporate bond funds usually exclude convertibles, preference shares and Pibs, and are generally classed as lower risk. Examples of funds in this sector include the Invesco Perpetual Corporate Bond Fund and M&G's Corporate Bond Fund, managed by Richard Woolnough who is regarded as one of the UK's top fixed income fund managers.

UK gilt funds

UK gilt funds invest most of their assets (at least 95%) in AAA-rated government-backed bonds (gilts). These are one of the safest forms of income funds and hence returns are often muted. Examples of funds which sit in this sector include the Schroder Gilt & Fixed Interest Fund and HSBC UK Gilt Index Fund, a tracker fund.

UK index-linked funds

These funds invest the vast majority of their assets into AAA-rated government-backed, index-linked securities. These funds are preferred in inflationary times as the bond payments are linked to the inflation rate. At the time of writing there were only six funds sitting in this sector with the Royal London Index Linked Gilt Fund and M&G Group Index-Linked Bond Fund boasting the most competitive fees.

High-yield bond funds

High-yield bond funds tend to offer higher income than, for example, corporate bond funds, by investing in riskier bonds. They therefore allow investors to access higher income returns without having to invest in equities.

[27] Note that IMA fund sector classifications are constantly reviewed and are subject to change.

Investments tend to be concentrated in bonds with lower credit ratings as well as convertibles, preference shares and Pibs. The risk of capital loss is higher and the fund manager needs to be skilled at steering clear of issuers likely to default on interest or capital payments. Examples of high-yield bond funds include the Marlborough High Yield Fixed Interest Fund and the Investec Monthly High Income Fund.

Strategic bond funds

A relatively new addition to the bond funds landscape, strategic bond funds are regarded as having greater investment flexibility. The manager of a strategic bond fund can invest across the fixed-interest risk spectrum with the ability to switch the asset allocation of these funds to where they see the most value in bond markets at any point. The risk profile of these funds can therefore change over a short space of time as investment changes are made. Top fund performers in this sector include the Legal & General Dynamic Bond Trust, M&G Optimal Income Fund (also managed by Richard Woolnough) and the Fidelity Strategic Bond Fund.

Global bond funds

Global bond funds invest the majority of their assets in fixed interest investments spread across different geographic areas. These funds have grown in popularity in the wake of the financial crisis as investors have sought to diversify their investment risk across different countries. GLG Global Corporate Bond Fund is a top performer in this sector. Other funds here include the BlackRock Global Bond and Newton Global Dynamic Bond Fund.

Table 7.10 gives a summary of the funds mentioned, their charges, the minimum investment requirements and whether the fund in question can be held in an individual savings account (ISA).

Table 7.10 – summary information about a selection of bond funds

Fund name	TER (from the FE)	Annual charge	Minimum lump sum (£)	Minimum monthly saving (£)	Can it be held in an ISA?
CORPORATE BOND FUNDS					
Invesco Perpetual Corporate Bond Fund	1.19	1	500	20	Yes
M&G Group Corporate Bond Fund	1.17	1	500	0	Yes
UK GILT FUNDS					
HSBC Gilt & Fixed Interest Fund	0.9	0.75	1000	50	Yes
Schroder Gilt & Fixed Interest Fund	0.56	0.5	1000	50	Yes
UK INDEX-LINKED FUNDS					
Royal London Index Linked Gilt Fund	0.43	0.4	1000	50	Yes
M&G Group Index-Linked Bond Fund	0.67	0.5	500	10	Yes
HIGH YIELD BOND FUNDS					
Investec Monthly High Income	1.36	0.95	1000	100	Yes
Marlborough High Yield Fixed Interest	1.56	1.5	1000	100	Yes
STRATEGIC BOND FUNDS					
Legal & General Dynamic Bond Trust	1.42	1.25	50,000	0	Yes
&G Optimal Income Fund	1.42	1.25	1000	10	Yes
Fidelity Strategic Bond Fund	1.22	1	1000	50	Yes
GLOBAL BOND FUNDS					
GLG Global Corporate Bond Fund	1.44	1.25	1000	50	Yes
BlackRock Global Bond	1.08	1	500	50	Yes
Newton Global Dynamic Bond Fund	1.38	1.25	1000	50	Yes

Source: IMA as at June 2011

EMERGING MARKET BOND FUNDS: AN ANSWER TO INCOME?

Emerging market bond funds invest in the government debt of the world's developing economies. Most of these funds sit within the IMA's Global Bond Fund sector.

A number of these funds were launched following the 2007-2009 financial crisis, as it became apparent that the finances of many of the world's emerging economies were in a much healthier position than those of the developed economies.

Emerging market companies are in a similar position of balance sheet strength, including banks which managed their books in a far more conservative manner than their counterparts in developed markets. But while many emerging market companies are characterised by better fundamentals they still trade on a higher yield given that emerging markets are still perceived by investors as high risk.

Table 7.11 shows the higher yields on the ten-year bonds of emerging markets such as Brazil, Columbia and Poland compared to developed markets such as the UK, Germany and Japan.

Table 7.11 – ten-year bond yields

Country	Ten-year bond yield (%)	Inflation YOY (%)	Real yield (%)	Credit rating (S&P)
Brazil	12.8	6	6.8	BBB+
Colombia	8.1	3.2	5	BBB+
Eqypt	15	10.7	4.3	BBB-
Hungary	7.3	4.1	3.2	BBB-
Indonesia	8.3	6.8	1.4	BB+
Malaysia	4	2.4	1.6	A+
Mexico	7.6	3.6	4	A
Peru	6.3	2.2	4.1	BBB+
Poland	6.4	3.6	2.8	A
Russia	7.8	9.5	-1.7	BBB+
South Africa	8.8	3.7	5.1	A+
Thailand	3.6	2.9	0.7	A-
Turkey	9.4	4.2	5.3	BB
US	3.3	2.1	1.2	AAA*
UK	3.5	4.4	-0.9	AAA
Germany	3.2	2.1	1.1	AAA
Japan	1.2	0	0.2	AA

Source: Aberdeen Asset Management using data from S&P, Bloomberg, 22 March 2011

* In August 2011 the USA's credit rating was downgraded to AA+.

In the past the focus has been purely on US dollar denominated emerging market bonds but increasingly fund managers believe the most attractive income opportunities lie in local currency debt. Investors in emerging market local currency debt can benefit from currency appreciation in emerging markets, while these investments offer broad diversification thanks in part to the modest correlations with developed asset classes. It is also a natural hedge against US dollar weakness. Asset managers launching these bond funds have billed them as an *investment-grade asset class*, offering high income often with less volatility than equity investments.

However, given that this is a relatively new asset class, there is a lack of research and dedicated analysts in this space. While this can mean untapped opportunities for the discerning investor, it is important to do your homework. The credit ratings of the underlying holdings of such funds need to be examined. It should also be established whether a fund is focusing on dollar debt, local debt, or whether it is investing purely in currencies. These are three very different propositions with different risk and return characteristics.

Funds such as the Barings Emerging Markets Debt Local Currency Fund and the Aberdeen Emerging Markets Debt Fund tend to favour local currency and credit markets while funds like the Schroder ISF Emerging Markets Debt Absolute Return Fund tends to buy emerging market debt via dollars although it also invests some in local currencies.

Other funds focused on emerging market debt include the Threadneedle Emerging Markets Bond Fund, Investec Emerging Markets Debt Fund (a top performer) and the Baillie Gifford Emerging Markets Bond Fund. It is worth noting that some of these funds are offshore vehicles and denominated in dollars which means you are exposed to currency risk and can not hold the fund in your ISA. Table 7.12 shows a number of emerging market bond funds listed in the IMA global bond sector, including the charges and whether the fund can be held in an ISA.

Table 7.12 – a selection of emerging market bond funds

Fund name	TER (%)	Annual charge (%)	Minimum lump sum (£)	Minimum monthly saving (£)	ISAable
Aberdeen Emerging Markets Bond Fund	1.79	1.5	500	50	Yes
Baillie Gifford Emerging Markets Bond Fund	1.3	1.3	1000	0	No
Investec Emerging Markets Debt	1.62	1.5	1000	100	Yes
M&G Emerging Markets Bond Fund	1.49	1.25	500	0	Yes
Threadneedle Emerging Market Bond Fund	1.7	1.5	2000	0	Yes

Source: IMA, as at June 2011

Exchange-traded funds

Exchange-traded funds (ETFs) in a similar way to tracker funds, track or mirror the performance of a particular index or basket of assets. This could be the FTSE 100 or a selection of shares of companies involved in a specific industry or sector. For instance, an ETF tracking the FTSE 100 such as the iShares FTSE 100 GBP ETF, will deliver the same performance as the index – if the FTSE 100 is up by 1%, the capital growth of the ETF will also be 1%.

The ETF market has grown exponentially since ETFs were first introduced in the UK with a number of players launching new funds almost on a weekly basis. The range of ETFs to choose from is therefore wide, covering an ever-expanding array of indices and sectors. For the income investor however, the ETFs of concern will be those that deliver income and distribute that income. Our focus here will therefore be limited to those ETFs tracking bond and stock market indices which distribute dividends.

ETFs are traded on the stock market just like ordinary shares – this means they can be bought and sold whenever the market is open, and their prices are subject to the same fluctuations as other shares on the stock market.

The advantages of ETFs can be summarised as follows:

- *Trading is easy and in real time.*
- You have the *convenience of holding a diversified portfolio* of bonds or equity investments without needing large amounts of money to invest or having to make the buy and sell decisions.
- It is possible to *achieve exposure to a whole index in one transaction.*
- *Charges are low* – the average total expense ratios of equity ETFs stands at 0.4% according to Morningstar/BlackRock figures. This compares favourably to passive equity open-ended funds, which charge on average 0.91% while actively managed equity open-ended funds charge 1.8%.
- *ETFs have a clear objective* – to track an index and deliver the same performance as that index. This limits the potential for style risk, which is the risk that a fund will change its objectives while you are invested in it. This would be a danger with actively managed funds if the fund manager changes the fund's investment process or underlying holdings.

But ETFs are not without their drawbacks, these include:

- *Commission.* Every time you buy or sell an ETF you have to pay trading fees.
- *Tracking error.* ETFs are designed to match the performance of the benchmark they follow as closely as possible but sometimes performance will deviate. This is known as tracking error and the reasons for this can be diverse. Tracking error can be negative (the ETF underperforms the benchmark) or positive (ETF outperforms the benchmark). If an ETF's tracking error is persistently negative and more than the ETF's total expense ratio the impact on returns can be detrimental.
- There is such a *wide range of choice* that investors could easily be overwhelmed. There are many ETFs which track identical or very similar indices – at one stage there were more than 20 ETFs in Europe tracking the Euro Stoxx 50 index.
- ETFs are *constructed in different ways* which can mean different risks. It is important to understand the difference in ETFs' construction and the exposure they offer, as we discuss next.

Table 7.13 provides a summary of the pros and cons of direct bond investments, and investments in bond funds and bond ETFs.

Table 7.13 – a comparison of corporate bonds, corporate bond funds and bond ETFs

Feature	Individual corporate bonds	Corporate bond funds	Bond ETFs
Income stream	Fixed	Income stream varies	Income stream varies
Management fees	None	Vary depending on the fund	Vary depending on ETF.
Returns	Not diminished by fees	Return reduced by fund's TER	Variable return, reduced by fees charged by ETF
Safety of principal	If a high quality bond held through to redemption, principal is returned	A chance that principal may not be fully recovered if share price of fund is below the purchase price when shares are sold	Fluctuating share price could result in a loss of principal
Holdings	Known	Not disclosed until end of the month/quarter	Depends on the structure of the ETF, but can change over time
Diversification	Need a large amount of money to build a diversified portfolio	Small investment buys a holding in a diversified portfolio	Small investment buys a holding in a diversified bond portfolio

Source: Esme Faeber, *All About Bonds, Bond Mutual Funds and Bond ETFs*

ETF CONSTRUCTION

If you are thinking about adding an ETF to your income portfolio, it is important to make sure you understand what type of tracking method the ETF is using to replicate the index it follows. In other words, how the ETF is constructed.

There are two main types of ETF strategies:

1. Direct replication
2. Swap-based replication

We will look at each of these in turn.

1. Direct replication

Direct replication, also often referred to as traditional replication, means the ETF has a direct investment in every security in the index it is tracking. This might not always be possible when an index contains many constituents, in which case the ETF provider will buy the most important shares that represent a big chunk of the index.

With direct replication, the investor gets daily portfolio transparency – you can see the exact holdings within the ETF. Also the assets are custodial which means they are held separately from the asset manager and held safe. The drawback of this method of replication is that it can at times and in certain markets be hard for the ETF provider to buy and sell underlying holdings.

2. Swap-based replication

If a security is difficult to buy or an index illiquid, the ETF provider may buy a financial instrument known as a swap to synthetically replicate the index rather than holding all the shares or a representative sample of shares in the index. ETFs constructed in this way are referred to as swap-based or synthetically replicated ETFs.

A swap is an agreement between two counterparties to exchange future cash flows. This form of index replication can be advantageous in the sense that the ETF provider does not have to incur the costs of buying all the shares in an index individually to replicate it. It can also mean that the fund's total return might match that of the index more closely than a vehicle which uses the traditional replication method.

However, the drawback of this type of replication is the lack of transparency as to what is actually held in the ETF. In an extreme situation you could, for example, have a UK corporate bond ETF where the underlying fund composition is actually a basket of Japanese equities. Investors can get information on an ETF's underlying holdings on its factsheet published online, but this information will usually only list the top 10 holdings and not the entire portfolio.

A further risk of these vehicles is that the swap counterparty backing the ETF, usually a financial institution such as a bank or insurer, could fail, leaving investors stuck in an illiquid instrument and unsure of whether their capital will be returned.

ETFs FOR INCOME

Equity ETFs

High-yield equity ETFs can range from the directly replicated iShares FTSE UK Dividend Plus, which tracks the 50 highest yielding shares in the FTSE 350, to vehicles covering a broad variety of income yielding asset classes such as the db X-trackers MSCI AC Asia Ex Japan High Dividend Yield Index ETF which offers exposure to Asian equities that aim to offer a higher than average dividend yield. The ETF offers exposure to an index-tracking basket of companies that have been screened for their dividend suitability. Securities entering the index must have a dividend yield at least 30% higher than the dividend yield of the MSCI AC Asia ex Japan Index.

Bond ETFs

Some bond ETFs are specifically set up to provide investors with access to income, for example the iShares iBoxx £ Corporate Bond ETF, which pays a quarterly dividend. As with direct bond investments, bond ETFs will be affected by changes in interest rates and inflation, while credit and default risk will depend on the quality of the underlying bond holdings of the ETF. An ETF invested in higher quality bonds or bonds with shorter maturities will be less susceptible to price volatility.

Tables 7.14 and 7.15 show some of the ETFs that distribute income.

Table 7.14 – a selection of db X-trackers ETFs that distribute income

ETF	TER (%)	Asset class	Base currency	Income treatment	Launch date	Exchange	Dividend frequency	Dividend yield (%)
db X-trackers FTSE 100 ETF	0.3	Equity	GBP	Distribution	05.06.2007	LSE	Annual	3.4
db X-trackers Euro Stoxx® Select Dividend 30 ETF	0.3	Equity	EUR	Distribution	01.06.2007	LSE	Annual	2.8
db X-trackers Stoxx® Global Select Dividend 100 ETF	0.5	Equity	EUR	Distribution	01.06.2007	LSE	Annual	3.3
db X-trackers FTSE All-Share ETF	0.4	Equity	GBP	Distribution	15.06.2007	LSE	Annual	3.1

Source: db X-trackers, **www.etf.db.com/UK**

Table 7.15 – a selection of iShares ETFs that distribute income

ETF name	TER (%)	Asset class	Base currency	Income treatment	Launch date	Exchange name	Dividend frequency	Distribution yield (%)
iShares FTSE UK Dividend Plus	0.4	Equity	GBP	Distribution	04-Nov-05	LSE	Quarterly	4.7
iShares Markit iBoxx £ Corporate Bond	0.2	Fixed income	GBP	Distribution	29-Mar-04	LSE	Quarterly	5.4
iShares Markit iBoxx £ Corporate Bond ex-Financials	0.2	Fixed income	GBP	Distribution	25-Sep-09	LSE	Semi-annually	2.9
iShares Barclays Capital £ Index-linked Gilts	0.25	Fixed income	GBP	Distribution	01-Dec-06	LSE	Semi-annually	3.7

Source: iShares, uk.ishares.com/en/rc

ADDING AN ETF TO YOUR PORTFOLIO

In a low interest rate environment, high-yield equity and bond ETFs may sound like a cheap and diversified income investment for your ISA or broader investment portfolio. But it is important to do your homework.

Here are some of the most important steps you should take before adding an ETF to your portfolio:

1. *Have a look at the ETF's dividend distribution policy*; is the fund *distributing or capitalising?* For example, the ETFX DJ Global Select tracks an index with a dividend yield of well over 5%, but on a net total return basis. This means dividends are automatically reinvested, not paid out. While this is not necessarily a bad thing given the power of dividend reinvestment to build your capital, you should be aware that you will not get a dividend payout. Also bear in mind that with a portfolio of directly held bonds you can choose to receive higher income by, for example, selecting high-yield bonds, but you don't have any control over the amount of income you receive from a bond ETF. Information on an ETF's distribution policy can usually be found on the fund's factsheet.

2. *Beware of currency risk.* Many ETFs – including the aforementioned ETFX DJ Global Select Dividend – are denominated in dollars, and some in euro, so movements in exchange rates might affect what dividend distributions are worth in sterling terms.
3. *Consider the legal status of an ETF.* If it does not have *reporting* or *distributor* status you may end up paying income tax rather than capital gains tax. This could be a big issue particularly if you are a higher-rate taxpayer. Again, this information should be stipulated on the ETF's factsheet, if not check with the provider of the fund.
4. *Find out where the ETF is domiciled.* This will be on the ETF factsheet or provider website. In some jurisdictions you may have to pay a foreign withholding tax charge on your dividends, even if you hold the vehicle within an ISA. You may be able to reclaim this, but this could be an extra piece of admin you wish to do without.
5. *Treat promises of low costs with caution.* While low charges are a major attraction of ETFs, remember that as these are traded like shares you will have to pay stockbroker dealing costs on top of the normal fee every time you buy or sell ETF shares. If you trade frequently, investing in an ETF can become expensive and so ETFs for income purposes should be regarded as long-term investments.

How to invest in funds

Now that you have a firm grasp of the different types of funds available and how these generate income, it is sensible to look at how you can invest in these vehicles. There are several ways: you can contact the provider of the fund you want to buy by telephone, on the internet, by returning the tear-off sheets from advertisements published in the financial pages of the newspapers, or you could buy the fund via an independent financial adviser (IFA). But usually the most cost-effective way of investing for those constructing their own investment portfolios is via a fund platform, otherwise referred to as a fund supermarket.

FUND PLATFORMS

Fund platforms have evolved rapidly from offering funds and not much else to having impressive ranges including everything from funds to shares, as well as comprehensive research and reporting services. The advent of the *wrap platform* has taken things even further, offering the traditional fund supermarket together with tax planning strategies and all the other financial services an investor may require.

It is worth noting that while some fund supermarkets sell direct to the investor, others are only available via an IFA (wrap platforms in most cases). When choosing a fund supermarket – the internet is a good place to start your search – make sure you opt for a platform which has a broad offering of funds to choose from. While most fund supermarkets offer access to a range of open-ended funds not all provide access to investment trusts and ETFs.

COST

Over time the charges that investors have to pay to invest in funds, especially actively managed funds, can significantly chip away at the income return from the investment.

In high-return years costs may not make a material impact; however, if the fund makes moderate or negative returns, costs can take a significant chunk of earnings. It is worth looking in more detail at the range of charges fund investors may have to pay.

Fund management charges and a fund's total expense ratio (TER)

The total expense ratio (TER) is regarded as the best measure of a fund's charges and, in its simplest form, this equates to the total fund costs divided by the total fund assets. The figure for the fund's total costs is an amalgamation of the annual management charge (AMC), which is the yearly fee the fund management company charges to run the fund, plus any other charges levied during the course of a year, such as audit, custodian and legal fees. The latter are considered hidden fees but will nonetheless be a drag on a fund's performance.

There are also a number of actively-managed funds which charge a performance fee on top of the other charges. Funds charging a performance fee will typically do so when the fund's return beats a particular benchmark or exceeds its previous high, known as a high-water mark. Performance fees can vary enormously from one fund to the next and may be included in the TER.

Active fund managers tend to bunch their annual management charges around 150 basis points, with the TER usually around 160 to 170 basis points. A basis point is a unit that is equal to 1/100th of 1%, so 170 basis points will equal 1.7%.

A number of closed-ended funds boast TERs below 1%. Table 7.16 below shows the AIC investment trust companies with the lowest TERs. On average both open-ended and closed-ended funds charge more than 1.5% when performance fees are included – see Table 7.17 for a comparison of fees between the two different fund types.

Table 7.16 – AIC members with the lowest TERs

Investment company	Sector	NAV TER (%)	NAV TER including perf. fee (%)	Performance fee in place	Performance fee paid during the period
Independent Investment Trust plc	Global Growth	0.36	0.36		
Edinburgh US Tracker Trust plc	North America	0.4	0.4		
Bankers Investment Trust plc	Global Growth	0.42	0.42	Yes	
Law Debenture Corporation	Global Growth	0.49	0.49	Yes	
City of London Investment Trust plc	UK Growth & Income	0.49	0.5		Yes
Mercantile Investment Trust plc	UK Growth	0.55	0.55		
Henderson Smaller Companies Investment Trust plc	UK Smaller Companies	0.56	0.56	Yes	
Scottish Mortgage Investment Trust plc	Global Growth	0.56	0.56		
Temple Bar Investment Trust plc	UK Growth & Income	0.56	0.56		
Electric & General Investment Trust plc	Global Growth	0.62	0.65	Yes	Yes

Source: AIC

Table 7.17 – comparison of fees between open-ended and closed-ended funds

	Simple average		Asset-weighted average		Average fund size (£m)
	TER	TER + performance fee (%)	TER (%)	TER + performance fee (%)	
Investment trusts	1.47%	1.59	1.16	1.24	218.3
Unit trusts/OEICs	1.68%	1.69	1.65	1.66	166.2

Source: Lipper, a Thomson Reuters company

Notes on Table 7.17

- Lipper does not include performance fees in the TER as standard, but a combined figure is also shown separately for completeness.
- Unit Trusts/OEICs include actively managed equity funds, excluding institutional funds and other additional share classes.
- Investment Trusts/Investment Companies exclude more specialised sectors, i.e. VCTs, Private Equity, Direct Property, Funds of Hedge Funds.
- A simple average treats each fund equally within the data set. An asset-weighted average is calculated using values that have been weighted to the size of assets managed - in this way, larger funds (by assets) contribute proportionally more to the average than other funds.
- Data based on calculations carried out in April 2010.

In stark contrast to active managed funds, the majority of passive funds – tracker and exchange-traded funds (ETFs) – boast TER's starting at as low as 15 basis points (0.15%).

The significant price competitiveness that passive funds have over their active counterparts is an attraction for cost-conscious investors, who question why they should pay so much more for an actively managed fund when most fund managers fail to outperform the index or stock market against which their fund is benchmarked. With a passive vehicle, the fund's performance will always be in line with that of the index or market which it tracks.

Impact of fund management charges on performance

Fund charges can have a massive drag effect on the performance of a fund, as the following example provided by funds data provider Lipper (**www.lipperweb.com**) illustrates.

Table 7.18 – example of two funds with different TERs

	Fund manager	Annual management charge (%)	TER (%)
Fund A	Mr Ash	1.5	1.55
Fund B	Mr Beech	1.5	2.25

If Mr Ash and Mr Beech both generate performance of 7% over one year, but Fund A has annual charges of 1.55% and Fund B has annual charges of 2.25%, then Fund A will return 5.45% to an investor over this year and Fund B will return 4.75% to an investor.

While Fund A and Fund B have different Total Expense Ratios (TERs), both have annual management charges of 1.5%. The TER reflects all annual operating expenses, not just the quoted management charge. Expenses additional to the management charge do not contribute to a fund's investment management – so be wary of a fund that justifies a higher TER relative to other funds by saying you are paying for fund management.

Fund charges, indirectly borne by the investor, have a cumulative drag effect over time. Figure 7.3 shows how a £7200 fund investment growing by 7% each year will reach £14,163 after ten years, before charges. Annual charges of 1.55% (Fund A) will reduce this to £12,240, while annual charges of 2.25% (Fund B) will reduce this to £11,452.

This drag effect becomes more pronounced over the longer term, as Figure 7.3 shows (page 176).

Figure 7.3 – the impact of the drag effect over the longer term

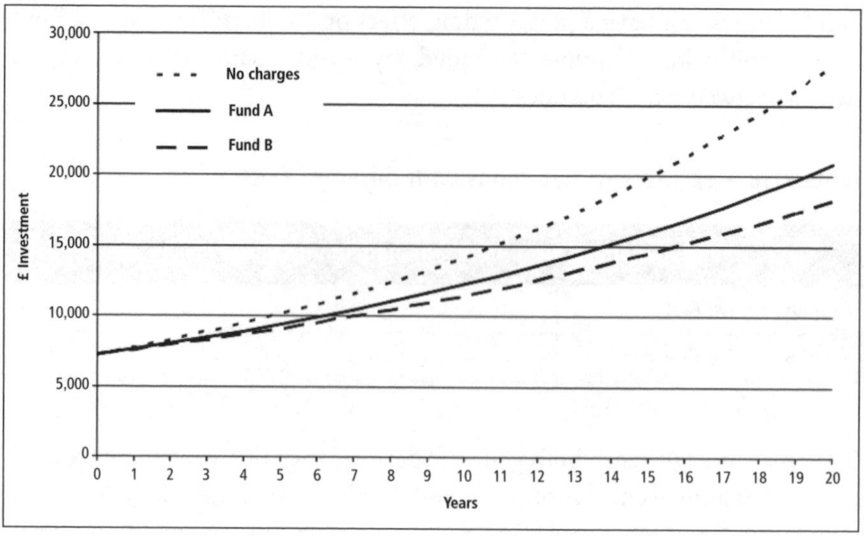

Fund supermarket charges

Probably the most enticing feature of a fund supermarket is the reduced cost on fund charges, which can make a significant difference to your investment portfolio over time. The sheer volume of funds sold by fund supermarkets enables them to offer attractive discounts on the initial charges and some discount on the annual management charges too. This is far more cost-effective than buying direct from fund managers.

Compare the charges and the fee structure of different fund platforms before you make a decision – competitive fees are important as these will impact the eventual income returns you get from your fund investment. Some providers, for example Alliance Trust Savings, rebate all commissions received from the fund management groups back to their customers. These rebates can be particularly significant for long-term investors due to the compounding effect on an increasing asset base.

ADMINISTRATION

Look for a fund supermarket which allows you to buy funds via tax wrappers such as Individual Savings Accounts (ISAs) and self-invested personal pensions (SIPPs). The wrapper will be administered by the supermarket, rather than by the individual fund manager. This enables you to spread your annual ISA allowance between different funds from different fund managers with much less paperwork.

If you have several different ISAs, unit trusts or shares, then you are probably receiving a number of valuations at different points throughout the year. One of the benefits of fund supermarkets is the convenience of receiving a single statement for all your investments.

RESEARCH

Look at the research capacity of the fund supermarket and the added value they offer. Many fund supermarkets boast comprehensive research teams which can provide valuable in-house research on funds and fund managers. They may also offer fund portfolio reviews and fund recommendations. The online presence of these platforms means you have the added benefit of viewing your portfolio whenever you wish.

THE MAIN PLAYERS

Currently the UK market is dominated by the so-called *big five*. These five main fund providers are Hargreaves Lansdown's Vantage service, Fidelity FundsNetwork, Cofunds, Transact and Skandia. You should note that the last three platforms mentioned are only accessible via an IFA. Table 7.19 compares the fees on different fund platforms in the UK available to private investors it includes Bestinvest Select, TD Waterhouse, Barclays Stockbrokers, Hargreaves Lansdown and Fidelity's offering.

Table 7.19 – comparison of different fund platforms available to private investors in the UK

	Bestinvest Select	Hargreaves Lansdown	Barclays Stockbrokers	Fidelity	TD Waterhouse
Choice					
ETFs	✓	✓	✓	✗	✓
Investment trusts	✓	✓	✓	✗	✓
Funds	✓	✓	✓	✓	✓
Shares	✓	✓	✓	✗	✓
Passive funds	✓	✓	✓	✓	✓
Low-cost active	✓	✗	✗	✗	✗
Research					
Proprietary rating system	✓	✗	✗	✗	✗
Model portfolios	✓	✗	✗	✗	✗
Share news and research	✓	✓	✓	✗	✓
Cost					
Share dealing	£7.50	£9.95 to £29.95	£6.95 (25 deals per month) to £12.95	Not available	£8.95 (15 trades or more per quarter) £12.50 for under 15 trades
Fund dealing commission	£0	£0	£0 to buy £15 to sell non-Funds Market funds	0.25% switch fee	£0
Initial charge on funds	most funds 0%	most funds 0%	Most funds min 0.5%	20% of funds have 0%, All fund in SIPP 0%	66% of funds have 0%
SIPP annual admin fee	£0	£0	£200 p.a.	£0	0.5% up to £200 p.a.
SIPP income drawdown set-up or annual fee	£0	£0	£275 p.a.	Not available	£150 p.a.

	Bestinvest Select	Hargreaves Lansdown	Barclays Stockbrokers	Fidelity	TD Waterhouse
Account fee – SIPP	£100 p.a.*	0.5% up to £200 p.a.	£200 p.a. (including SIPP annual fee)	Not applicable	0.5% up to £200 p.a.(including SIPP annual fee) & £40 p.a. inactivity fee
Account fee – ISA	£50 p.a.*	0.5% up to £200 p.a.	£50p.a.	Not applicable	£30 p.a. (up to value of £5100) & £40 p.a. inactivity fee
Account fee – Investment Account	£50 p.a.*	£0	£48p.a. (inactivity fee)	Not applicable	£40 p.a. inactivity fee
Annual loyalty bonus					
SIPP	Up to 0.5%	✗	✗	✗	✗
ISA	✓	✓	✗	✓	✗
Investment account	✓	✓	✗	✓	✗
Number of funds offering rebate	1706	1397	0	1672	0

Source: Bestinvest

Notes on Table 7.19

* Only charged when holding investments not paying an annual commission (ETFs, Shares, Investment Trusts & non-trail paying funds).

Factors to consider when investing in funds for income

When selecting a fund in which to invest for income, investors may intuitively look to buy the last year's top yielding fund or the fund that has posted the highest return for the current year, but this can be a huge mistake.

Past performance figures in isolation give no indication of a fund's performance going forward – a previous year's figures only show that you should have bought the top performing fund a year ago, which does not help an investor trying to decide what to buy now.

To make the figures around a fund's past performance and its yield – the quantitative factors – meaningful, you will need to carry out some qualitative analysis to find out how this performance was achieved. The points to look at are as follows:

1. Fund manager competency and style
2. Security of underlying holdings
3. Country influence
4. Currency exposure

1. FUND MANAGER COMPETENCY AND STYLE

When choosing an actively-managed fund (a fund managed by a fund manager) part of your investment decision will be based on the fund manager's ability to deliver outperformance, but there is always the risk that the manager will be ineffective.

Look at the manager's track record and experience. Has the manager been producing in different cycles, or only in rising markets? How stable has their career been? Also consider the constraints set by the investment house, and how the manager's performance is judged and remunerated. A number of companies such as Morningstar (**www.morningstar.co.uk**), OBSR (**www.obsr.co.uk**) and Standard & Poor's (**www.standardandpoors.com**) research and allocate ratings to funds which can be a good starting point when researching a particular manager and their investment style. These ratings can be found on their websites.

The other risk with fund managers is that of *style drift*. This is the risk that the fund manager will diverge from the investment strategy and process that was originally set out for the fund.

A change in the manager heading up a fund you have invested in can also introduce an element of risk. Fund managers often switch jobs, which can reflect unfairly on a fund's quoted performance figure as a new manager can erode the performance delivered by a predecessor. If a fund has recently had a change of manager past data is not going to tell you how the fund may perform going forward.

When a fund's manager changes this may also cause a shift in investment style and an investor will have to decide whether they are still happy to be invested in the fund under the tenure of the new manager.

The advantage of investing in funds is that your investments are chosen and managed by a professional. The caveat is that you are giving up some of the control. You won't always be able to know the exact make-up of the fund's underlying portfolio and neither will you be able to influence the fund manager's investment decisions or the timing of these.

2. SECURITY OF UNDERLYING HOLDINGS

The biggest risk with funds is the loss of part or all of the initial capital invested as the fund's underlying holdings fluctuate. The risk of investors losing the original amount they invested is known as *principal risk*. A fund's underlying holdings may fluctuate depending on factors such as the broader economy, the stock market (in the case of equity funds), interest rate movements and changes in the fund's investment style or process. This may in turn impact the fund's ability to maintain dividend payments or the size of its dividend yield.

Never make assumptions about the underlying holdings of a fund based on the fund's name – always check this carefully yourself.

3. COUNTRY INFLUENCE

Political, natural or economic events can have a significant impact on the value of a fund which invests in the companies of a particular country, or companies which derive a significant proportion of their earnings from a particular country. Examples include the civil unrest and political turmoil in North Africa and the Middle East in 2011 which put pressure on funds focused on companies earning revenues in these regions. Similarly the earthquake disaster and subsequent tsunami in Japan in March 2011 had a major effect on the Japanese stock market and funds invested in Japanese shares.

4. CURRENCY EXPOSURE

Funds, such as global equity funds, may invest in a range of companies which earn their income in currencies other than the investor's home currency. Depending on exchange rate movements this can result in a reduction in returns for the investor, or alternatively help boost the returns. Some funds offer a hedged share class which is a way to mitigate the risk of currency movements impacting the value of the fund's returns.

8

PROPERTY

Property is classified as an alternative asset class. This means it is regarded as a non-traditional investment because it tends not to be correlated to the main asset classes of cash, bonds and equities. It can therefore provide valuable diversification to a portfolio.

Some might suggest that a house should be a home, not an investment. The argument which follows this is that a house should be somewhere to enjoy a lifestyle – a safe and comfortable place of residence. It should be seen as an asset to use and enjoy but one which can depreciate in value and incur costs. An investment, in contrast, is a place for money to appreciate, there are risks involved and the aim is to generate an income and show a profit. As such, an investment and a home do not equate and so some argue that you should not include your home when calculating investment capital and assets from which to generate an income.

The counterargument to this is that buying a house is more likely than not the biggest investment most of us will make in our lifetime. The purchase of a house does effectively represent a direct investment in the residential property market and for most individuals their home will probably be worth more than all of their other investment assets put together. Also, as we will see, there are ways of drawing an income from property without leveraging off of the capital tied up in the home where your family lives.

Property has performed well over the years. Figure 8.1 shows the rise in UK house prices since 1952.

Figure 8.1 – changes in UK house prices since 1952

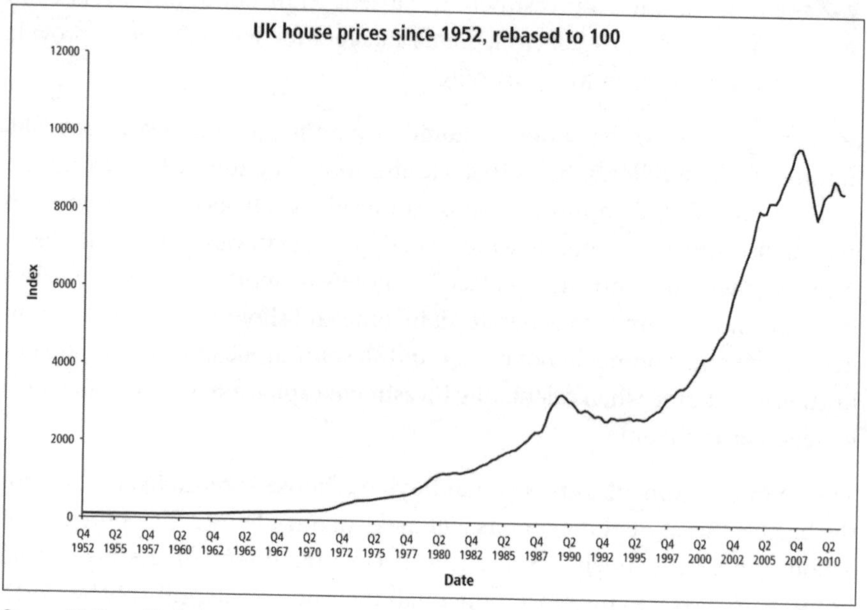

Source: Nationwide Index

Drawing an income from your home, and other property, is the subject of the following section.

Yield

Investing in a property and then renting it out to a tenant is a relatively simple way of receiving an income return from property. There are also various investment vehicles linked to property which can provide you with an income stream that diversifies from the more mainstream asset classes such as equities and bonds. Examples include property funds which invest in **land, commercial properties** such as offices, shops and factories, and **property development**.

Yield within the context of property investments is the annual rental income expressed as a percentage of the property purchase price – i.e. the capital value of the property. As with bonds and equities, the yield from property and a property's price share an inverse relationship.

If the capital value of property falls, rental yields are pushed up and property becomes an increasingly attractive source of income. However, if property prices rise, rental yields will fall and so will the income return offered by property. This is illustrated by Figure 8.2.

Figure 8.2 – capital values versus yields

Capital values ↓ = **Yields** ↑

Capital values ↑ = **Yields** ↓

Yield generated by property can be split into *gross yield* and *net yield.*

Gross yield is calculated by dividing a property's annual rent by its market value.

```
gross yield = (annual rent/property value) x 100
```

So if a property's annual rent is £5000 and the market value of the property is £100,000 then the gross yield will be:

```
(£5000/£100,000) = 0.05 x 100 = 5%
```

Net yield takes into account all the operational costs involved with the property, such as maintenance bills, etc. It is seen as a more accurate assessment of the investment. The formula for calculating *net yield* is:

```
net yield = ((annual rent - annual costs)/property value) x
100
```

The return you get over the long term from a property-based investment will depend on changes in capital value of a property as much as from the rental yield.

Unlocking income from the family home

A homeowner looking to unlock an income stream from their home has broadly two options:

1. If they have a sizeable chunk of their mortgage repaid they can downsize, selling their home and purchasing a smaller, cheaper property. The

capital released in this way can then be invested with the income returns used to supplement their pension and/or help fund their living costs.

2. *Equity release* is another option. This has the advantage that the family does not have to move out of the property. Also called lifetime mortgages, home reversion or home income plans, equity release plans enable investors of a certain age (usually over 60) to borrow against the current value of their home, having the cash value paid to them in a lump sum, regular income payments, or both. The debt is then repaid from the sale of your house after your death. Equity release schemes can however be notoriously complex and could result in extra tax. These schemes should not be considered without consulting a qualified financial adviser with knowledge in this area.

Releasing equity from your home, whether by downsizing your property or opting for an equity release plan, is a very concentrated investment strategy. If things go wrong, the investor risks not only losing the income return they had bargained on, but also the family home. This doesn't mean that property should not be considered as part of an investment portfolio but just that the risks need to be borne in mind.

Investing in property aside from the family home

A way of using property to generate an income without putting your family home at risk is to invest in the asset class as part of a broader investment portfolio. This can be done in two basic ways:

1. *Direct investment* – the purchase of a property or portfolio of properties which you can then rent out.
2. *Indirect investment* – the purchase of one or more types of financial vehicles, such as property-based funds, where the underlying investments are a spread of physical properties or shares in property companies.

We will now look at these in turn.

1. DIRECT INVESTMENT

The first way to invest in property is to directly purchase it. This purchase would usually be made with the aid of a loan or mortgage. If you have £25,000 in capital a mortgage provider may lend you £175,000 to help you purchase a property worth £200,000. You then have to make a mortgage payment each month to the mortgage provider, which will include interest on the loan. A regular income can then be drawn from this property investment by letting it out to tenants, and ensuring that the rent they pay covers all costs, including the loan repayment.

Investing in property in this way can have attractive income generating prospects. There lies a contractual obligation for tenants to pay their rent, which ranks ahead of the obligation for bond and equity holders to be paid their income by the bond/share issuer.

Given that rental income from property investments, in particular commercial properties, involves long leases and annual indexation of rents in line with inflation, some regard the income from property as more predictable and safer than dividend income from shares.

Gearing and mortgage debt

When a loan or mortgage is taken out to assist in the purchase of a property, this can lead to negative or positive gearing. Gearing refers to the borrowing (debt) on a property relative to its capital value and income earnings. A positively geared property is one where the income received from the property exceeds the interest being paid on the property loan and any other costs of holding the property.

Thus a property that delivers an income of £500 per month, where the monthly loan repayments are £400, is positively geared (if all other costs are ignored). A negatively geared property is one where borrowing costs exceed the rental income and the property's capital growth.

Returns on property can be magnified by gearing up – in other words increasing borrowing to amass more properties. If the property market is in a downward cycle and property prices fall, the effect of gearing up is reversed: the property loan will become a larger percentage of the value of the property and you could end up in a situation of negative equity, where the value of the loan taken out to buy a property is greater than the value of the property.

Liquidity

Liquidity presents one of the biggest risks of investing in property, especially with direct investments into physical property. The only way to realise a profit from a direct property investment is by selling the asset, but property does not transact quickly and easily. Even in a healthy market it can take months, sometimes even years, to sell a property and the risk is that investors become stuck in their investment – this is known as the property liquidity trap. The risk of liquidity is twofold: first, you cannot always find a buyer when you want to sell; Second, with a direct property investment you cannot sell your investment a little bit at a time as needs dictate (unless you own a massive portfolio of individual properties).

Liquidity, as we will discuss, is also a major risk with open-ended property funds (especially bricks and mortar funds) as the fund manager will need to buy and sell holdings to meet any fund outflows.

Different types of direct property investment

Direct property investments can be further subdivided into purchases of:

1. Residential property
2. Commercial property

As we will see, these represent quite different investments.

1. Residential property

A residential property is, fairly obviously, one where people live. The income return on a residential property is generated by the rent paid by tenants, although typically the biggest element of total return will be the growth in the capital value of the property. This means that any appreciation in the capital worth of a residential property, realised when the property is sold, will usually make up more of the total return on the initial investment than the income from rents received in the period when the property was owned.

Traditionally, buy-to-let is the preferred way for private investors to access direct property investments. This means buying a property with the specific intention of letting it out to someone else, rather than living in it yourself. However, the barriers to entry into a buy-to-let arrangement are often too high for many investors.

Buying to let can be expensive given the high costs of properties and securing a mortgage can be difficult (especially in the wake of the 2007-2009 financial crisis). Lenders now require larger cash deposits and most apply rigorous credit checks to ensure the finances of borrowers are such that they can afford to pay back the loan.

Concentration risk is another issue: most people will find it difficult (given the costs involved) to buy more than one or two properties, which does not make for a well diversified investment. Then there are also the risks of ongoing and unexpected maintenance costs and that of tenants defaulting on rents or damaging the property; all of these will eat into your investment returns. If the market is saturated with too many buy-to-let properties, finding tenants to fill the property could be a challenge in itself. Liquidity – when it comes to selling the property – is another issue.

Given the many risks, residential property is best viewed as a long-term investment for those who can afford to take on the risks involved.

2. Commercial property

Commercial property is real estate designed for use by retail, wholesale, office, hotel, or other service users. It can include office buildings, restaurants, shopping centres, hotels, industrial parks, warehouses, and factories, which must usually be zoned for business purposes. For the income investor, the attraction of commercial property lies in the enticing rental incomes, which are usually subject to long-term leases and annual rental reviews.

As with residential property, there are investment issues to be conscious of. Commercial mortgages work in a different way to residential ones – the costs are higher and it is generally harder for investors to secure loans to raise the high amounts of capital required. The prices of commercial property can also fluctuate greatly depending on factors such as location – property in central London can demand higher rentals than property in North East England for example. The amount of rent that can be charged is related to planning regulations, the supply and demand of commercial property in the area, and whether the building is occupied or not (an occupied property will have a higher value than an empty property).

Holding commercial property in a SIPP

Tax charges can take a huge chunk out of the investment returns from commercial property, but by holding commercial property in a Self-Invested

Personal Pension (SIPP) this tax burden can be mitigated. Within a SIPP, no capital gains tax (CGT) has to be paid on profits made when the property is sold and no income tax has to be paid on rental income.

Placing commercial property into a SIPP is usually only an option for those with a large pension pot, as a commercial property purchase will require a large amount of capital. However, it is possible to form a syndicate with other SIPP investors to buy a commercial property.

Besides the tax advantages, there are other benefits to holding commercial property in a SIPP. If you are a business owner it can be a cost effective way to hold your business premises – rather than you purchasing the property yourself or renting it for your business, your SIPP buys the premises and you pay rent to the SIPP. Instead of the rental income going to a landlord it goes into your pension, and is untaxed. In this way your commercial property investment can be a good long-term, income-producing asset for your SIPP.

If you are struggling to get finance for your business, purchasing a commercial property outside of your business's balance sheet and adding it to your pension fund will inject cash into the business. You can also use the property as security to borrow additional funding via the SIPP. You can borrow up to 50% of your net pension fund against your SIPP to purchase commercial property.

The rent you pay to the SIPP can be used to pay back capital on the loan, and because this is untaxed it can cut the time it takes to repay the mortgage.

When buying a commercial property via a SIPP you should call in the help of a solicitor and accountant.

You will also have to choose a SIPP that allows you to invest in commercial property as not all SIPP providers offer this facility. Examples of SIPP providers which do allow commercial property as an investment include Mattioli Woods, Standard Life and James Hay.

2. INDIRECT INVESTMENT

Property investing does not necessarily have to mean a direct purchase of a physical property. Indirect investment in property can either involve investing in the shares of a property company (similar to an equity investment) or via a property fund, where underlying investments are a spread of physical properties or shares in a property company. The latter tends to be a more affordable way of getting exposure to the property market and a good way of spreading the risk.

Different types of indirect property investment

Property funds are mainly distinguished based on their underlying investments, the two main types are:

1. *Direct property funds*, or bricks and mortar funds, invest in directly-held physical property (usually commercial property).
2. *Indirect property funds*, or listed property funds, invest mainly in the shares of property companies quoted on the stock market. These are also often referred to as property securities funds. Real Estate Investment Trusts (REITs) introduced in 2007 are an example of an indirect property fund. These can contain commercial and/or residential property and are attractive to the income investor given that they are required by law to distribute at least 90% of their taxable income as dividends to shareholders. Examples of REITs include British Land, Hammerson and Land Securities.

There are advantages and disadvantages to both structures. Indirect property funds which invest in property equities or shares tend to be more correlated to the stock market than direct bricks and mortar funds. Direct property funds are therefore a better means of adding diversity to an investment portfolio.

Indirect property funds in turn tend to benefit from greater liquidity. If lots of investors want to disinvest at the same time, a direct property fund will be forced to sell its underlying holdings to meet redemptions (returning an investor's money). It can take time to buy and sell properties and investors can be left waiting for their money. Bricks and mortar (direct property) funds got caught out by this during the financial crisis and crash in the property market in 2007-2008 when investors withdrew large amounts of money from these funds. This forced many fund managers to sell properties in a falling market, only to buy them back at inflated prices when demand picked up again.

Other open-ended property funds had such difficulty in selling the buildings that they did not have the cash to return to investors – these funds closed to redemptions, leaving investors' money locked in the fund. While listed property funds were also hit by the downturn, they did not encounter redemption issues to the same degree because these funds invest in shares which are much easier to buy and sell than physical property.

Property funds for different geographical areas

Property funds also differ by the geographical areas in which they invest. Over recent years commercial property has increasingly become a global market, and as a result many funds with a global investment mandate have been launched. The advantage of a property portfolio spread across different geographies is that global property markets generally do not move in sync.

A skilled property fund manager can therefore enhance investor returns by increasing a fund's weighting in the better performing markets and moving out of the poor performers. Investing in the property markets of the world's emerging economies is also becoming increasingly popular, but there are risks involved – see the note 'Investing in emerging market property'.

The First State Global Property Securities Fund is an example of an open-ended fund which invests in the shares of REITs and property companies around the world. Figure 8.3 shows the fund's geographical breakdown as at 31 March 2011. As you can see, the fund, which is benchmarked against the UBS Global Real Estate Investors Index, has a portfolio of investments spread across the globe, including exposure to the emerging markets.

Figure 8.3 – geographical breakdown of the First State Global Property Securities Fund

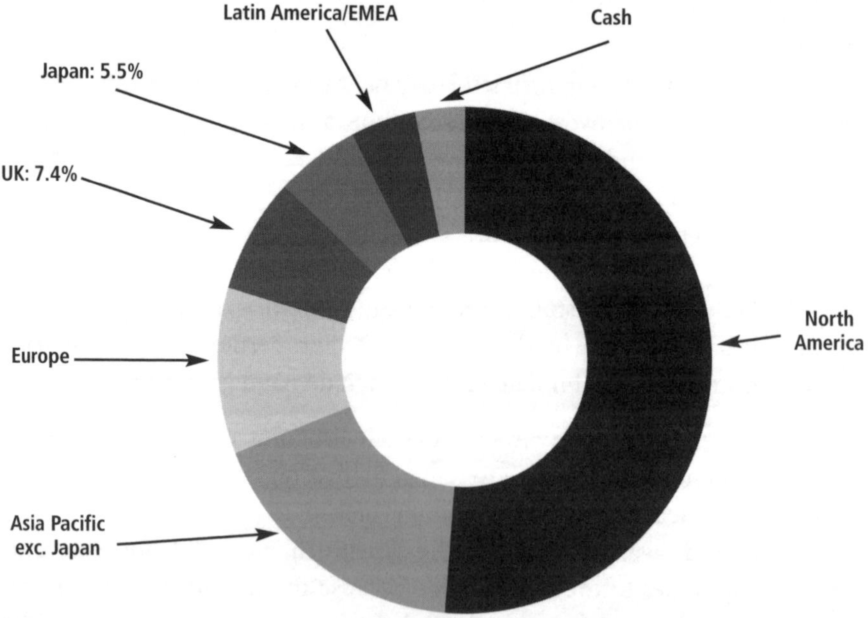

Source: First State Global Property Securities Fund, March 2011

Structure of property funds

It is not just the underlying holdings and geographic focus which distinguishes different property funds. The fund structure – whether the fund is actively or passively managed – can also have an impact.

Actively managed property funds can be split into open-ended vehicles (unit trusts and OEICs) and closed-ended vehicles (REITs and property trusts). Closed-end property funds have the same attributes as other closed-ended funds which we looked at in chapter 7.

Remember that the shares of closed-ended funds can trade at a premium or discount to the fund's net asset value (NAV). This is significant for property investors because if fund shares are trading at a premium to NAV it usually means the market is anticipating a rise in property prices while if shares are trading at a large discount to NAV (typically greater than 15%) the market anticipates a fall.

Many open-ended funds meanwhile, invest globally and advocates suggest these funds offer the highest yields and boast the most diversified portfolios. A drawback however, is that the fund manager's strategy can be heavily impacted by inflows into a fund, and redemptions to those leaving the fund.

To minimise your risk with direct property funds you should pick an unleveraged fund which is well diversified and prudently managed. A good starting point is the fund's factsheet and prospectus, which should be available online. Look at factors such as the fund's gearing ratio and the spread of investments held. Is the fund well diversified across sectors? How about different geographies? Also assess the fund manager's track record. How long have they been managing the fund? What is their investment style and performance track record? Does the fund provider have experience in providing property fund investments? Fund rating agencies such as S&P and Morningstar can be a good place to look for this information.

Property ETFs

Finally, there is the option of passive property investments in the form of exchange-traded funds (ETFs) which track property indices. These can offer more diversified access to exchange-listed REITs and real estate companies with fees markedly lower than active funds. There are a number of ETFs offering exposure to real estate shares across Europe, American and Asia, many with dividend yields on par with their actively managed counterparts.

ETF provider iShares property ETFs include the iShares FTSE EPRA/NAREIT Asia Property Yield Fund, the iShares FTSE EPRA/NAREIT UK Property Fund and the iShares FTSE EPRA/NAREIT Developed Markets Property Yield Fund. Most of iShares' products make use of direct index replication techniques. The FTSE EPRA/NAREIT indices replicate the performance of equity REITs and real estate companies offering diversified coverage of the real estate market in different regions.

Swap-based ETF provider db x-trackers' offering includes the db X-trackers FTSE EPRA/NAREIT Developed Europe Real Estate ETF, the db X-trackers FTSE EPRA/NAREIT Eurozone Real Estate ETF and the db X-trackers FTSE EPRA/NAREIT Global Real Estate ETF. The drawback of the db x-trackers' products is that these capitalise rather than distribute income, so all dividends are reinvested into the funds. Table 8.1 below gives a summary of a selection of property ETFs which distribute income.

Table 8.1 – a selection of property ETFs that distribute income

ETF	Index tracked	TER	UK distributor status	Domicile	Base currency	Distribution of dividends	Dividend yield
iShares FTSE EPRA/NAREIT Asia Property Yield Fund	FTSE EPRA/NAREIT Developed Asia Dividend+ Index	0.59%	No	Ireland	USD	Quarterly	3.15%
iShares FTSE EPRA/NAREIT UK Property Fund	FTSE EPRA/NAREIT UK Index	0.40%	Yes	Ireland	GBP	Quarterly	2.36%
iShares FTSE EPRA/NAREIT Developed Markets Property Yield Fund	FTSE EPRA/NAREIT Developed Dividend+ Index	0.59%	No	Ireland	USD	Quarterly	2.65%

Source: iShares, uk.ishares.com/en/rc as at May 2011

The advantage of a property ETF is that the investment can be readily liquidated, so there is no risk of getting stuck in the asset class. The drawbacks are that ETFs cannot invest directly in individual properties and are not governed by rules on income distribution. While the REIT structure dictates that 90% of profits have to be paid back to investors in the form of income, ETFs can choose to reinvest profits in the fund rather than pay income to investors. Another danger is that the ETF may be concentrated in certain companies if these constitute a large part of the index.

EMERGING MARKET PROPERTY

The world's emerging markets, in particular those in Asia, are increasingly on the radar of property investors owing to the improving fiscal position of these economies and their consumers, relative to the debt-burdened West.

There are of course risks attached to investing in emerging market property. These markets are generally more volatile and often market prices are driven by factors other than real-estate fundamentals. Many stock markets are still developing and have different reporting requirements, while the legal processes are not always as robust as in developed economies.

There are also corporate governance issues and political risks, including the threat of government intervention. For example, in 2010, as fears mounted of a speculative bubble in China's real estate market, the Chinese government implemented policy measures to slow down the market. Even in jurisdictions which are regarded as more accountable, government intervention can swing property markets – the Singapore government has great control over the ability to release land for development. At times when rental prices are too high and tenants are being lost to neighbouring Malaysia, the government of Singapore has been known to release more land for development, thereby artificially pushing prices down.

Property as an inflation hedge

As a real asset (one which has intrinsic value) property has been regarded a powerful hedge against the income-eroding impacts of inflation.

This is a contentious issue though, as research supporting property as an effective inflation hedge depends heavily on the time frame over which it is conducted. By using selective time periods, as is often done with financial research, it is possible to prove almost any investment case.[28] Robert

[28] R. Pemberton, 'HFM Columbus Investment Strategy newsletter' (1st Quarter 2011), p. 14.

Pemberton of wealth manager HFM Columbus says that the status of property as an inflation hedge may date from the 1970s and 1980s when inflation averaged 10% and was at 25% in the worst year; 1975.

There are, though, a number of arguments that back property as a powerful hedge against the detrimental effects of rising prices. The first lies in the fact that property is regarded as a real asset, with an intrinsic value that will be retained regardless of economic fluctuations. Property is also favoured as a hedge during inflationary times thanks to the growth in its underlying income – rent. Most rental contracts operate in the landlord's favour as rents tend to be negotiated up, not down, and may tie tenants in for long periods. Thanks in large part to upward-only rent reviews, income from property has risen over time more or less in line with inflation.

The time period, type of inflation and type of property investment all impact the effectiveness of property as an inflation hedge. Real estate's relationship with inflation can also fluctuate if economic activity slows and corporate tenants and rental growth come under pressure. The many different ways an investor can hold property – which were covered above – will also further complicate the relationship between inflation and property.

Factors to consider when investing in property for income

Property investments can vary greatly. You have to distinguish between residential and commercial property, owner occupation or a letting proposition, to name but a few. In the case of property funds, there is a variety of structures each with its advantages and disadvantages.

It is important to understand the type of investment you are getting into, how it will deliver income and how this income will be taxed. The investment structure will also dictate how easily the manager can sell investments – if a direct property fund is faced with a number of redemptions, it may have to sell assets to meet these which could take months or years, whereas property shares can be traded on a daily basis.

Other factors which you should consider when investing in property include:

1. Gearing & access to credit
2. Investment costs
3. Rental prices
4. The property cycle

Let's look at each of these in turn.

1. GEARING & ACCESS TO CREDIT

Given the large amounts of money required to make a direct property investment, most people buy property with money they do not have, in other words they borrow to invest. This is known as gearing. While gearing can magnify gains, it is high risk. If interest rates rise above the rental income or you cannot sell your property at a price sufficient to cover you borrowing, you will end up in trouble, possibly even bankrupt.

Gearing should also be a concern when investing in indirect property vehicles such as funds. A number of property funds landed in trouble during the 2007-2009 financial crisis due to high levels of gearing.

If investing in a property company directly or via a fund always make sure the balance sheet of the company is under control. While gearing can benefit an investment in rising markets, if markets turn it can be a major drag on returns.

It is also important to determine whether the gearing is priced into the dividend. If it is this may be presenting a skewed picture of the company's true ability to generate an income – remember gearing may magnify gains. Gearing can be a great illusion which makes investors think the underlying investment is much better than is actually the case.

Also look at a property company or fund's ability to secure funding. Access to credit will be an important factor in enabling it to tap into new investments. This may be tricky to assess but a good starting place will be the company's relationship with its creditors and the state of its balance sheets – the company's year end results showing this information will be available on its website or via Companies House. Lenders will be reluctant to lend to a company which is already heavily indebted.

2. INVESTMENT COSTS

Investing in property, especially via a direct investment, is not cheap. The costs involved are high and numerous. First you need to contend with the borrowing costs – will you be able to service the debt on your property investment if interest rates rise? The transaction costs involved with property deals can be substantial whether you are buying or selling a property. Then there are the running costs to contend with, such as replacing fixtures and fittings as well as services charges, insurance premiums and letting agency fees should you use an agency to help you rent out your property.

It is important to determine whether the yield generated by the property investment is enough. Does it cover the mortgage and other related costs? Alan Dick, chartered financial planner at FortyTwo Wealth Management points out that people often make the mistake of looking at the increase in the price of a property over time, thinking that it is a lucrative investment but forget about the cost of the interest they have had to pay on the debt used to buy that property.

If investing in property indirectly via a fund, remember that the fund's fees will impact the income return received.

3. RENTAL PRICES

The income from property will increase over time if the market rental prices increase. This can happen when local supply/demand dynamics change and/or where the market is able to capture fundamental changes in economic activity. When the economy grows, employment and consumer spending grow too, contributing to a greater demand for space resulting in higher rents.

How readily tenants can be found and vacancy levels in other properties in the same area as a property you are seeking to let are two factors to consider as this will determine how secure the income from a direct property investment will be.

Your property investment can quickly become unsustainable if you cannot find a tenant. Most properties have periods of non-tenancy known as void periods but it is important that the mortgage can still be paid during these periods. If not you run the risk of defaulting and in the worst case, after an extended period of not making your mortgage payments, the mortgage lender may reclaim the property.

Diversification of investments can better secure the income stream as you will not be relying on one investment alone to pay you an income. Here, property funds, investing in a spread of different properties or property companies, have the advantage.

4. THE PROPERTY CYCLE

The state of the property market and broader economy will have an impact on the income you receive from a property investment. Residential and commercial property are cyclical assets which means they are subject to downturns and upturns as demand and supply fluctuates.

Property prices and yields will rise and fall depending on the property cycle. Property cycles are marked by periods of boom and bust. A boom period is characterised by soaring economic growth which pushes up property prices and increases tenant demand. This increase in demand pushes up property rents and, in response, property developers (those individuals or businesses buying land and developing properties) plan more investments in real estate. Eventually this leads to an oversupply of property, rents start to flatten and eventually again fall. Boom then turns into bust and developers suffer capital losses on new developments and a fall in rental income on occupied properties.

Historically, this pattern of boom and bust has tended to be uncorrelated to stock market ups and downs as property is believed to have its own demand and supply cycle, but this has not always been the case. In the run up to the 2007-2009 financial crisis, commercial property prices were driven to unsustainable levels as investors, fuelled by cheap and widely available credit, bought into the asset class *en masse*.

This pushed prices higher and drove yields down. When the economic downturn hit, rents came under pressure, undermining property values and forcing many investors to sell property assets at low prices to pay off the debt. The commercial property bubble burst dramatically, striking a huge blow to perceptions of property as a safe investment which is less volatile than shares and counter-cyclical to the broader equity market.

Given the cyclical character of property it is important to have a long-term time horizon when investing in this asset class. Although typically less volatile than shares, property does not come with the promise of a fixed income return as is the case with the safer asset classes such as cash or bonds.

9

ALTERNATIVE INCOME INVESTMENTS

This chapter identifies three slightly more unusual asset classes which can provide a route to income. For each of the three, the investment fundamentals, risks and the different ways to invest are identified, along with an explanation of why these investments could make a good addition to your income portfolio. The three investments are:

1. Structured products
2. Infrastructure
3. Timber

We will now look at these three investments in turn.

1. Structured products

Structured products are fixed-term investments sold by high street banks, insurers and investment firms that offer a return based on specific circumstances related to an index, such as the FTSE 100, or other underlying assets.

This is an increasingly popular investment area – growth in the sector over the decade to the beginning of 2010 has averaged 20% per year[29]. To understand their popularity you need to understand how structured products work.

THE INVESTMENT FUNDAMENTALS

The main features of structured products are as follows:

- They can be used to deliver an *income*.
- The *risks and returns* for each product are defined in its literature at the outset before you buy.
- *Return of initial capital* and income payments are linked to an index, such as the FTSE 100, and dependent on the counterparty not defaulting.
- The *investment term* – often five or six years – is defined at the outset. Structured products are designed to be held until their maturity date. This means you are locking away your capital for a number of years.
- Structured products can be placed in a *tax exempt wrapper* such as an ISA, provided the investment falls within the maximum allowance of the ISA.

[29] www.structuredretailproducts.com.

The attraction of structured products lies in the predictable returns they provide and the element of capital protection they offer – there are very few other investments that can offer both. Structured products can also offer enhanced returns which might not be achievable for direct investments in equities or funds, such as in markets that are trading sideways or falling.

Let's now break down the structured products area into different varieties of these products in order to get a better idea of how they can be used.

TYPES OF STRUCTURED PRODUCTS

There are two main categories of structured products:

1. Structured deposits.
2. Capital-at-risk products.

1. Structured deposits

Structured deposits are cash-based term deposits mainly sold by banks and building societies. These pay an income in the form of an interest payment linked to the performance of a given index or other underlying instrument such as interest rates, fixed-income instruments, foreign exchange or commodities.

The original investment capital is guaranteed to be returned, providing the firm that issued the product does not default.

An example of such a product is the Meteor FTSE Income Deposit Plan 2 (**www.comparestructuredproducts.com/Structured-Product-Information.aspx?&ID=2876**). This plan's features are:

- A term of six years and two weeks.
- Stock market-linked performance: 7.5% annual or 1.5% quarterly gross income paid, provided FTSE 100 Index closes between 4500 and 7500 each day.
- Deposit returned at maturity, independent of stock market performance.

Another example is the Investec FTSE 100 Income Deposit Plan 20 (**www.investecstructuredproducts.com/products/launch27/ftse100_income_deposit_plan_20.html**). The features of this product are:

- Five-year term.
- Stock-market linked income payments.
- Deposit returned at maturity, independent of stock market performance.

UK-based structured deposits are normally eligible for compensation from the Financial Services Compensation Scheme (FSCS), as an ordinary savings or current account would be, should the issuer of the product fail or default on its payment obligations. But it is not guaranteed that you will receive this compensation – you should research this carefully before investing.

2. Capital-at-risk products

Capital-at-risk structured products (or *structured investments)* are not cash-based. These are packaged financial products typically based on a note (a fixed-term loan), derivatives or a warrant. These are complex financial instruments. As they are not deposit-based they are not protected by the FSCS – so the promise of a return of capital is only as strong as the bank behind the product. If it fails, investors could lose all of their capital. Also note that these vehicles do not benefit from share dividends, as would be enjoyed from equity income investments for example, because they do not invest in shares.

As investing in these products entails putting capital at risk, the returns they offer can be higher than with other structured products or investment assets of other types.

As an example, the return of initial capital from a structured product might be based on a predetermined provision such as, when the plan matures, the FTSE 100 (or any other index) must not have fallen below a pre-determined level and be at or above the level it was when the plan was started.

For instance, it might protect capital and repay it in full on the maturity date unless the FTSE (or other underlying index) falls below 50% of the price it was at on a given date. If this situation occurs then the product might, say, reduce the amount of initial investment capital by 1% for every 1% fall in the index over the investment term. Thus investment capital is at risk because its repayment is subject to certain criteria.

Income payment may be payable irrespective of the performance of the index (unconditional), or provided the index stays above a certain level or within a certain range (conditional). Plans which offer conditional income often provide a higher income than unconditional income plans.

An example of an unconditional income plan is the Morgan Stanley UK Inflation-Linked Income Plan 2:

www.comparestructuredproducts.com/Structured-Product-Information.aspx?Name=Morgan-Stanley-UK-Inflation-Linked-Income-Plan-2

The features of this product are:

- Five-year term.
- Inflation-linked income payments each year; there is a fixed payment of 5.25% in the first year and then four annual payments of 1.5 times the increase in the Retail Prices Index (RPI) year-on-year.
- Initial capital returned subject to the performance of the FTSE 100 index and the continued solvency of Morgan Stanley & Co. International plc.

You can see that such a product could be used to balance your portfolio against rising inflation, as it performs better the higher inflation rises.

Autocall arrangement

One particular form of structured products that is popular are those with what is known as a kick-out or autocall provision – they can be either deposit-based or capital-at-risk products. They can be employed by income investors to potentially generate high returns.

An autocall (or kick-out) product can offer higher returns than standard income-paying structured products within a shorter investment term. For example, a standard five-year FTSE 100 structured product might offer an income of 5% per year, but an autocall product might offer 10% for each year held.

The autocall works by setting out a return that will be paid based upon certain circumstances. For instance, the terms might state that if the FTSE 100 has risen the 10% return is paid and the product matures, and if the FTSE 100 has fallen the product rolls on to another year.

How an autocall works is best explained with an illustrative example.

Autocall product example

Let's say our autocall product has a maximum term of six years and will pay a potential return of 10% for each year held. A start date is given to the product and the level of the FTSE 100 is taken on that date.

After one year, if the FTSE 100 is above the level it was at on the start date then the product matures and the original capital is repaid along with the return of 10%. If the FTSE 100 is lower after one year than it was on the start date then the investment rolls into year two.

At the end of the second year, if the FTSE 100 is above the level it was at on the start date then the product matures and the original capital is repaid along with a return of 20% (twice the annual return). If the FTSE 100 is lower after two years than it was on the start date then the investment rolls into year three.

This continues until the final year. After six years, if the FTSE 100 was lower than its level on the start date each year but has now climbed above that rate, then a 60% return is paid along with the original capital. If the FTSE 100 is lower than it was at the start of the six-years but by no more than 50% down, then the original capital is repaid but there is no additional return. If the FTSE is more than 50% down then the investor will suffer an equivalent loss.

An example of a structured product with an autocall provision is the Walker Crips Annual Growth Plan Issue Thirteen:
www.comparestructuredproducts.com/Structured-Product-Information.aspx?Name=Walker-Crips-Annual-Growth-Plan-Issue-Thirteen-Kick-out

The features of this product are:

- Maximum six-year term; the plan matures on the first anniversary that the FTSE 100 is higher than it was at the start date or at the end of six years if that comes first.
- Stock market linked payments of 8% for each year the plan has been in force, providing the FTSE 100 is at or above its initial level at the end of one of the years in which the plan is active.
- Return of original capital subject to FTSE 100 performance; capital returned in full if the FTSE 100 index is at the same level, or higher, as the initial level on a plan anniversary or, if not, provided the index isn't more than 50% down at the end of the sixth year, and the continued solvency of Santander UK plc (the plan's counterparty).

Recently, *defensive* autocall products have become more popular. With these products the gain is payable if the underlying index has fallen by up to a specified percentage (for example, 90% of its initial level), although plans of this nature offer lower returns. Autocall plans can also be linked to two or three indices, offering higher returns than single index plans due to the increased risk of the plan not maturing early.

Gains on autocall capital-at-risk products are typically subject to capital gains tax (CGT) and this could prove very favourable for investors who do not ordinarily utilise their CGT allowances.

CHOOSING A STRUCTURED PRODUCT

The range of structured products available is large; and new structured investments are also constantly being launched, most with limited offer periods.

For a rundown of structured products currently offered on the market, a good source is provided by Lowes Financial Management. This site enables you to filter the current market offering by type of structured product, counterparty, underlying index and a range of other parameters. It can be found at: **www.comparestructuredproducts.com**.

So how do you choose which structured product to invest in?

Ian Lowes of Lowes Financial Management advises that the first important step is to fully examine what products are available before deciding upon one. You should check the products of all banks and firms, not just those you already use, to see what is on offer.

There are lots of companies offering similar products but a good place to start in weighing up structured products is the credit rating of the organisation offering the product. Remember that while the risk of a bank defaulting may be very low, those that have poorer credit ratings carry a greater risk of default. These credit ratings are provided on the Lowes Financial Management website. Remember that firms with a credit rating of Baa have a 3% chance of defaulting in a five-year period and a firm rated higher than this will default with a lower frequency.

When thinking about structured products, consider how they would perform relative to other investments in various market conditions. For example, if a structured product offers some degree of protection from negative market movements, this can be used to balance your portfolio as some of your other investments – such as equities or ETFs – may be adversely affected by falls in the stock market. Similarly, an inflation-linked structured product may provide comparable protection against rising inflation to that provided by an inflation-linked bond, but with greater upside potential for income payments.

Regulation requires that you buy structured investment plans from a financial adviser or execution-only broker rather than directly from the provider.

How much to invest

Guidelines from the regulator advise that an investor should not have more than 25% of their overall portfolio invested in structured products, or more than 10% invested in any one product. However, there is no law or regulation which says you cannot have an entire portfolio of structured products provided that you understood the risks involved and accepted the risks were appropriate for you. Of course, the usual principles of diversification still stand – a balanced portfolio should ideally contain a mix of assets and a portfolio of only structured investments will generally not achieve this aim.

Utilising structured investments as part of a well balanced income portfolio can provide you with defined income at pre-defined dates which could help tax planning and potentially enhance your income returns while reducing the risk of loss. These benefits do, however, have to be offset against the drawbacks and risks of these products.

THE RISKS

The risks of investing in structured products are:

1. Investment risk
2. Counterparty risk
3. Inflexible, fixed-term contracts and liquidity
4. Complicated investment class

Let's look at these four risks in some more detail.

1. Investment risk

You could lose some or all of your capital. Those products that do provide capital protection may do so by limiting the income payments generated by the product.

2. Counterparty risk

Counterparty risk is the risk that the company backing the plan will be unable to repay your initial investment and any returns. The structured product plan provider splits your money into two parts, with most of it buying the loan note from a counterparty. This collateral funds the repayment of all or part of your initial investment when the fixed term ends. The rest of your money is invested by the counterparty in derivatives to produce either income or growth, depending on the structure of the plan. If the counterparty gets into financial difficulty you could lose some or all of your investment and compensation is not guaranteed.

Counterparty risk of structured products during the credit crunch

The biggest single risk of structured product plans is that of the counterparty backing the plan defaulting – this is because the plan's return relies on this entity, which is usually a bank. In the run up to the 2007-2009 financial crisis a number of investors bought these plans from the now defunct companies NDF, Defined Returns Limited and Arc Capital & Income. The counterparty to some of these plans was Lehman Brothers. When Lehman Brothers collapsed in late 2008 many investors lost out on their structured investments and eventually all three providers went into administration after they were unable to meet the cost of complaints from investors in Lehman-backed investment plans.

An investigation by the regulator later found that investors who were sold Lehman Brothers-backed structured products by NDF, Defined Returns Limited and Arc Capital & Income had been adequately warned about the risk of a counterparty default in the marketing material supplied by the three structured product providers and thus these investors were not entitled to receive financial compensation. Compensation was however due from the providers where they had made errors in the brochures and this has prompted a significant tightening up in the quality of product literature.

3. Fixed terms

As these are fixed-term investments, investors may face penalties if they withdraw from a plan before its term is finished and in some cases early withdrawal is not permitted at all. This makes structured product plans relatively illiquid as they often require investors to lock away their money for several years with limited opportunity to realise their investment until maturity. The inflexibility of structured products often makes them unsuitable for investors with a high risk appetite who prefer to have greater control over their investments or investors who might need the capital within the term period. Structured products should therefore never be seen as an alternative to cash.

4. Complexity

The product literature attached to structured product plans needs to be studied carefully. There is a risk that investors can be lured in by high headline rates of return, often not understanding the risks. The structure of the plans can also be opaque and it is often unclear how much of an investor's subscription goes into the plan's guarantee, the option that delivers the return, or into the charges. However, charges are normally accounted for in the structure so do not affect the amount being invested as they have been taken into account in the terms of the investment. So, for every £100 invested, the return, provided the investment is held until maturity, should be £100, plus or minus the gain or loss in accordance with the defined terms.

2. Infrastructure

Infrastructure development is a key growth driver in any economy. There are broadly two types of infrastructure:

1. Economic
2. Social

Economic infrastructure has income which is based upon the level of demand, and includes both transport infrastructure, such as ports, railways or toll roads, and public utilities such as water and electricity distribution.

Social infrastructure is normally available as an investment through public private partnerships (PPPs) or private finance initiatives (PFIs). Common investments are schools, hospitals and prisons, and revenues are based not upon usage but upon provision and service levels. Typically the contracts are backed by governments, and annual adjustments to income and some costs are made according to an inflation-linked agreement. The cash flows are relatively high and paid regularly. This last mentioned form of infrastructure is what the income investor will be interested in.

As establishing and maintaining infrastructure is an expensive exercise which involves very large amounts of money, government and companies are often left facing a funding gap. This opens up an opportunity for investors to become involved by investing in infrastructure companies and developments. A number of funds have been set-up for this purpose. These, similar to equity income and bond funds, pay dividends and can boast attractive dividend yields.[30]

[30] B. Weber and Hans Wilhelm Alfen, *Infrastructure As An Asset Class* (John Wiley & Sons, 2010), p. xviii and pp. 21-54.

INVESTMENT FUNDAMENTALS

Infrastructure boasts a number of compelling investment fundamentals.

As a start, the fixed contracts linked to infrastructure investments are agreed far in advance – these long lead times and the fact that infrastructure development is essential (it can't just be called off in a downturn) gives a degree of protection to revenues from changes in the economic cycle.

Infrastructure provides a natural hedge against inflation as most revenues are combined with an inflation adjustment mechanism either through regulated income clauses, guaranteed yields or other contractual agreements.[31]

Companies in the infrastructure space benefit from high barriers to entry given that their services are usually difficult to duplicate and start-up costs are high. This gives companies the benefit of strong pricing power, sustainable growth and predictable cash flows. Regulatory support also means prices are fixed and infrastructure investments provide minimum payment guarantees, making income more predictable.

Typically the contracts to provide infrastructure are regulated by government and are long-term, and define significant parts of both revenues and costs. For an investor the key attraction of infrastructure lies not in the physical assets but in the risk/return profile. In this regard the asset class has a mixture of the attributes of equity, debt and real estate.

HOW TO INVEST IN INFRASTRUCTURE

Given the large amounts of capital involved and the complexities of the underlying investments, a direct investment in an infrastructure project may be too risky or practically impossible for most investors. The most affordable way for an investor to gain exposure to infrastructure and spread their risk is via funds vehicles. Funds spread the cash of a number of investors across a pool of infrastructure projects, each with different maturity dates.

The infrastructure funds universe has grown rapidly over a short period – as at November 2009 there were 100 infrastructure managers and more than 150 unlisted funds globally. If you include managers investing in clean energy

[31] Weber and Alfen, *Infrastructure.*

infrastructure assets the figure swells to well in excess of 200 managers and 300 unlisted funds globally.[32]

Infrastructure funds can invest in two principal ways, via a closed-ended fund or an open-ended fund.

Closed-ended funds

A closed-ended investment company may take equity stakes in or inject debt into individual infrastructure projects – such as bridges, toll roads, airports and so on – usually via a public private partnership (PPP) or the private finance initiative (PFI). These schemes design, finance and construct the asset and then maintain it for a long period – usually between 25 and 40 years.

In return, the investing fund gets payments from the public sector. Payments are agreed up-front and linked to the physical availability of the asset, rather than the level of demand or use. The investing fund is expected to meet the finance and subcontracting costs from this income, and keeps the difference.

There are a number of players within the closed-ended space investing in social infrastructure – these include HSBC Infrastructure and Gravis Capital Partners (GCP) Infrastructure Investments Limited, which focus almost exclusively on the UK, International Public Partnerships (IPP) and 3i Infrastructure which include overseas projects in their portfolios, and the John Laing Infrastructure Fund. Closed-ended funds tend to benefit from higher dividend yields. Table 9.1 below shows the yield on these funds.

Table 9.1 – yield on closed-ended infrastructure funds

Fund	Dividend yield (%)
HICL Infrastructure	5.7
John Laing Infrastructure	5.6
International Public Partnerships	5.1
3i Infrastructure	4.7
GCP Infrastructure Investments	4.3

Source: Association of Investment Companies (AIC) website (based on annual yields as at 31 May 2011)

[32] Weber and Alfen, *Infrastructure*.

Open-ended funds

Open-ended funds invest in the shares of infrastructure companies – these are more liquid investments as they are listed publicly. A fund manager can therefore adjust their strategies at short notice, although this does go against the long-term nature of these investments.

There are a number of funds which invest in global infrastructure many, with a broad spread of investments in both developed and developing economies. Most of these funds are listed in the IMA's specialist sector and examples include the First State Global Listed Infrastructure Fund, JPMorgan Emerging Markets Infrastructure Fund and Macquarie Global Infrastructure Securities.

The drawbacks of investing in listed investments include high volatility and correlation with the equity markets.

What to look out for with funds

Most of these funds have short track records which can make it difficult to assess the expertise and performance of the managers. Two factors that you can watch out for when investing in an infrastructure fund are strategy drift – this occurs when the fund manager fails to adhere to the agreed investment strategy – and high charges, including performance fees, as these can significantly reduce your net yield. Also, make sure the fund manager has investment experience and understanding of the segment in which he or she is investing.

INCOME FROM INFRASTRUCTURE

For an income investor the most attractive characteristic of infrastructure is its ability to provide stable and consistent income returns with moderate risks and volatility, relatively independent of the macroeconomic environment.

Social infrastructure in particular is a good route to income given that revenues are based not upon usage but upon provision, and most contracts for schools, hospitals, etc., tend to be backed by the government. Investing in this form of infrastructure can provide good yields of around 5%, positively correlated with inflation.

As mentioned, with infrastructure the costs of finance are fixed at the outset; however, income streams and operating costs from mature concessions are often inflation-linked with limited exposure to economic cycles or competition. There is no simple rule of thumb across all infrastructure projects but most have some link to inflation. Typically the link is to the Retail Prices Index (RPI), in whole or in part.

There is also longevity to the income generated by infrastructure investments given that concessions are normally long-term – anything up to 20 to 50 years and in a few cases even longer. You should therefore always regard infrastructure as a long-term investment to allow time for investments to come to fruition – expect to hold an infrastructure fund for at least five years.

THE RISKS

- It makes sense to invest in this asset class via an infrastructure fund where decisions are left to the fund manager. But *make sure the manager heading up the fund has the necessary experience* to invest in this area and thus understands the market and the risks. As infrastructure funds are a relatively new development, managers of the funds may lack operational experience in the area.
- Infrastructure's position as a long-term, comparatively low risk investment depends on the *structure of the specific investment in question.* In some cases, infrastructure investments can entail risks equal to those of equity investments.
- There is also the thorny issue of *contract renegotiation* and the effect that this would have on longer term cash flows.
- Infrastructure projects can involve huge levels of debt and if interest rates rise this could place pressure on the balance sheets of the companies involved.
- Given the public nature of these assets, these projects can fall prey to *government intervention* – for example funding, regulation or price setting.
- Investment companies investing directly in infrastructure often need to subcontract construction or management which can add a significant degree of *third-party risk*. The possible failure of any of the counterparties, whether for building, facilities management, finance or insurance, is always a risk but these are not specific to the infrastructure sector alone.

3. Timber

AN EVERGREEN INVESTMENT

Investing in trees might sound like an esoteric way of unlocking an investment income but commercial tropical timber plantations have been around for more than 300 years, having first been used by the Dutch East India Trading Company for shipbuilding and repair. While there are risks, timber is regarded as a relatively safe route to predictable income returns. The obvious reason for this is that trees will grow regardless of economic conditions and, as such, forestry tends to be less volatile than other assets and can bring an important element of diversification to an investment portfolio.

During the economic downturn in 2008, timber was one of the few asset classes in the UK to emerge relatively unscathed by the collapse in markets. The IPD Forestry Index, calculated from a sample of private sector coniferous plantations of predominantly Sitka spruce in mainland Britain, indicates that an investment in forestry outperformed domestic commercial property and equities, as Table 9.2 shows.

Table 9.2 – The Investment Property Databank (IPD) UK Forestry Index. Figures to December 2010.

	1 year	3 years	5 years	10 years	18 years
Forestry total return (%)	20	12.6	17.7	10.4	6.3
Timber price changes (%)	38.5	1.5	12.7	4.5	-0.5
Other assets (total returns)					
Equities (%)	14.5	1.4	5.1	3.7	8.2
Gilts (%)	9.1	7.7	5.9	5.9	7.7
Commercial property (%)	15.1	-2.5	1.1	6.8	9.2

Data sources: FTSE All-Share Index, FTSE UK Gilts Index 5-15 yrs, IPD UK Annual Index, Forestry Commission Nominal Price Index of Coniferous Standing Sales (for Great Britain)

THE INVESTMENT FUNDAMENTALS

Timber offers diversification benefits for investors because it is not affected by movements in the traditional investment markets. It is also supplied as a raw material to industry sectors that are not strongly correlated with each other. There is the potential for regular cash generation from tree harvesting, licensing, water rights and carbon credits, along with capital appreciation from timber growth and land sales.

Other favourable characteristics include strong demand and supply fundamentals – global demand for timber is growing thanks to population growth and rising disposable incomes, especially in the world's emerging economies. China, for example, imports vast amounts of timber each year to build homes for people moving to the cities.

Meanwhile, the supply of timber is constantly on the decline. This is due to reduced arable land on which to grow timber while forest coverage in timber-producing regions such as Africa, Asia and Latin America has been declining as a result of increased environmental awareness and policies to tighten wood supply.

Timber also qualifies as a green and socially responsible investment as timberlands consume carbon dioxide and produce oxygen, while wood is a renewable resource because more trees can be planted if there is space to plant them in. Making wood-based products consumes less energy and generates less pollution than most substitutes. Renewable energy incentives, backed by climate change commitments, are expected to increase demand for wood.

HOW TO INVEST IN TIMBER

There are two main ways to invest in timber:

1. A direct investment in woodlands.
2. An indirect investment via pooled funds such as exchange-traded funds (ETFs) or timber real estate investment trusts (REITs).

Investing directly

Investing in timber directly is costly and usually requires a very large commitment of capital. Few investors can afford the high minimum costs involved with directly investing in timber.

These investments also tend to be illiquid and require investors to lock up capital for long periods – anywhere between 10 and 12 years. When investing directly, investors also need to buy insurance against the physical risks such as adverse weather conditions, fires and pest infestations.

The attraction of a direct investment in timber, however, is in the tax advantages such an investment can bring. To encourage private ownership of woodlands in the UK and investment in forestry, there is relief from income tax, capital gains tax and inheritance tax. The benefits of these tax breaks should be judged in connection with the overall commercial benefit of the investment.

Investing indirectly

For most an investment in a collective vehicle such as a forestry or timber fund, or exchange-traded fund (ETF) may represent a more affordable entry point into the asset class. These investments will work in the same way as an investment in any other fund or ETF; they invest in a spread of timberland assets or timber-related companies.

As this is a specialised area, fund choice is limited and many of the funds are unregulated non-UK collective investment vehicles. Timber funds registered offshore are not regulated under UK law, which means there is no investment protection from the Financial Services Compensation Scheme (FSCS).

It is also not possible to hold these funds within your Individual Savings Account (ISA), although they are permitted within a SIPP.

These funds also tend to demand higher fees. An example of a more affordable and liquid option is the iShares S&P Global Timber & Forestry ETF. It follows an index of the 25 largest and most liquid listed companies globally that are involved in the ownership, management or the upstream supply chain of forests and timberlands, and comes with a competitive total expense ratio (TER) of 0.65%.

Table 9.3 provides some examples of timber funds.

Table 9.3 – examples of timber funds

Fund name	Manager	Domicile	Structure	Launch date	Fees
Cambium Global Timberland	CP Cogent AM LB	Jersey	Closed-ended	06-Mar-07	1% AMC
iShares S&P Timber & Forestry ETF	BlackRock Asset Mangement	Ireland	ETF	15-Oct-07	0.65% TER
Phaunos Timber Fund	FourWinds Capital Mangement	Guernsey	Closed-ended	30-Dec-06	1.5% AMC, 3.47% TER

Source: Factsheets of respective funds

INCOME FROM TIMBER

Timber is generally regarded as an investment for capital growth but it can produce income as well. This income is influenced by three factors:

1. Biological tree growth
2. Timber price changes
3. Changes in the value of the underlying land asset

Though the income stream from an investment in timber will fluctuate depending on these factors, trees tend to grow predictably year-on-year and as a tree's price grows as it grows, timber tends to be a fairly consistent cash-generative investment. Once a plantation holds mature timber it can generate a steady income stream each year through the harvest and sale of that timber. This means that timber can pay a fairly fixed income stream over time and this often sees it compared to bond investments.

As a defensive, real asset, timber can also be a useful shield against inflation and market price fluctuations, providing valuable income protection to a portfolio. The main difference between timber and other asset classes covered in this book is that the performance of forestry assets is driven primarily by the natural growth rate of trees rather than what's happening in the markets or the broader economy. This makes timber a much less volatile investment over the long term.

That said, timber is not entirely immune from outside factors. For instance, in the 12 months to March 2009 timber prices fell by 29%, the sharpest decline in a decade, due in part to a drop in the number of new homes being built, an increase in the recycling of wood and a flood of low cost imports of forestry assets.

Positive carry

Timber also provides protection against market price movements by positive carry. This means if a tree grows 8% in a year and the price of timber rises 2% then the worth of the asset has grown 10% in total.

To benefit from positive carry investors can hold off selling while market prices are low, safe in the knowledge that the underlying value of their investment is still rising as trees grow.

THE RISKS

Timber is regarded as a relatively low-risk investment but it is certainly not risk free.

Timber and forestry assets involve a lot of work – keeping the forest clean, patrolling for pests and managing any problems that might occur before they become real hazards. Even the best management can not protect against the risk of natural disasters such as fires, floods and pest infestations destroying plantations. Any of these problems could affect the forestry assets a fund is invested in.

Valuing timber can also be tricky because essentially the value is vested with the tree but, if investing via a fund, the investment will only start to pay an income once the tree has been cut down as income is generated from the sale of harvested timber. If you're investing via a timber fund, you will also enjoy income diversification benefits as managers tend to invest in timberland with different harvest maturities.

PART C:

BUILDING AND MANAGING AN INCOME PORTFOLIO

Understanding how investment income works, the different shapes and forms it can take and how the different investment vehicles can be used to generate income is useful but you also need to know how to apply this knowledge to construct an investment portfolio for income.

In Part C the focus shifts from the theoretical to the practical. This section explains how to apply what you have learned in the first two parts of the book. We look at the steps you need to take to build an investment portfolio suited to your specific circumstances and income requirements.

Model income portfolios suited to different life stages, from the young to those in retirement, are presented, along with thoughts on how these can be tweaked to fit with your individual circumstances, risk appetite and income needs. In each case we will look at a worked example showing how an investor should go about dividing up their capital and constructing a portfolio, looking at hypothetical incomes that can be earned and the asset allocation mix for different types of investors.

We then go on to look at pensions and the different ways in which you can draw down an income from your retirement pot. Lastly we consider the tax vehicles, reliefs and tax-efficient investment strategies that you can use to help you retain as much of your investment income as possible.

10

BUILDING AN INCOME PORTFOLIO

As we saw in Part B, there are a number of asset classes and investment vehicles that can generate income. Putting these together to achieve your targeted income stream is the ultimate goal. This chapter will look at how investments can be blended together to build a portfolio that generates an income.

There are a number of important steps to this:

1. Create an *income strategy*.
2. *Asset allocation*: Determine your ideal asset mix based on your age, investment goals and risk appetite.
3. *Investing*: Find individual investments to hold within each asset class. Determine how much capital you have to invest, the investment platform or wrapper you are going to use to invest, how many different investments you intend to hold within each asset class, and your investment timing and style.
4. *Drawing income*: decide when, how and how much income you want to draw from your portfolio.
5. *Monitoring*: Review and rebalance your income portfolio.

Let's discuss each of these points in turn.

1. Income strategy

Before investing, if you are to be successful, you need an income strategy. The planning process need not be overly complex. It has three basic steps:

1. *Target returns* – what yield do you want to achieve?
2. *Establish your time horizon* – how long are you intending to invest for?
3. *Your return expectations* – what is the balance between income and capital growth you would like to achieve?

Let's look at each of these in turn.

1. TARGET RETURNS

Establish how much capital you have to invest and use this to work out what yield you are targeting.

For example, if you want £5000 in income a year and you have capital of £100,000 to invest, you should be aiming for an income return or yield of 5% on that capital. If you have £50,000 to invest, you would need to aim for an income return of 10%. To achieve this higher return, you will need to take on more investment risk.

You may just be looking to beat the interest rate paid by your bank account on savings. If this is, say, 2%, you will be looking to earn a higher yield than this.

2. ESTABLISH YOUR TIME HORIZON

Your investment time horizon – how long you intend to hold your investments for – will determine whether your ideal income return is achievable or not. An income investor should have a time horizon of at least five years, but it is often the case that different time horizons apply to different income needs. You will probably find that you need income now to fund short-term expenses as well as income in the future for your retirement.

The way to address these immediate and future income needs is to build a portfolio with a blend of investments, including some that will pay an income immediately and some to grow your capital now and then pay an income in the future. You could even create two separate portfolios – one focused on meeting your immediate income needs and one which will grow your income for future needs, although you need to be wary of the costs this may incur.

Let's think about what sort of investment classes are suited to delivering incomes on various time scales.

- Investments used to finance your *immediate income* needs should be liquid – in other words, you should be able to convert them into cash easily without suffering a loss of capital. If, for example, you want income in six months' time to buy a new home or car you should not be investing in the most speculative, volatile investment for those six months. In this case you should consider safer, more conservative investment such as cash-based deposit accounts and money market funds, which are readily convertible into cash and provide better protection for your capital invested.
- For your *intermediate income* goals – the income needed to cover annual or triennial expenses – you will need investments that generate slightly

higher returns than your average savings account. Bonds offer a constant income stream with the return of capital at fixed date.

- Finally, investments best suited to meet your *long-term income* requirements, such as income in retirement or money for a child's university education will be those with long-term growth prospects, which can also provide a hedge against inflation, such as equities or property.

3. YOUR RETURN EXPECTATIONS

You might be able to determine that you need an income return of 5% on your investment but how do you know if 5% is a reasonable income return? Besides the amount of capital you have to invest and your investment time horizon, this will depend on the asset class or investment vehicle you are investing in.

A higher risk investment, for example an equity investment, might comfortably deliver this return but of course you will need to contend with the increased risk to your capital. How much or how little risk you take will determine the amount of return you can expect. This is why it is crucial to understand the risk associated with different asset classes and investment strategies. Another factor will be the economic environment at the time. For example, if interest rates are low and inflation high, achieving a return of 5% might be more challenging.

When assessing your return expectations, you also need to decide the balance between income and capital growth you wish to achieve. While income will be your main goal, it is still important to keep an eye on maintaining your capital. If your income needs aren't immediate you might consider making investments which will see your capital grow or rolling up your income returns via compounding or reinvesting dividends. In this way you grow your original capital invested and so increase any future income payments.

2. Asset allocation

The fundamental premise behind asset allocation is that by diversifying your investments you should be able to limit losses and reduce volatility in income returns without giving up too much in gains.

Your asset allocation will be the most significant determinant of your income portfolio's performance over time; countless research studies have found asset allocation to account for the majority of returns from different portfolios over the long term. This means that timing the market - when you choose to buy and sell your investments - and stock-picking - the individual equities you choose to invest in - pale into insignificance compared to the importance of achieving the right balance of cash, fixed interest and shares in your portfolio.

DECIDE WHAT PROPORTION OF YOUR CAPITAL GOES INTO WHAT ASSETS

Your first step is to decide what percentage of your capital you will put in these asset classes in order to maximise the income return for the level of risk you are willing to take.

But how do you decide how much goes where?

Unfortunately there is no rigid formula that can be applied to find the ideal mix. But there are a number of criteria which an individual investor should consider in order to construct the asset allocation balance that is right for them. These include:

- Age of the investor
- Investment goals
- Risk appetite

Age

A younger investor with a long investment time horizon and many years of earnings capacity ahead can afford to take more risks and deal with greater volatility as their portfolio has more time to smooth out returns and recoup any investment losses. Their asset mix might therefore be heavier weighted towards the more risky asset classes such as equities, and equities at the higher risk end, such as global markets.

Older investors or those nearing retirement with less time to recoup any investment loss should focus more on capital protection. They will want to maintain the value of their investment capital in order to be able to draw the maximum income from it when they retire and can no longer rely on income from a salary or wage. As such, these investors might prefer to allocate more of their capital into the safer asset classes such as cash and fixed interest.

Investment goals

Your investment goals will also play a role in your asset allocation plan. The main question you need to ask yourself is to what extent you are willing to accept a possible capital loss to achieve a higher level of income. If you are not prepared to accept any risk of capital loss you should confine yourself to a bank or building society deposit account and be content with the lower interest returns on offer. You should also be content with being a saver, not an investor.

Equally, while you may think to yourself that you want as much income as possible, you will need to compromise between the level of income you want to achieve and the risk you are willing to take. If interest rates are low, cautious investors who prefer to hold their investments in cash will either have to contend with a lower level of income or take on more investment risk and move into higher-risk assets to secure a higher level of income.

The gap between your current income and your investment goals will also determine how risky your asset allocation will be. If you are far off from achieving your ideal income you may have to allocate more of your investment portfolio to the riskier asset classes with the aim of achieving a higher income return.

Risk appetite

The risk built into a portfolio needs to be at a level at which the investor is comfortable, while the reward needs to be matched to the investor's income goals. Your asset allocation will therefore also be a function of your risk appetite – how much risk are you willing to take with your capital.

Risk profiling

The more risk averse you are, the greater the percentage of your portfolio that will be allocated to cash and the safer asset classes. Financial advisers and investors often use questionnaires and risk scales to determine risk appetite. This process is known as risk profiling. There are a number of risk profiling tools available online that you can use to determine your ideal level risk such as FinaMetrica's risk profiling system (**www.finametrica.com**), which is often used by financial advisers.

As can be expected, risk profiling is a highly subjective process – one person's idea of low risk could be another's idea of high risk. Risk profiling tools should therefore be used with a pinch of salt.

If you are willing to take on a fairly large amount of risk in the search for a higher income, you will weight your asset allocation mix more towards the riskier asset classes such as equities, funds and property. If you are more risk averse, you should tilt your portfolio's asset allocation mix more towards the safe asset classes such as cash and bonds. But remember that to maintain a balanced portfolio it is important to always have a mix of all the traditional asset classes and possibly some alternative assets, within your portfolio.

Figures 10.1, 10.2 and 10.3 show how the asset allocation plan will vary between low risk, medium risk and high risk portfolios. As you can see the high risk portfolio has substantially more allocated in equities while the lower risk portfolio has a high proportion in the safe asset classes, cash and fixed interest.

Figure 10.1 – asset allocation for a low-risk investor

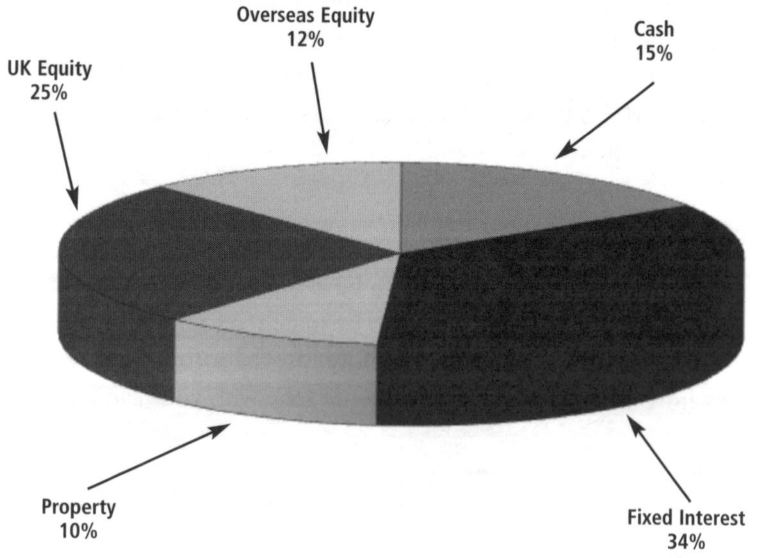

Figure 10.2 – asset allocation for a moderate-risk investor

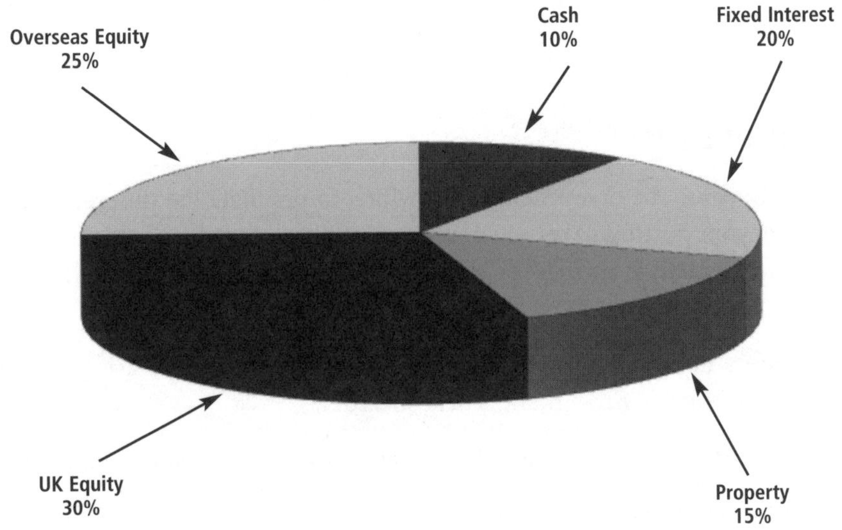

Figure 10.3 – asset allocation for a high-risk investor

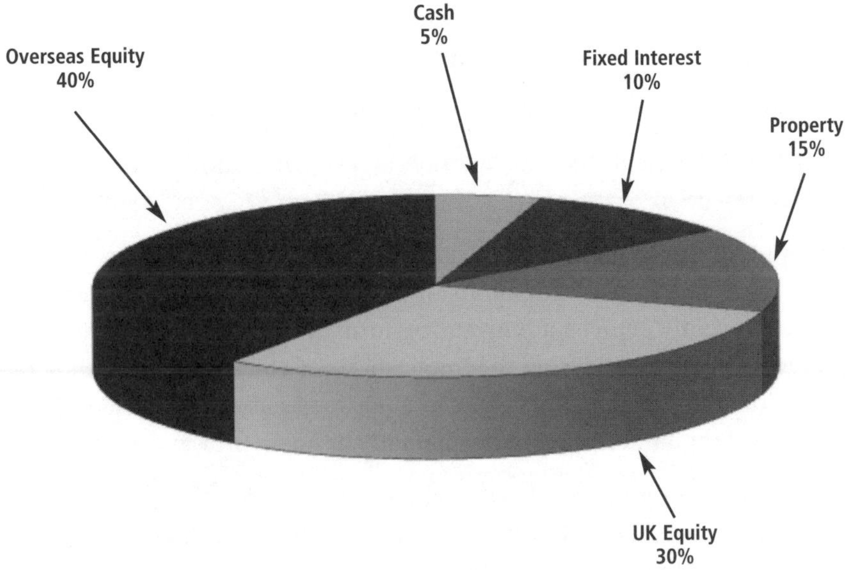

Asset allocation is not a pre-determined, rigid process – your asset split will depend on various factors and may shift as your circumstances, risk appetite and income goals change. Allowing for some flexibility is therefore important.

Once you have decided what proportion of your money is going to be invested in which asset class you can begin to implement your asset allocation strategy by selecting specific investment vehicles.

3. Investing

When choosing the investments with which to populate the different asset classes in your portfolio, you will need to carefully assess which vehicles allow you to implement your income strategy in the most efficient and effective way.

There are a number of important questions that you should ask yourself before you make an investment. These include:

- What exposure do I want to this area and do I already have too much?
- What is the yield of this investment – is the historical record good or is this yield variable, and what are the future prospects for the yield?
- What is the risk (high or low)?
- How much do I invest?
- How long do I intend to hold this asset for?
- What return do I expect over this period?
- What if the yield drops below my target – when do I reconsider the investment?

The approach that should definitely not be taken is to spread capital randomly within asset classes, allocating funds to shares that are fashionable or funds that have recently enjoyed a buoyant performance. By adopting a random approach without considering the implications of your investment choices, you could end up being overweight in a particular asset class, leaving you overexposed should that asset perform poorly or not in the way you expected.

The idea of building a portfolio is to achieve a level of diversification that fits with your risk appetite and meets your income objectives. Taking a random approach will not have this desired effect. Some of the most important factors you will need to consider before you start investing are:

1. *Your available capital.* How much money do you have to invest? The amount of capital you have will influence the type of investments you buy and can have a bearing on the amount of risk you are able or willing to take.
2. *Your investment platform or wrapper.* How are you going to invest? There are various ways of setting up an investment portfolio and you need to weigh up the costs and benefits of these before you part with your money.
3. *Portfolio construction.* How many investments are you going to hold in each asset class?
4. *Timing and strategy.* Are you going to invest via a lump sum or regular contributions? Will you buy and hold your investments for the long term or actively manage your portfolio?
5. *Tax.* Take time to structure your portfolio in the most tax efficient way.
6. *Advice.* Are you going to adopt a DIY approach to selecting investments or will you call in the help of an expert?

1. AVAILABLE CAPITAL

The amount of capital you have to invest will determine the investments you choose and how much risk you are willing and able to take. For example, an investor with a smaller capital pot might be more likely to invest in funds and exchange-traded funds (ETFs) as opposed to shares. This is because funds, being invested in a spread of different securities, will enable them to access the full range of asset classes needed to achieve diversification with relatively modest investment sums.

If you have a small amount to invest you need to be careful about having too much invested in the more risky assets such as equities. If the stock market suffers an extended period of falling prices this might force you to sell your holdings to fund your income needs and in the worse case, could wipe out a significant chunk of your capital. It therefore follows that investors with a limited amount of capital tend to be more risk averse – while investors with more capital may be more willing to take more risk.

Of course, the opposite can also be true – just because you have a large pool of investment capital does not mean you will be more willing to lose it than someone with a smaller capital pot.

2. INVESTMENT PLATFORM/WRAPPER

There are various ways to hold a portfolio of investments. You can opt for a stocks and shares ISA or choose to hold your investments within a SIPP portfolio; both are explained in chapter 12. Fund platforms such as Alliance Trust Savings and/or execution brokers such as Hargreaves Lansdown will usually offer these vehicles along with a range of investments to put into them.

You could also consider investing in an investment trust savings scheme, either via regular monthly savings or lump sums at any time. Each scheme has its own features – you can find about about these and apply to the funds on their respective websites. Examples of the providers are BlackRock (**www.blackrock.co.uk/IndividualInvestors/FundCentre/InvestmentTrusts**) and the Scottish Investment Trust (**www.sit.co.uk**). You can find a directory of investment trusts on Trustnet (**www.trustnet.com/InvestmentTrusts.aspx**).

Refer to Table 7.19 on page 178 for a comparison of fund platforms.

Costs

The costs of your investments can significantly reduce your returns; the cost of making an investment – the commission and fees incurred – needs to be considered. The fees for ETFs might be less than those for actively managed funds, but if you buy and sell ETFs regularly the trading costs will mount up.

3. PORTFOLIO CONSTRUCTION

You will have already decided upon your asset allocation, but you now need to decide how to spread your investments within asset classes.

Cash

For example, you could hold the cash element of your portfolio in one deposit account. How much you hold in cash will be a function of your risk appetite, but all investors should hold some of their capital in cash and never more than the FSCS compensation limit with any one institution.

Your cash holding can be used to provide an ongoing income. It also enables you to take advantage of new investment opportunities as and when they arise. Cash is flexible and unless you are holding it within a term deposit account it can be moved into a new investment quickly and easily.

Cash is also an important balancing tool – if higher risk investments such as equities are delivering a low or uncertain income, an investor may want to shift more of their portfolio into cash to balance this and reduce the overall risk.

Shares

With shares, it is good to have a spread of investments across different industries; in other words don't restrict your investments to only one sector or industry. Let's say two-fifths of your portfolio is invested in just three companies: Vodafone, GlaxoSmithKline and National Grid. How will you know if your portfolio is adequately diversified?

Firstly, this will depend on the other investments you hold within your portfolio – perhaps you are getting exposure to other shares via an investment in a UK equity income fund. It is also worth noting that the specific three shares noted are among the least volatile in the market, which means the risk of a large loss on any one is smaller than it is for most shares. These three shares are also poorly correlated with each other – they are in different industries and affected by different economic circumstances – which means a loss on one is likely to be offset by a gain on another.

Important considerations when investing in shares are:

- What is held in the broader portfolio?
- How volatile the shares are.
- How correlated different share investments in your portfolio are with each other.

Funds

Funds are already diversified, given the spread of assets they hold, so you might not need to hold as wide a spread of these as you do with shares. As a general rule, holding four to six funds can add diversification and allow you to gain exposure to a range of different areas. If you do decide to hold two funds in the same sector, for example two UK equity income funds, make sure you look at the funds' underlying holdings. If these are very similar, it will defeat the object of holding more than one fund.

Holding funds that utilise different investment strategies also makes sense – for example, for your property exposure you could choose to hold a bricks and mortar property fund investing in physical properties along with a property fund or real estate investment trust (REIT) investing in the shares of property companies.

Whatever investment vehicles you choose the important thing is to ensure that every asset class is represented in your portfolio and an adequate level of diversification is being maintained.

4. TIMING AND STRATEGY

There are two main ways to time investments:

1. You can invest a lump sum in your chosen investments as soon as you have decided you want to invest in them.
2. You can look to strategically time your investments, for instance investing in a company when its share price is cheap relative to its long-term average, or when a certain industry or sector has fallen out of favour.

There is a lot to be said for the first approach. Once you have done your research and decided that the long-term income prospects of an asset are good, it makes sense to invest then. Timing the market strategically, as in the second approach, can be a risky strategy and one which few investors get right. The problem with both of these approaches is that you might invest at precisely the wrong time.

As such, a better approach is to invest a portion of your capital regularly through a dividend reinvestment plan (DRIP) (see page 119) and by using the process of *pound/cost averaging* (see page 156).

It is also important to decide on your investment style. Some investors may choose a *passive investment style*, which essentially means leaving your portfolio to ride out the ebbs and flows of the market. In other words: you adopt a buy and hold investment strategy. Such a strategy is preferred by those who do not have a lot of time to spend managing their investments or have a long investment horizon ahead of them and can afford to take a more static approach with their investment, allowing portfolio returns to smooth out over time.

Others may prefer an *active investment style* which involves actively managing the assets in the portfolio and regularly reviewing holdings. It will also involve rebalancing the portfolio from time to time, which we will look at in greater detail later.

5. TAX

When you start investing you might still be a basic rate tax payer but tax will become an increasingly relevant as your career progresses and you have more money to invest. It is important to shield your investments from being subject to HMRC tax charges where this can be done legitimately.

An individual savings account (ISA) will allow your investment to grow tax free while still allowing you access to your money. Remember that you have a limit on how much you can commit to an ISA in any one tax year. A pension fund also comes with enticing tax advantages and the earlier you start saving for your retirement the better; but remember that with this vehicle you will not be able to get the funds out until your retirement. We discuss these and broader tax planning in greater detail in chapter 13.

6. ADVICE

Those who feel they do not have the knowledge or expertise to make their own investment decisions might prefer to call in the help of an expert. A qualified financial adviser or planner will be able to give you guidance on the different investment options available and how to these weigh up. Make sure the adviser is independent – not tied to a certain provider or bank – and provides advice on a fee basis rather than commission linked to the financial products.

4. Drawing income

In order to draw income effectively from your investments you need to think about:

- When you will draw income.
- How much income you will draw.
- How to draw your income.

WHEN TO DRAW INCOME

You should consider how often you will take income from your portfolio. Do you require the money monthly, quarterly, annually, or simply as and when required?

If you need income each month, there are various ways to structure your portfolio holdings in order to match income payment dates with your needs. Glyn Williams, an investment funds analyst suggests matching income from index-linked gilts with income funds which pay their income on regular cycles. This should give you the beginnings of a portfolio that will deliver a healthy, rising income over time.

Let's say, for example, the City of London Investment Trust pays out income in months February, May, August and November and an index-linked gilt pays out in January and July, and April and October. These two investments can be blended to make sure your portfolio is delivering a consistent monthly income for you to draw down.

You might then fill in the remaining months with an open-ended income fund, for example Artemis Income, which pays its dividend in June and December. Midas Balanced Income Fund would also be a good fit, as it pays income mid-month in March, June, September and December (on the 15th of each). Or you can cover your income requirements in the remaining months by buying a conventional bond or gilt. You can see that with this range of investments you have some form of income for every month of the year. These steps are shown in Table 10.1.

Table 10.1 – a range of investments that pay income in different months

Month	Asset paying income in this month
January	Index-linked gilt
February	City of London investment trust
March	Midas Balanced Income Fund
April	Index-linked gilt
May	City of London investment trust
June	Artemis Income, Midas Balanced Income Fund
July	Index-linked gilt
August	City of London investment trust
September	Midas Balanced Income Fund
October	Index-linked gilt
November	City of London investment trust
December	Artemis Income, Midas Balanced Income Fund

Think carefully about the times when you need income and then review when the investments you are considering pay income. This could determine whether you invest in a cash savings account which pays interest yearly or monthly, or an income fund which pays out dividends on a quarterly basis or twice yearly. Alternatively you could choose to buy bonds with different maturing dates and then match these payments with the specific time periods when you need income. Shares also pay dividends on a regular schedule.

You might chose to withdraw a portion of the income generated by your portfolio at regular intervals into a cash account to meet your longer-term income requirements, such as purchasing a car or paying for a wedding or anniversary. So, income payment dates are a useful indicator in structuring a plan to draw down income. This should not be your only consideration though – you also need to think about how much income you will take at a time.

HOW MUCH INCOME TO DRAW

No matter how much capital you have or how well you invest, your investment portfolio will produce a finite level of income. Therefore you also need to think about how much income you want to take out, and as a corollary how long your money will last if you draw certain levels of income.

You will need to decide which of the following approaches is most suited to your objectives:

1. Maximum income with capital erosion.
2. Sustainable income with capital preservation.
3. No income with capital appreciation.

Under the first option you will be drawing 100% of the income earned every year and possibly more. This will eat into your capital invested and could, over the long term, deplete your capital pot. The second approach will see you varying your income withdrawals depending on how well your investments have performed – how much income they have yielded. You would take a higher income in good years and a lower income in less good years, so as to not dip into your capital pot to meet an income shortfall, thereby preserving capital. Or you can decide to follow the third approach and delay drawing an income, instead allowing income returns to roll up alongside your original capital.

It is important to regularly review the income you are withdrawing from your portfolio. For example, if your portfolio has performed well (i.e. delivered the yield you were targeting within your income strategy and more) you might choose to increase your income withdrawals or else take some profits from your portfolio and bank these. Alternatively you can choose to reinvest excess income back into your portfolio.

If your portfolio is missing its yield target, you will also have to review the income you are taking from it. If it is important that your capital is preserved, then income withdrawals might have to be reduced or suspended for a period, to allow your portfolio time to recover lost capital.

Too high a withdrawal rate can significantly erode your capital invested, as Figure 10.4 shows.

Figure 10.4 – how different withdrawal rates could erode your capital

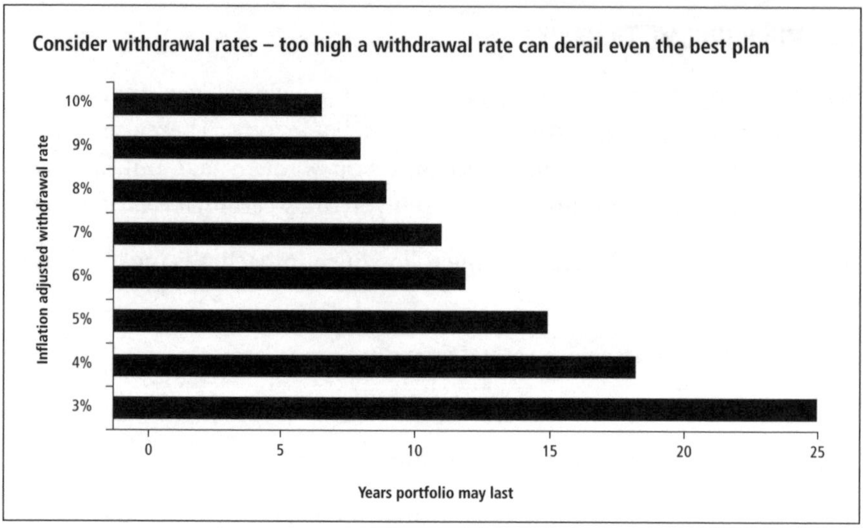

Source: Fidelity

Notes: Time for which a hypothetical untaxed portfolio of 50% UK equities, 40% UK government bonds and 10% UK cash might be expected to last with a reasonable degree of certainty. Rates of return are based on historical index returns for the period 31.12.69 to 31.12.05. Actual rates of return may be higher or lower. This chart is for illustrative purposes only and is not indicative of any actual investment.

If your portfolio is consistently failing to meet the income target you have set it might be the case that you need to make changes to your portfolio's underlying holdings. Perhaps you need to sell a fund or share that is not performing and replace it with another fund or it might just be that you have to allow time for your holdings to recover.

HOW TO DRAW YOUR INCOME

There are various ways to withdraw income from your portfolio. If you are investing via a stocks and shares ISA this could involve writing to the provider and stipulating the amount you wish to withdraw.

A number of fund providers offer regular withdrawal facilities which pay you a specified amount from your investment accounts, transferring the money directly into your bank account. To ensure you benefit from a constant income stream, such a withdrawal facility will automatically sell some of your holdings if the yield on your investments is not achieving the income amount you need. Of course this runs the risk of eroding your capital invested if your returns are too little to meet the yield stipulated.

If you are retired, you might have to choose between receiving income from an annuity, via a drawdown arrangement or from another scheme. The merits of each of these will be discussed in detail in chapter 12. Cash also plays an important role, not only in providing you with an immediate income, but also in covering any fees and costs involved in managing your investments.

5. Monitoring your income portfolio

Once your portfolio is set up you can't just ignore it. You need to monitor it.

As different asset classes perform at different rates, your investment in certain asset classes can grow at a faster rate than others, while you may suffer losses in others reducing your holding in these. Over time an investment portfolio can become unbalanced and drift away from the original allocation that matched your risk profile. It is therefore important to revisit your portfolio from time to time, perhaps every three to six months depending on time constraints, to ensure your asset allocation is still in line with your investment objectives.

REBALANCING

The circumstances when you might need to rebalance are thus as follows:

1. Your portfolio is not delivering the yield you planned for and you need to make changes to improve this.
2. The make-up of your portfolio has changed, perhaps through fund strategy shifts, and you need to reconsider your asset allocation.

3. You investment goals have changed and you need to realign the portfolio with these – you might want to take more or less risk, or seek higher or lower income.

The frequency of your rebalancing will depend on whether you adopt a passive or active investment style.

The advantage of rebalancing is that your portfolio remains aligned with your financial objectives, risk tolerance and income goals. The drawback is that rebalancing a portfolio can incur trading costs as you are likely to be buying and selling investments.

How to do it

There are a number of options available for investors to rebalance portfolios. Investors can either manually rebalance their portfolio, a process which is made easier with facilities for online switching between investments available from some brokers, or it can be carried out automatically via some fund platforms.

Alternatively, rebalancing can take place automatically within funds. For example, multi-manager funds are typically rebalanced regularly to match asset allocations within defined parameters. The frequency at which they are rebalanced varies by fund.

The challenge with rebalancing is ensuring that a given asset allocation is appropriate and ensuring that the asset allocation is populated with the best investments in a tax-efficient manner.

11

MODEL INCOME PORTFOLIOS

There is no fixed formula for how you should put your income portfolio together as financial objectives, risk appetite and income goals differ from one individual to the next. That said, life does follow a natural progression and for the different life stages there are a few guidelines to investing for income that can make a positive difference to your financial well-being in the long run.

The model income portfolios discussed in this chapter have therefore been compiled so as to address the income needs of investors at different life stages, from the young to those in retirement.

These are general guidelines and not rigid formulas. Individual circumstances and goals may dictate something different, for example not everyone starts a family in their thirties or begins to think about retirement in their fifties. For this reason, the models below are not exclusively of use to the age ranges suggested. If you are in your fifties and looking to take on high risk, you may find the young investor's model portfolio to be more suited to your needs. Likewise, if you are in your thirties with low risk tolerance, you may find one of the 'later life' portfolios more suitable.

1. Income for the young

The earlier you start investing, the more time there is to reap the rewards; if you're in your twenties or early thirties, time is on your side and you can afford to take a long-term approach to your investing. You can also afford to take more risk.

Taking on more risk will mean your income returns are exposed to greater volatility – in other words you might earn strong income returns in one year and then less income in another. Higher-risk investments will fall and rise depending on factors such as the health of the economy, movements in the stock market and other factors but at this stage of life you have got time to take considered risks and ride out these ups and downs.

With student debts most likely having to be paid off, and having just started out in your career, you may have a relatively small amount of money to invest. Growing your capital will be one of your main priorities: seek out income-growth investments with a successful track record of progressively growing yields year-on-year. Also, given the aim of increasing your capital, you should try to take advantage of the power of compounding by rolling-up interest on your cash investments and reinvesting as much of your income returns as your circumstances will allow.

ASSET ALLOCATION BREAKDOWN

A young investor's income portfolio should have a significant weighting in the high-risk investments such as shares and equity-based funds with less in the more cautious asset classes such as cash and fixed interest. In the example portfolio in Figure 11.1 the investor has 80% invested in equities with exposure split between UK and overseas investments, but only 10% has been allocated to the safer asset classes (cash and fixed interest).

There is also room for some exposure to alternative asset classes. Given that you might not yet own a house an investment in a property fund (around 10%) with an attractive yield could be a suitable addition to your portfolio.

You might have a limited amount of savings to commit to an investment portfolio and funds which require small minimum initial investments and spread risk across a number of asset classes could be a good way to gain both your equity and fixed interest exposure. In chapter 7 we looked at the different types of fund investments available and the fund platforms where you can buy these. Multi-manager funds are another option; these will diversify your exposure beyond the talent of any one fund manager by investing in a spread of funds.

Investing directly in shares for your equity exposure is another option, but this will require time, commitment and research. You will need to monitor your investments closely and have a certain amount of knowledge about companies and the market. If you're in your twenties, you may have priorities in your life that you place ahead of investing – such as having fun with friends, finding a partner, establishing a career and travel. Thus, leaving investment decisions to a fund manager and balancing your portfolio so as to ride out market volatility could be an appropriate strategy.

Figure 11.1 shows an example of the spread of assets in a model portfolio for a young income investor.

Figure 11.1 – model portfolio for a young income investor

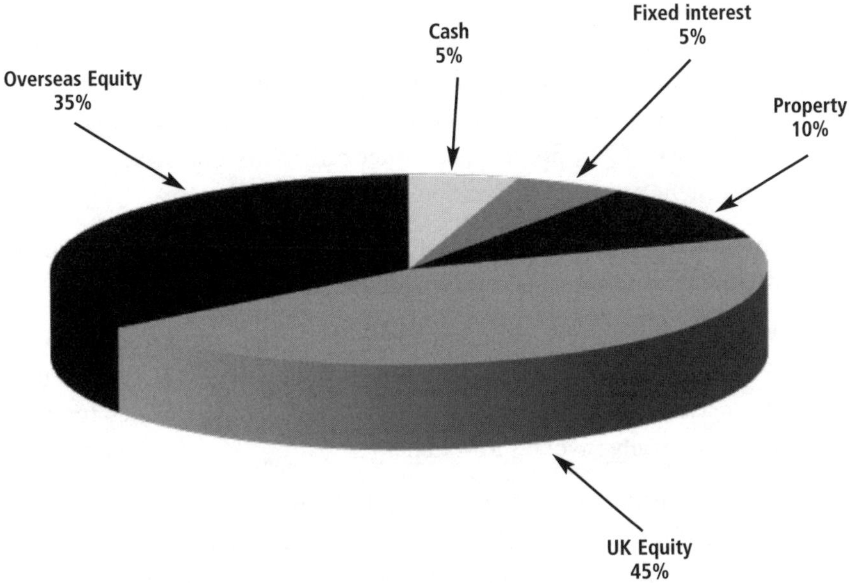

CHOOSING INVESTMENTS WITHIN THE ASSET CLASSES

Once you have decided what proportion of your capital to put into each asset class, the next task is to decide which investments to make within each asset class.

- Your cash exposure could be a money market fund or you could hold money in a bank or building society account.
- For your fixed-interest exposure, you might look for more flexible, slightly higher risk investments – perhaps a strategic bond fund where the fund manager has greater power to move between different offerings in the bond markets. Alternatively a high-yield bond or bond fund which will ensure you are receiving a decent income.
- Your equity exposure could be split between shares and equity income funds. Financial advisers usually suggest holding between 8% to 10% of

your equity exposure in one fund but again this can vary depending on individual circumstances.

- Overseas equity exposure can be gained via an investment in a global income fund or an emerging market fund with an income mandate. An emerging market bond fund with a healthy yield, skilled manager and robust investment process is another possibility but these are high risk investment products, so caution should be used.
- Investment trusts which boast a successful track record of growing dividends year-on-year can provide income growth.
- When you are an investor starting with a small amount of capital and plan to invest over the long term, investment charges start to add up. For this reason it could make sense to opt for an exchange-traded fund (ETF) which typically involves lower charges.
- Your property exposure could be split between two funds – around 5% in each. Opt for funds that have a different investment focus, perhaps one which invests in direct properties and one which invests in the shares of property companies.

CASE STUDY: A YOUNG INVESTOR

Let's have a look at an example of a young investor in their twenties who wants to make an income generating investment. We will assume the investor is 25 years old and earns a salary of £23,000 a year that covers outgoings but little more. They have just inherited £30,000 and want to invest this to provide some extra income.

Glyn Williams, investment funds analyst says:

> "At this age you have plenty of time ahead to make up for any early mistakes, so you should take advantage of this to learn about investment overall. A really good starting point is to start learning how to build an increasing income stream over time.
>
> Hold your investment in a tax wrapper to ensure you do not pay unnecessary tax. Depending on the amounts involved and whether or not you wish to draw any income early on or are willing to wait until you reach retirement, you would typically use a pension or an ISA for this purpose.

If you do not need to have access to all the capital invested it will make sense to concentrate on finding investments which have consistently delivered growing income, and also growing earnings, over the years.

Investment trusts are an excellent source of increasing income, as their structure enables them to smooth out the better and worse years by topping up or dipping into their revenue reserves, thus smoothing your income stream over the years. The City of London Investment Trust is a good example, delivering an ever-growing income stream rising from 1.05p per share in 1980 to 12.66p per share in 2010, with commensurate gains in capital value along the way. That is more than three times RPI inflation over that period. This fund pays income at the end of February, May, August and November."

You could easily make a monthly income schedule by adding other funds which pay in the other months to your portfolio. Table 11.1 provides an example of how the £30,000 might be invested in a number of funds.

Table 11.1 – £30,000 invested in a series of funds. Yield data based on figures from March 2011.

Fund name	Investment amount (Capital)	Yield (%)	Income	Pay dates (months)
Troy Income & Growth Trust	£10,000	3.73%	£373	Jan, April, July, Oct
City of London Investment Trust	£10,000	4.64%	£464	Feb, May, Aug, Nov
Temple Bar Investment Trust	£5000	4.12%	£206	March, Sept
Lowland Investment Company	£5000	3.05%	£175	June, Dec
Total	**£30,000**		**£1218**	
Average income per month (£1218 /12)			£102	

Table 11.1 shows that this selection of funds gives a net income of around £1200 a year and thus about £100 a month.

2. Income for families

Your thirties and forties is probably the time when you start to settle down and make permanent commitments such as getting married, starting a family and buying a home.

At this stage, family and property are likely to be your main financial concerns, and these will have to be balanced with the need to get an income portfolio off the ground. Time is still on your side at this point, because you have perhaps 25 or 30 years until you retire. You can still afford to take a fair amount of investment risk, albeit with more moderation than younger investors.

Intermittent but large expenses – be it home improvements, education, a family car or child care – are characteristic of this life stage and having ready access to a liquid asset such as cash to cover such costs will be important. Given the many financial commitments, investing at this time of your life can be challenging. Ideally, you should maintain a seperate cash savings account – a *rainy day* fund if you like – outside of your investment portfolio from which to draw to meet such costs as they arise.

ASSET ALLOCATION BREAKDOWN

At this stage you are still some way off from retirement and should be making the most of the stock market by having at least 70% of your income portfolio's assets in shares or equity-based funds in order to benefit from the superior returns offered by this asset class over the long term. The usual caveat applies of course: higher returns mean higher risks and you will still have to contend with a fair amount of volatility.

You should slowly be upping your exposure to fixed interest and cash – if interest rates are attractive enough – as these asset classes provide more stable income returns. As you can see in Figure 11.2, this portfolio has a 25% exposure to fixed interest and cash combined against only 10% exposure to these classes for the younger investor.

If you have a specific income target in mind, investing a small amount regularly in your thirties means you don't have to save as much in your fifties, and the total can build up slowly over the duration of your career. As an example of the benefits of starting to invest as early as possible, consider that an ongoing investment return of 7% per annum makes any contribution that is made 30 years before retirement worth almost four times more than the same amount invested with just ten years until retirement.

If you need to draw regular income payments from your portfolio to meet your expenses it is important to keep an eye on your capital and keep withdrawals moderate – you do not want to make an unnecessary dent in your overall capital now, with the result that you earn less income later. Try to reinvest as much of your income returns back into your portfolio as possible.

Figure 11.2 provides an example of how a family investor's income portfolio might be divided between asset classes.

Figure 11.2 – model portfolio for a family income investor

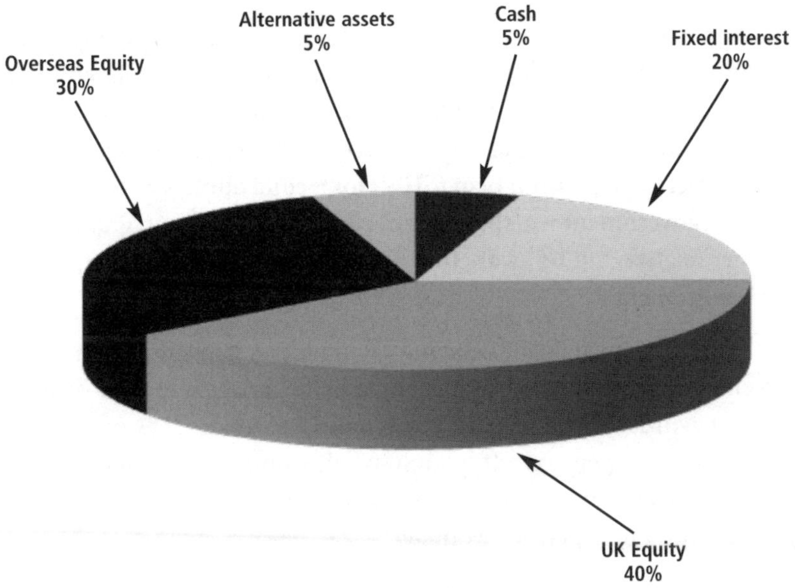

CHOOSING INVESTMENTS

- Your equity exposure can be in blue chip shares which usually pay solid dividends. If you do not have enough time to research the stock market opt for two or three UK equity income funds or an equity income fund with a global mandate. These will ensure diversification but make sure you choose one with a decent dividend yield.

- Your fixed-interest exposure should ideally be at the safer end. A corporate bond fund is a good option. If you understand the bond market you could opt to buy directly into three or four bonds. The pros and cons of investing into a bond fund versus directly buying bonds were discussed in chapter 5, page 94.
- You may now have a mortgage and so you might not need additional exposure to the property market and may opt to further increase your fixed-interest exposure instead. Opting for an investment in infrastructure via an investment trust which promises regular dividend payments is another possibility.
- An income paying structured product which pays out at a predetermined period in the future can be a useful investment if you want to time an investment payment to meet a future income need, for example a child's university tuition.
- Children have the same basic allowance for income and capital gains tax as adults and it is possible to build an income portfolio for your children, holding assets in their name. Other options include a trust-based savings plan or a junior individual savings account (ISA). Investing in a self-invested personal pension plan (SIPP) for a child attracts a contribution from the government whether the gift comes from a parent, grandparent or other relative, but be aware that this will only be accessible once they reach retirement.
- Don't make the mistake of delaying saving into a pension. Aim to put a percentage of your income equivalent to half your age into your pension. In other words, if you are 30, you should be saving 15% of your net income into a pension. If you have the option to make tax-free contributions via an employer's salary sacrifice scheme use this. If not, look at setting up a pension yourself.
- Ideally your pension savings should be complemented with a portfolio of investments but if you can't afford to contribute to a pension and an investment portfolio, prioritise your pension and manage this as an investment.

CASE STUDY: AN INVESTOR WITH FAMILY COMMITMENTS

Let's look at an example of an investor in their forties with various financial commitments. They are now facing redundancy. How will this investor generate additional income to support their family during this time?

The investor is aged 40 and married with two children aged 8 and 11. The family earns £60,000 per annum, has an existing mortgage of £120,000, pension arrangements from previous company schemes, £20,000 in cash ISAs and £100,000 in shares ISAs which are focused toward long-term growth. Table 11.2 shows the breakdown of this investor's ISA portfolio.

When the investor is out of work they will need to generate additional income from the assets to supplement the family's total income. They are keen to retain the capital values as these assets are required for longer-term retirement planning.

Table 11.2 – breakdown of investor's current shares portfolio, yield figures as at March 2011

Fund Name	Weighting (%)	Weighting (%)	Yield (%)
UK Equities		**34**	
Newton UK Opportunities	14		1.8
AXA Framlington UK Select Opportunities	12		0.9
M&G Recovery	8		1.0
Overseas Equities		**43**	
Neptune US Opportunities	10		0
Threadneedle American	8		0
Cazenove European	6		1.5
Fidelity South East Asia	9		0.2
GLG Partners Japan Core Alpha	3		0.6
Aberdeen Emerging Markets	5		0.4
Fixed interest		**15**	
M&G UK Optimal Income	8		3.5
Newton International Bond	7		2.1
Property		**10**	
M&G Property Portfolio	10		2.9
Total	**100%**	**100%**	**1.3%**

Patrick Connolly of AWD Chase de Vere Wealth Managers offers the following thoughts:

Extracting income with capital preservation

Income cannot be generated from pensions until you are at least 55 years old. You can start to draw an income from your cash ISAs but will also need to look at your shares ISAs.

The portfolio in Table 11.2 is diversified and growth-orientated. This focus on growth means that the yield is only 1.3%, effectively producing a natural income of £1300 per annum on the £100,000 portfolio.

There is less risk to underlying capital if you take the natural yield from investments and so higher-yielding funds should be considered, such as Artemis Income and Schroder Income Maximiser. If the existing UK equity income funds are replaced with a combination of the Artemis and Schroder funds this would have the effect of increasing your overall income from £1300 each year to around £2747 each year.

Extracting higher income

To extract a higher income you should look to replace more of your existing holdings with those that generate a greater natural yield. While doing this it is important that you retain an overall mix of assets that is appropriate for your attitude to risk and can still maintain the value of your underlying capital.

In addition to the Artemis Income and Schroder Income Maximiser fund, you could look to replace existing equity holdings with Newton Asian Income, Jupiter North American Income and Ignis Argonaut European Income.

Lowering risk

If you want to take a lower risk, changes should be made to the asset allocation of the portfolio. Currently 75% is invested in equities which means that while there is good growth potential there are significant risks that the value of your portfolio could fall, particularly in the short term. The equity weighting could be reduced to 40%, the fixed interest exposure could be increased to 40% by including funds such as Legg Mason Global Multi Strategy Bond and Kames Strategic Bond, and the property exposure could be increased to 20%.

Taking more risk

There is already 75% invested in equities in this portfolio, which is at the top end for what would be considered reasonable. This investor does have other cash and pension savings not included in the portfolio though, which provides something of a safety net.

AWD Chase de Vere would recommend a diversified mix of equity funds is maintained. To generate a higher income you may consider replacing your fixed-interest exposure with funds that pay a higher yield such as L&G High Income, which yields 6.8%, and M&G High Yield Corporate Bond, which yields 5.6%. Bear in mind that these are higher risk investments.

3. Income in your fifties

Once you reach your fifties and early sixties, your active income is likely to have increased significantly and your investment goals may now be shifting from growing your investment portfolio to securing your income. Your aim is not just to generate income, but also to safeguard that income for your retirement and for the benefit of future generations.

With the likelihood that you may have moved into a higher rate tax band, tax considerations are more important than ever. Your children are likely to be more financially independent – you could be at the empty nest stage – while your mortgage might be paid off or at least reduced. Preparing for your retirement should now top your list of financial planning priorities.

At this stage, your pension should be building up nicely and you should be giving serious consideration to your retirement plans. There are a number of important questions you should be asking yourself, such as:

1. What type of retirement are you expecting to have?
2. Will you be selling your property and downsizing to help fund your retirement?
3. Are you likely to need care in your old age?
4. Will you be working part-time in retirement?

5. Are you planning on running down your capital pot completely or do you want to leave some income for your heirs?

Revisit your financial plan and redefine your financial goals and time horizon in light of your answers to these questions. Getting professional financial advice is vital.

Work out how much income you might need to live on in retirement and compare this with the projected benefits from your pensions. If you identify a shortfall, put a plan in place to close this gap. The RetireEasy software, available from the RetireEasy website (**www.retireeasy.co.uk**), can help with this. You should also look into your retirement options (see chapter 12) and decide which arrangement is most suited to your income needs.

When you reach your fifties, your income is likely to be higher than it was earlier in your life and you will need to look at ways of managing your tax liability. Consider tax-efficient products such as ISAs, pensions, venture capital trusts (VCTs) and Enterprise Investment Schemes (EIS). Make use of tax allowances and reliefs, and any tax-free investments. These are explained in detail in chapter 13.

It is also worth considering making lump-sum contributions into your pension fund to take advantage of the tax relief available and to give your fund a boost.

ASSET ALLOCATION BREAKDOWN

As you age and your investment horizon shortens, the balance of your portfolio should be directed towards safe assets such as gilts and bonds, and you should gradually be reducing your exposure to the more volatile assets. Given that retirement is not too far off you may not have enough time to recover capital lost through exposure to risky assets. You may also wish to increase your holding in cash.

Maintain a diversified approach and utilise other asset classes – while it is important to play it safe at this stage, you also need to get your capital pot as large as possible to provide a better income during retirement.

The extent to which you lower your income portfolio's risk profile will depend on your investment time frame: the further away you are from retirement the more you can afford to hold in equities, but as you get closer to retirement it becomes more important to start taking risk out of your portfolio. Figure 11.3 provides an example of how the income portfolio of an investor in their fifties might be divided between asset classes.

Figure 11.3 – model portfolio for an income investor in their fifties

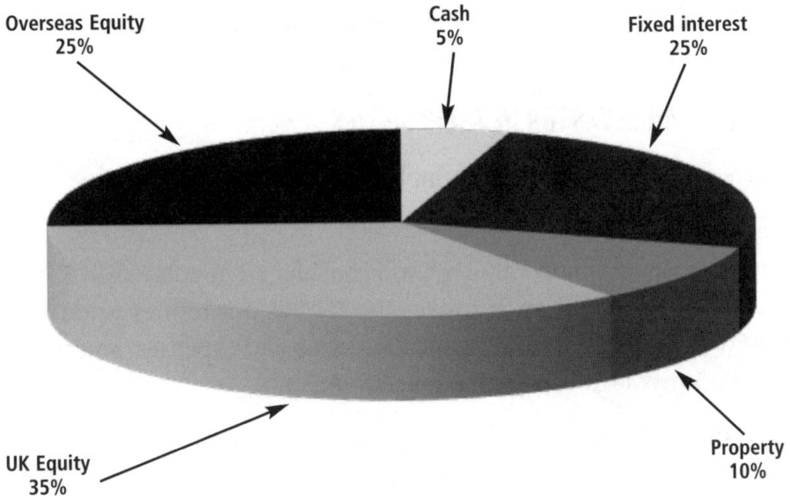

CHOOSING INVESTMENTS

Consider holding an index-linked gilt or inflation-linked corporate bond fund as part of your fixed-income exposure to shield against the capital-eroding effects of inflation.

If you can, hold your cash exposure in an NS&I index-linked certificate to shield your cash against inflation and avoid paying tax.

With the children out of the house and retirement beckoning, you may now have more time to manage your buy and sell decisions rather than leave this to a fund manager. You may therefore prefer to access your equity exposure by investing directly into shares rather than buying collective investment vehicles such as funds and ETFs.

If you have paid off your mortgage and don't hold any direct property investments, it might be worth upping your exposure to the property market again via a property fund with an attractive yield.

Consider adding an infrastructure investment – this could provide yield and also provide a natural inflation hedge.

You should now be redirecting funds that may previously have been spent elsewhere – such as on the mortgage and school or university fees – into your retirement savings pot.

Think about any pensions you have from previous employment and consolidate them if necessary – a SIPP is a good vehicle to facilitate this.

CASE STUDY: AN INVESTOR IN THEIR FIFTIES

Let's have a looked at a worked example of an investor in their fifties and how they might structure their income portfolio.

For the purposes of this example we will consider an investor aged 55 who is married with two children at university. He has put money aside to help support the children with their education costs and expenses, and the main financial priority now is planning for retirement.

The investor currently earns £50,000 per annum and his wife earns £25,000. Their mortgage has been paid off. He has pension funds worth £400,000 which he does not wish to access at this time, cash of £50,000 on deposit and an ISA portfolio worth £300,000. He wishes to move into part-time employment, which will mean a drop in income and would also like to partly subsidise this by taking an income from the ISA portfolio. Table 11.3 shows the breakdown of the ISA portfolio.

Table 11.3 – current ISA portfolio breakdown. Yield figures as at March 2011.

Fund name	Weighting (%)	Weighting (%)	Yield %
Equities		**50**	
Schroder UK Alpha Plus	10		0.5
L&G UK Index	5		2.4
Invesco Perpetual Income	15		4.1
Invesco Perpetual High Income	15		3.9
First State Global Emerging Market Leaders	5		0.3
Fixed interest		**40**	
M&G Optimal Income	10		3.5
L&G Dynamic Bond	10		5.1
Investec Strategic Bond	10		4.3
Kames Strategic Bond	10		3.9
Property		**10**	
M&G Property Portfolio	5		2.9
Aviva Investors Property Trust	5		2.4
Total	**100**	**100**	**3.33**

Patrick Connolly of AWD Chase de Vere provides the following suggestions:

Extracting low income

As this investor is aged 55 he may be able to take tax-free cash benefits from the pension schemes. He could also consider taking an income from cash savings. Regardless, he should aim to move cash savings into a cash ISA wrapper as annual allowances permit. This will ensure that all interest is received tax free.

The existing ISA portfolio will already generate a natural yield of £9900 each year (£300,000 x 3.33%). This may be suitable to meet requirements and with 50% invested in equities he still has reasonable growth potential to help maintain the value of the underlying capital should inflation increase.

If this investor starts withdrawing the income from the Invesco Perpetual and fixed interest holdings only, leaving the other income to role up in the portfolio, this will produce a yield of 2.88%, converting to £8640 per annum (£300,000 x 2.88%).

Extracting high income

To extract a higher income the investor should review the investment funds which are not producing an attractive level of income and see if these can be replaced by suitable funds which will generate a higher natural yield.

You could look to replace the Schroder, L&G Index and First State funds with funds such as Schroder Income Maximiser and Newton Global Higher Income. The fixed-interest holdings are focused on strategic bond funds. This should provide a reasonable mix of sovereign, investment grade and high-yield credit and so it may be sensible to retain these rather than looking at funds with a slightly higher yield but where risks are likely to be greater.

Taking low risk

Currently 50% of the ISA portfolio is in equities with the remainder in fixed interest and property. This seems like a reasonable mix, especially as there are separate cash holdings and pension funds. If the investor is particularly cautious he could reduce the equity weighting still further.

There is about £90,000 invested in two Invesco Perpetual funds which are run by the same manager. While this is a proven manager who adopts a defensive approach, risk could be spread further by halving this holding and considering other UK equity income funds such as Artemis Income and Neptune Income.

Taking high risk

The investor could decide to take a higher level of risk in the hope of achieving better performance or a greater level of income. The equity holdings are very focused on the UK and you could look to diversify into other regions which may have more growth potential and where you can still generate income. You could use the Newton Asian Income fund, for example.

To achieve this the equity weighting could be increased, with the view that it is reasonable to take extra risk because there are other cash savings and pension investments. However, no more than around 70% of the ISA portfolio should be held in equities – this will provide at least some protection if stock markets fall.

4. Income in retirement

Once you reach retirement, your income needs change drastically. You are now likely to be dipping into your pension fund and investments as opposed to just adding to these. The income you receive from your pension arrangement, be it an annuity, drawdown or a state pension, needs to be taken into account along with any income you could be receiving from other investments such as a second property or an ISA. It is important to draw down these various incomes in the most tax efficient manner and in keeping with your financial goals.

Pension arrangements can be notoriously complex and it is important to seek professional advice to make sure you opt for the right retirement solution and match this as effectively as possible with any other incomes. A pensions adviser can help you to re-evaluate your income requirements and reassess how you can meet any shortfall.

As you approach the time when your main income will come from your investments, you need to reduce the risk in your portfolio. If you prefer to keep risk as low as possible you should start doing this around ten years out from the point when you will draw income. If you are prepared to take more risk you can wait until around five years from the point when you will draw income before you start to move more of your investment into safer asset classes.

ASSET ALLOCATION BREAKDOWN

In retirement, the largest proportion of your assets will be invested in asset classes such as fixed interest and cash. Fixed-interest investments such as bonds can be particularly vulnerable to inflation and it would be wise to build some inflation-proofing into your portfolio, perhaps via a property fund. Also look at the merits of buying an inflation-linked annuity.

Financial advisers suggest that a defensive, risk averse investor such as an individual in retirement should hold around 10% in cash, but this will vary depending on your pension arrangement and the size of your retirement fund. You should ideally have secured your first two years' income in cash arrangements to avoid having to sell investments to meet income needs.

Figure 11.4 provides an example of how the income portfolio of an investor in retirement might be divided between asset classes.

Figure 11.4 – model portfolio for an investor in retirement

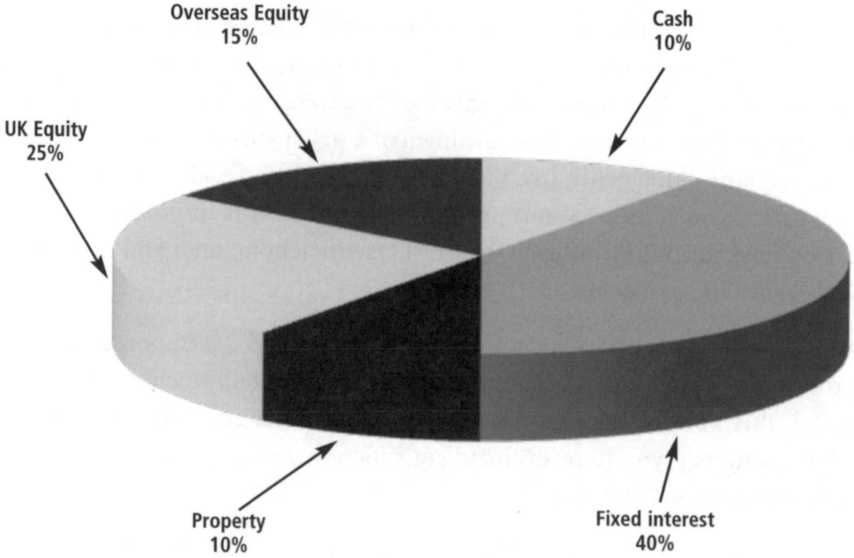

CHOOSING INVESTMENTS

Your retirement options

Of all the life stages, the period leading up to retirement is arguably the time when you will have to make the most important financial planning decisions. These decisions are likely to impact your income for the remainder of your life. It is important to make sure you have a good look at the options available to you for drawing income from your pension before your reach retirement.

This could be a conventional annuity option or a drawdown arrangement where you continue to make the investment choices for your pension capital. Each option comes with advantages and drawbacks and you should get advice from a financial adviser qualified in retirement and pensions advice before committing your retirement savings.

Never just accept the default pension you are offered from your current pension provider. Use your right to the open-market option, which allows you to take your pension fund to whichever provider you choose; preferably the one that will pay you the most income. See chapter 12 for more details.

Maintaining flexibility

It is important to maintain flexibility in your investment decisions. Your circumstances may well change over the course of your retirement, for example you may need to pay for a care home or help your children through a difficult financial patch, and it is important not to lock yourself into a fixed income with little flexibility. You will also need to arrange your investments in such a manner that should you pass away prematurely your family and dependents can still benefit from your accumulated pension savings.

If you are considering semi-retirement, think about moving your pension funds to a flexible plan that will allow you to draw on them in part, as and when you require, in order to top up any reduced income without the need to start a completely new plan.

If you intend to secure a pension in the short term, such as by buying an annuity, move your investments into cash to protect them from any sudden market falls during the period in which you are arranging the new plan.

Make the most of your cash lump sum

When you start drawing your pension fund, you have the benefit of taking a cash lump sum to the value of 25% of your pension fund. Some investors might use this to clear debts such as paying off the mortgage, while others might use it for a special holiday or a large purchase such as car. Others might keep it in a cash-based deposit as their rainy day fund. Either way, it is important to use this tax-free income wisely and remember that it can be a useful income generator.

One strategy could be to use the cash lump sum to purchase an annuity, while keeping the remaining pension fund in drawdown. In this way you will have a secure core income, while keeping exposure to the market and allowing your pension fund the opportunity to grow further.

Alternatively, you can invest your cash lump sum into investments held within a stocks and shares ISA where you still have control over the capital and can generate an extra income stream.

CASE STUDY: A COUPLE IN THEIR SIXTIES DRAWING DOWN INCOME

Let's have a looked at a worked example of a couple, both in their sixties, and how they structure their investments to draw an income.

This couple are in their mid-sixties and about to retire; they now wish to live comfortably from the savings and investments that they have accumulated. Over the years they have been very careful to use their ISA allowances each year and now have built up ISA funds between them of over £300,000. Mr A has built up a pension pot of £650,000 over his working life and between them they have built up other investments of £300,000 with cash of £100,000. They also have £60,000 in National Savings (NS&I) Index-Linked Savings Certificates, which they do not require the income from, but know the funds are there should they require them.

They are now looking for a tax efficient income to see them through their retirement years, without having to take excessive investment risk, having always been fairly cautious investors.

Zoltan Molnar, independent financial planner at WH Ireland Wealth Management suggests the following strategy:

Firstly, Mr and Mrs A should take the maximum tax-free cash from the pension plan – £162,500, at 25% – in order to take control over the funds, which ultimately gives them more flexibility with regards to using the cash in the future, but also giving them a more tax efficient way of taking the income.

From the remaining funds in the pension (£487,500), Mr A. is recommended to go into a pension drawdown plan taking an income of 4.75% (£23,156 pa), which is taxable at the basic rate of tax only and he has the flexibility to take more income from this fund should he wish to. With sensible investment planning, in a diversified portfolio of funds with an overall cautious risk approach, with approximate yields/income of 4% pa, he can attempt to maintain the income, keeping it tax efficient and allow for potential growth of the overall fund over time. This should allow gradual increases to his income in line with inflation throughout retirement.

With the ISAs, Mr & Mrs A can invest in a similar manner, being cautious with risk, again with the aim of providing steady yields and income at 4% (around £12,000 pa) free of tax.

They are also advised to invest in a portfolio of unit trusts and OEICs. This means that the income would be paid as a combination of interest and dividends. Should they obtain growth over and above the income taken, then both of their capital gains tax allowances (up to £21,200 between them at the time) are available to utilise each year.

Figure 11.5 provides a summary of this course of action.

Figure 11.5 – a summary of the strategy of Mr and Mrs A

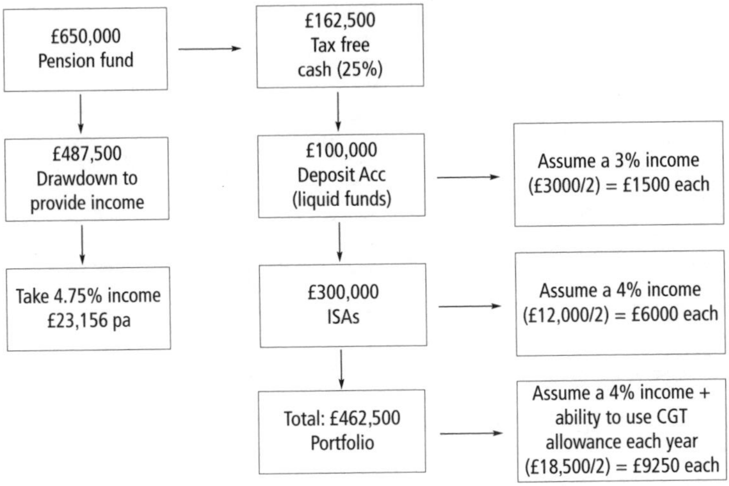

Putting these plans in place would give the approximate gross annual income as shown in Table 11.4 (please be aware that this will fluctuate and is only an example).

Table 11.4 – approximate gross annual income from Mr and Mrs A's plan

	Mr A	Mrs A
State pension	£9984	£5400
Pension drawdown	£23,156	
ISA (tax free)	£6000	£6000
Interest	£1500	£1500
Portfolio income (50% dividends + 50% Interest)	£9250	£9250
Gross income	**£49,890**	**£22,150**

This plan can provide a gross annual income of around £72,040 (£49,890 + £22,150) for the couple.

Summary

The sample portfolios in this chapter are not intended to be followed precisely, but should give an indication of the sorts of strategies that might be used at different life stages to generate an income.

12

PENSIONS

In this chapter the focus is on the different retirement options which investors can use to draw money from their pension fund. Having the right strategy in place is important not only to ensure that you do not deplete your pension pot prematurely, but also to guarantee that you get the most income possible from your retirement savings.

Securing a consistent income in retirement

THE STATE PENSION

Securing a consistent income for old age is an important part of every individual's financial planning. Many people wrongly assume that the state will take care of their financial needs when they have retired but unfortunately relying solely on a state pension will leave you with a level of income that will hardly suffice to cover your basic living costs. In 2011-12, a single person could get up to £102.15 a week basic state pension, hardly enough to cover a weekly grocery bill, with most receiving even less depending on how many national insurance contribution years they have completed. You should therefore plan to provide entirely for yourself in retirement and then treat any income you may receive from the state as a bonus.

More information and resources on the state pension are provided on the Directgov website:

www.direct.gov.uk/en/Pensionsandretirementplanning/StatePension

DEALING WITH INCREASED LIFE EXPECTANCY

Arguably, the biggest hurdle when it comes to securing a sufficient income in retirement is that of life expectancy (longevity), which is rising in the UK. Figures published by the Department of Work and Pensions (DWP) in 2010 show that more than 10m people in the UK can expect to live to see their 100th birthday – 17% of the population.[33] Chances are you're likely to reach an older age than your grandparents, and even your parents, and as such your retirement income will need to last for longer.

---

[33] Department of Work & Pensions, 'Over ten million people to live to 100', press release (30 December 2010). Available at: **http://bit.ly/hPE1iD**. [Accessed 17 January 2011.]

Making sure you have enough income to last you for the duration of retirement and ensuring it is sufficient to maintain a decent standard of living is not an easy task. This is especially the case in an environment where rising inflation continually pushes up living costs and interest rates remain at low levels, and where many pension schemes and the contribution levels into these are still based on life expectancy rates of yesteryear. Research by asset manager Fidelity shows that even with moderate inflation averaging at 3.1%, securing an income with the same purchasing power as £10,000 in September 2010 will cost you £334,000 in 20 years time.[34]

VARIABLES THAT AFFECT PENSION INCOME

If you have the sense to set up a private pension or are fortunate enough to have your employer provide you with a pension fund, the income you receive from this arrangement in retirement will depend on a number of variables:

- When the pension fund was originally set up.
- How much was contributed both by you and your employer over the lifetime of the pension.
- The performance of the pension fund's underlying investments.
- How income is eventually drawn from the pension fund (this last point is very important).

As such, for those who have a private or company pension fund, there are a number of important decisions you need to make once you reach retirement. These include whether you would like to take a tax free cash lump sum from your pension fund, how you would like to invest or utilise this cash, and how you are going to draw the rest of your pension pot. There are various retirement investment strategies that you can use to enhance the income available.

Let's start by discussing the option most investors are likely to go for in retirement: an annuity.

[34] Fidelity, 'Home truths: six things we all need to accept about retirement', press release (October 2010). [Accessed 17 January 2011.]

Annuities

HOW ANNUITIES WORK

Annuities are the best known and most widely used vehicle for unlocking an income from a pension fund. The concept of an annuity is simple: you accumulate a pension pot over the course of your working life then at retirement you use this money to purchase an annuity from a life insurance company. Rather than being a direct investment, you are handing over your pension capital to the life insurance company, which will invest your money in low-risk investments such as government bonds.

In return for handing over your pension capital, the insurance company then pays you regular income payments which can be monthly, quarterly, semi-annual or annual. The income can be paid in advance or in arrears depending on the arrangement with your annuity provider.

An annuity is therefore essentially an insurance policy which guarantees you an income for life. This income can be fixed or, if you opt for an annuity linked to inflation, it can vary in accordance with the prevailing inflation rate.

In the UK, annuities are provided by life insurance companies like Aviva, Canada Life, Legal & General, Prudential and Standard Life, to mention just a few. Different types of annuities will also pay out different income.

A good way to get an idea of how much an annuity will pay you, based on your specific needs and the size of your pension fund, is to make use of websites providing annuity best buy tables such as:

- William Burrows Annuities
  www.williamburrows.com/atables.aspx
- AnnuitySearch
  www.annuitysearch.co.uk/annuity.cfm
- Hargreaves Lansdown
  www.hl.co.uk/pensions/annuities/annuity-best-buy-rates

THE TYPES OF ANNUITIES AVAILABLE

The biggest drawback of an annuity is that when you pass away, the life insurance company gets to keep all the money you used to fund your annuity purchase. There are ways to mitigate this risk though: some annuities provide a guarantee that in the event of death the income will continue to be paid to your beneficiaries for the balance of the guaranteed period – this is known as a guaranteed annuity. If you apply for a five-year guarantee and were to die after two years of annuity payments, the annuity will continue to pay out income for the next three years.

A joint-life annuity is another option. This product will continue to pay an income to your spouse, partner or financial dependant after you die for the rest of their life.

Table 12.1 shows the different annuity rates as at 2 June 2011, for a man, based on a fund value of £100,000 after taking his 25% tax-free cash with payments made monthly in advance. As you can see, depending on the type of annuity purchased and the age of the individual, the income payments will differ.

For example, a single-life annuity will pay a higher income than a joint-life annuity. Similarly, whether you opt for a guarantee or not will also influence the income paid.

Table 12.1 – the annual income paid by different annuities for a man at various ages

	55 years of age	60 years of age	65 years of age	70 years of age	75 years of age
Single-life, level, no guarantee	£5443	£5786	£6354	£7266	£8600
Single-life, level, five-year guarantee	£5437	£5771	£6337	£7231	£8513
Single-life, 3% escalation, five-year guarantee	£3525	£3983	£4574	£5383	£6689
Joint life 50%, level, no guarantee	£5115	£5499	£5978	£6467	£7452
Joint life 50%, 3% escalation, no guarantee	£3179	£3552	£4028	£4650	£5624

Source: Hargreaves Lansdown, as at 2 June 2011

Key to terminology:

- **Single-life.** This means the income is payable to you only and will not continue to be paid to your spouse upon your death.
- **Joint life 50%.** This means that upon your death 50% of the income will continue to be paid to your spouse. Different percentages are available up to 100%. Where a joint life annuity is shown, this is based on a named spouse where the male is three years older than the female.

- **Level.** This means the income will remain level and not increase over time.
- **RPI.** This means the income from your annuity changes in line with inflation as measured by the Retail Price Index.
- **3% escalation.** This means the income from your annuity will increase by 3% every year.
- **Guarantee.** This means the annuity will continue to pay an income for at least that period of time (i.e. five years), even if you should die before that time. Guarantee periods of up to ten years are available. Guarantees on protected rights are limited to five years.

ANNUITIES AND UK LEGISLATION

For more than 30 years from 1976 to 2011, anyone in the UK with a personal or workplace pension was effectively forced by law to buy an annuity once they reached the age of 75. An alternatively secured pension (ASP) was the other choice but because of heavy tax penalties involved almost no-one opted for it. The requirement to buy an annuity at age 75 fell away in April 2011 and investors now have the freedom to choose between either buying an annuity or, if they meet the necessary requirements, opting for a *drawdown arrangement*.

Increased longevity was the main driving force behind this significant change to the UK pension landscape.[35] In 1976 the average life expectancy of a healthy 65-year-old male was 13 years. By 2010, a healthy 65-year-old male could, on average, expect to live for another 21 years, and a 65-year-old female for another 24 years. With longevity increasing, and more people working longer into their lives, the requirement to annuitise by age 75 had become too restrictive for many and the decision was made by government that people should have more choice over how they could use their pension savings.

While the decision to scrap the age 75 rule was for the most part welcomed by pensions experts and the public, the truth is that for many investors, in particular those with smaller pension funds, purchasing an annuity still

[35] HM Treasury, 'Removing the requirement to annuities by age 75', consultation document (July 2010), p. 5. Available at: **www.hm-treasury.gov.uk/d/consult_age_75_annuity.pdf**. [Accessed 17 January 2011.]

remains the most suitable option for securing an income in retirement. An annuity guarantees an income payout for the life of the annuity holder, which means there is no danger of your pension pot running out of money (which, as we will see, is one of the risks of a *drawdown arrangement*).

The alluring promise of an income for life does not mean that you should automatically assume an annuity purchase is the best option. Buying an annuity is arguably one of the most important financial planning decisions you will make in your lifetime. If you get it wrong, you risk being stuck with a lower pension income than you might otherwise have enjoyed for the rest of your life.

To understand the factors influencing the income you will receive from an annuity, you need to understand how annuity payments are calculated.

HOW ANNUITY INCOME IS CALCULATED

The two main factors that will impact an annuity income are:

1. The size of your pension fund (at the time of purchasing the annuity).
2. The annuity rate offered by the insurance company.

The annuity rate is the factor used to convert a pension pot into a pension income. Hence, if you want to determine the income you will receive from an annuity, the calculation is relatively simple:

```
annuity income = pension fund x annuity rate
```

The size of the pension fund will logically depend on how much money you have contributed over the lifetime of the pension. The annuity rate is a bit more complex.

What affects the annuity rate?

Pension annuity rates are calculated by actuaries using factors such as mortality (how long you are likely to live in retirement), your age, health and even where you live – in the UK life insurance companies use your postcode to determine if you are statistically likely to live longer. Areas such as Glasgow and Manchester have lower life expectancy rates than, for example, Kensington and Chelsea, which means if you live in Glasgow you're likely to receive a higher annuity payout per year than if you live in Kensington.

If you are older, or if your health is impaired, your annual annuity payments are likely to be higher as these factors are believed to reduce your longevity and hence the insurance company expects to not have to pay out for as long. If you live much longer than mortality rates suggest, the life insurance company loses out as it will have to continue paying you an income; if you pass away soon after buying your annuity, it is the insurance company that benefits. In recent years increased life expectancies have forced insurers to lower annuity rates, as annuities will have to be paid for longer.

Interest rates

The annuity provider, who is investing your pension capital, will primarily invest in low-risk gilts, which means that medium-term interest rate movements and inflation expectations will also have an impact on the annuity rates. A rise in interest rates will mean annuity rates will also rise. If interest rates are low, as they have been in the UK for three years from 2009 to 2011, gilt yields will be low and annuity rates will also be low.

In 2010, the combination of low interest rates and rising longevity saw annuity rates fall to their lowest level in 20 years. As Table 12.2 illustrates, in April 2008 interest rates were 5%, long-dated gilt yields were 4.6% and William Burrows' benchmark annuity was paying £6547. By April 2011 interest rates had fallen to 0.5%, the gilt yield stood at 3.9% and the benchmark annuity paid £5943.

Table 12.2 – falling annuity rates, based on gilt yields as at 27 April 2011. Benchmark annuity based on male aged 65, female aged 60, £100,000 purchase, joint life two-thirds, guaranteed for five years and level payments.

	Bank rate	Gilt yield	Annuity
April 2008	5%	4.6%	£6547
April 2011	0.5%	3.9%	£5943

Source: William Burrows Annuities

If you are considering buying an annuity and expect interest rates to rise you might think it worth delaying the annuity purchase until the rate rise. But, generally, pension experts don't advise this. Even if interest rates do rise it is unlikely that the full benefit will be passed on to customers given factors such as life expectancy and gender neutral annuity pricing which will impact the income life insurers can pay.

"Investors who delay their annuity purchase in the hope that they will get a higher income are generally disappointed. Timing an annuity purchase is a complex thing because not only are annuity rates moving, but fund values can also be volatile," says Billy Burrows of William Burrows Annuities.

Laith Khalaf of Hargreaves Lansdown adds that even if you can get a better rate by delaying your purchase this might not make up for the income you have missed out on in the meantime. He says: "You could hedge your bets by annuitising in stages, or wealthier investors willing to take investment risk might consider a drawdown plan to provide them with a flexible level of income."

Inflation

Finally, expectations of a rise in inflation, in turn, can have a positive impact on annuity rates. If inflation is expected to increase, the attractiveness of bonds as an income generating investment will diminish and with it investor demand for bonds will weaken. In response, bond prices will fall and yields will rise, pushing up annuity rates.

* * *

While factors such as mortality rates, interest rate and inflation movements will heavily impact annuity rates, and hence the income you receive from your annuity purchase, it is important to realise that the annuity market is broad and there are a number of variants of the traditional annuity model that can be used to generate a better income return.

THE BROAD ANNUITY MARKET

To benefit from the different annuity products available, it is important to shop around before you finalise your annuity purchase. A good place to start is the best buy tables provided by Hargreaves Lansdown and William Burrows. These websites can also provide you with a free instant annuity quote based on your individual needs and pension fund.

The chances are your current pension provider or providers won't offer you the best annuity returns. Shopping around for a better deal is referred to as exercising your right to the *open market option*. The importance of the open market option (OMO) in securing the best possible income stream from your annuity purchase is discussed in further detail below.

If you do take the time to shop around you might find that you qualify for a *lifestyle annuity*, or an *enhanced or impaired annuity*, which can significantly boost your income.

- *Lifestyle annuities* take into account behavioural factors such as: smoking (ten cigarettes a day for the last ten years, or the equivalent in cigars or tobacco), high alcohol consumption, obesity, high cholesterol and/or diabetes that may impact your life expectancy. If you qualify for such an annuity, it could boost your annual income significantly.
- *Enhanced* and *impaired annuities* pay out an even greater income than a lifestyle annuity, depending on lifestyle factors and health conditions. An enhanced annuity will, for example, pay more for those whose health is impacted by conditions such as mild angina, multiple sclerosis or chronic asthma. High levels of blood pressure – when taken together with other lifestyle or medical conditions – can also increase the enhancement in income received. Impaired annuities likewise pay out more income for individuals with a medical condition that may significantly reduce their life expectancy such as heart and kidney disease, cancer, or a stroke.

The main difference between an enhanced and an impaired annuity lies in the underwriting. For enhanced annuities the insurance company will only require the information provided on a medical questionnaire, whereas for an impaired life annuity the insurer will require a medical report from your doctor, although you may not need to have a medical examination. Typically an enhanced annuity quote can be produced more quickly.

A combination of illnesses can also achieve some form of enhancement, for example raised blood pressure, along with raised cholesterol and perhaps an issue with weight. There are over 1500 conditions that count towards an enhancement and tapping into the higher annual retirement income offered by these annuity products is relatively straightforward.[36]

The difference this can make to your income can range from a few percentage points right up to 100% uplift – doubling the income you receive from your annuity. Table 12.3 provides a sample of how certain health conditions can impact annuity rates – the percentage increases given are compared to the best standard rate for a person that does not declare any medical conditions and assumes they have used the open market option.

---

[36] According to enhanced annuity specialist, Just Retirement, Steve Lowe.

Table 12.3 – how certain health conditions can increase your annuity income

Conditions	Age	Gender	Just Retire- -ment quotes (£)	Best standard (£)	Worst standard (£)	Percentage improvement – best standard compared to worst standard	Percentage improvement – JR Enhanced Annuity compared to worst standard
Mini stroke four years ago, hospitalised, blood thinning medication taken daily	65	Male	3421	3204	2930	9%	17%
Epilepsy, occasional fits, frequent seizures and two tablets a day	65	Male	3606	3204	2930	9%	23%
Lifelong asthma, takes daily inhaler; type one diabetes, takes insulin daily; high blood pressure, cholesterol medication daily	60	Female	3217	2787	2469	13%	30%
Chronic kidney failure, end stage disease, daily medication, dialysis, hospitalised and waiting for a transplant	65	Male	4197	3204	2930	9%	43%
Heart-bypass operation seven years ago; depression; used to smoke 30 per day gave up after heart-bypass operation; sleep apnoea and leg pain – claudication	60	Female	2812	2787	2469	13%	14%
Smokes ten cigarettes per day	65	Male	3606	3204	2930	9%	23%
Drinks 36 units per week	65	Male	3421	3204	2930	9%	17%
High blood pressure and high cholesterol: one medication for both conditions	65	Male	3421	3204	2930	9%	17%
Obese (5'9, 22 stones); drinks 36 units per week	65	Male	3693	3204	2930	9%	26%
Bowel cancer diagnosed within the last six months, treated with surgery and radiotherapy	60	Female	3242	2787	2469	13%	31%

Source: Just Retirement, August 2011. Based upon a £50,000 purchase price and post code RH2 7RU.

Not everyone will qualify for an enhanced or impaired annuity, but if you do it could make a marked difference to your income in retirement. It is important to remember that when it comes to purchasing an annuity, if you want the best income you should do your homework and tweak your annuity purchase to suit your situation.

THE OPEN MARKET OPTION

When buying an annuity, many people take the first deal offered to them which is usually presented by the life insurance firm they are holding their pension with. There is no going back once you have transferred a pension fund, so your annuity purchase needs to be right. The best way to ensure this is by exercising your right to the open market option (OMO). This piece of pension jargon means shopping around for a better annuity deal. OMO has been around for many years but pension providers have not always made it clear to customers that they do have the option to shop around for a higher annuity.

While best-practice guidelines now dictate that investors should be sent all the information they need to shop around effectively at least four to six months before they retire, many industry campaigners want OMO to be made the default option for all investors. This is largely due to the fact that the number of individuals who do shop around remains low.

As a result many people in poor health never find out that they could achieve much higher income with an impaired or enhanced life product than the one they are offered by their pension company.[37] According to annuity provider Just Retirement, an estimated 55% to 65% of those retiring might have conditions that qualify them for an enhanced or impaired annuity, yet only 12% of annuitants buy enhanced products.

If you do not shop around you might end up with the default: a single-life level annuity which does not protect against inflation. Married individuals who take a single-life annuity instead of a joint-life annuity will leave their surviving spouse without access to any continued annuity payments if they die, as the annuity returns to the life insurance company.

Factors you should be taking into account when considering an annuity include the potential effects of long-term inflation, a spouse's pension and building in guarantees via a guaranteed annuity which pledges to make payments for a minimum period even if the annuitant should die during that period. To find the right annuity, one which fits with your individual circumstances, shopping around and getting the right advice is essential.

---

[37] Just Retirement, 'Health statistics suggest many more might qualify for increased income from their pension funds', (20 September 2010). Available at **www.justretirement.com/About-us/Media_Centre/Press_Releases**. [Accessed 17 January 2011.]

Drawdown

WHAT A DRAWDOWN ARRANGEMENT INVOLVES

For many the idea of handing over their pension funds to a life insurance company to then be tied into an income payment based on the interest rate prevailing at the time of purchasing an annuity does not appeal. Then there is the risk of passing away earlier than expected and your life savings ending up in the hands of the life insurance company that sold the annuity. Many investors find it hard to stomach these risks and demand greater flexibility and choice when it comes to their pension income. This is where a drawdown arrangement comes in.

The appeal of drawdown lies in the greater investment control it gives you over your pension capital – you can tailor your retirement assets to your investment preferences and protect against inflation. If you make good investment decisions, your pension fund will continue to grow. The flexibility of income withdrawals and the ability to leave a lump sum to a beneficiary on death (although there will be tax charges involved) are other appealing features of a drawdown arrangement.

Most people use a self-invested personal pension (SIPP) to run a drawdown so that they can invest where they want. This can be in shares, in bonds and gilts, property, or cash. Although, conventional wisdom suggests that you should look for at least some exposure to equities, otherwise you might as well buy an annuity where the insurance company invests in bonds and gilts on your behalf. A typical drawdown portfolio would be around 60% invested in equities with the remaining 40% in bonds, gilts and some cash to cover income withdrawals, although this will vary depending on the investor's risk appetite.

With a standard drawdown arrangement, known as *capped drawdown,* the maximum cash you can take each year is determined by the government actuary's department rates.

Government Actuary's Department (GAD) rates

GAD rates are calculated and published by the Government Actuary's Department. The GAD rate varies depending on three factors: gender, age, and prevailing gilt rates (15-year gilt yields are used).

The rate is then applied to your capital. So, for instance, the current 15-year gilt yield is 4% and for a man aged 60 the GAD rate is 5.9%. If you have

£200,000, the maximum income you can withdraw each year is therefore £11,800 (5.9% of £200,000). This income level is set for three years (annually from age 75), after which it is reviewed again based on your new fund value and the GAD rate at the time of the review. There is no minimum withdrawal amount for income drawdown, so you could choose to withdraw zero income if you wish. Figure 12.1 shows the historic GAD rates.

Figure 12.1 – historic GAD rates

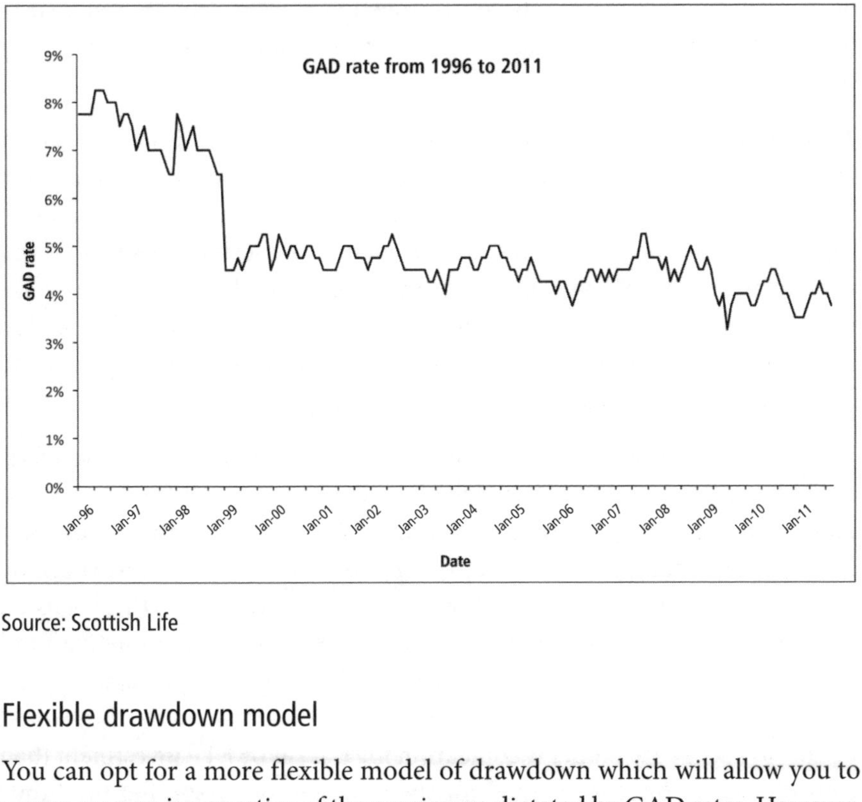

Source: Scottish Life

Flexible drawdown model

You can opt for a more flexible model of drawdown which will allow you to access money, irrespective of the maximum dictated by GAD rates. However, under the flexible model you will need to prove you have secured a pension income of at least £20,000 a year. This can include state pensions, most employer pensions and private pension annuities. This £20,000 per year is considered sufficient additional pension income to mean that you would not need to fall back on the state if the stock market did wipe out your pension money invested under the drawdown arrangement.

THE RISKS OF A DRAWDOWN ARRANGEMENT

There are number of risks attached to drawdown. While an annuity guarantees you an income for life there is no such assurance with drawdown. Furthermore, you will be a hostage to the state of the markets when you start drawdown. As you are keeping your pension fund invested, in a rising market your pension fund will increase while in a falling market the value of your pension fund will shrink. Your income will therefore be subject to both positive and negative market performance and may increase significantly or be eroded. In 2008 many retirees in drawdown arrangements watched in horror as the stock market nosedived, taking a significant chunk out of their pension's savings.

There is also the risk of running out of funds during drawdown – a danger which increases with advancing age. If you choose a drawdown arrangement rather than an annuity and end up living beyond the life expectancy of someone in your position, you will miss out on the effective subsidy that you would have received from other annuity buyers who die early on. To make up for the forgone subsidy from not buying an annuity you might need to hold higher-earning, risky assets within your drawdown arrangement to ensure that your funds do not run out before you die.

With drawdown the high charges of investing – including commission fees, dealing charges and the costs attached to active investment funds – can eat away at your pension pot. In this regard, passive funds tend to be more cost effective. For example, if an investor aged 65 invested in a fund charging 0.27% (the typical charge of a tracker or exchange-traded fund) their pension pot would last until they were aged 88. If they invested in an active fund charging a 1.66% annual total expense ratio (TER) the pension capital would run out three years earlier, when they were aged 85. Alternatively, they would be able to take a 15% higher income from the tracker or ETF investment than from the active fund if invested for the same period, assuming the funds perform the same.[38]

As a caveat to this, a good fund manager running an active fund should beat the market and justify the additional charges, whereas a tracker fund is certain to underperform the market because it is designed to produce the same returns as its benchmark index and then deducts charges.

[38] Vanguard, 'Impact of High Charges on Pension Pots', press release commentary (3 August 2010).

Drawdown arrangements can also be complex, with a raft of rules and cumbersome administration surrounding them.

HOW TO USE A DRAWDOWN ARRANGEMENT

If you have thought about the risks and decided that drawdown is the best option, you need to consider how much income to draw from your plan. If you take the maximum income permitted this increases the chances of depleting your pension fund prematurely. Investors may wish to pursue a strategy of drawing as much income as they can as soon as they can. However, a more sustainable approach would be to draw the dividend and interest payments from your investments, leaving the capital untouched until later.

Many drawdown investors opt for a mix of equities and bonds, typically in line with a cautious managed fund's portfolio breakdown of 60% in equities and 40% in bonds. This can be achieved by either investing into such cautious managed funds yourself or using individual equity and bond investments to reach the appropriate ratio. The benefit of the latter is that it broadens the investment options available to you – as opposed to investing in a single fund where the underlying portfolio will be chosen by the fund manager and you will have no control over where exposure lies. Building your own portfolio of investments also allows you to tweak the asset allocation according to your personal attitude to risk.

Remember that if you are drawing an income from your plan you will need to have cash available to withdraw, otherwise you will be forced to sell investments to provide your income when it may not be the right time to sell. Depending on the level of income you are drawing, the cash in the drawdown arrangement should typically equate to between one and three years' worth of income. Your investments may generate dividends and interest which you can draw out and if this is all you are taking then you may not need much of a cash buffer.

You should make regular reviews of income withdrawals, your investments' performance and your investment strategy during the drawdown arrangement to check that assets can be moved when needed for encashment and your pension pot is not being depleted prematurely.

PHASING YOUR DRAWDOWN

When constructing your drawdown arrangement it is worth taking note of the tax charges which apply. If you die before taking an income from your pension, your pot will be entirely free of tax as long as you are under age 75. But if you have started to draw an income from your pension via drawdown, any lump sum remaining in the pension when you die will be taxed at 55%. This tax charge on pension benefits also applies to investors aged 75 or older at the time of death. One way to ensure that your family receives a greater proportion of your pension on your death is by using a phased drawdown plan.

Under phased drawdown, you move your pension into drawdown in a number of chunks, depending on the income you need from it. If you die before age 75 and want to bequeath your pension pot as a lump sum, the bit which is in drawdown would be subject to a 55% charge, whereas the bit that has not been moved into drawdown is deemed untouched – and can be passed on to your family as a lump sum tax-free.

Phased drawdown means that you cannot take all of your 25% tax free cash right away. If you do, this will mean that your entire pension fund will be crystalised and on your death 55% of the fund will be taxed before it passes to your dependants. Rather, you create a situation where you elongate the period of drawing out your cash lump sum so that you do not crystalise your entire fund in one go. You draw your tax free cash in small amounts over a period of time, in this way maximising the capital that will be passed to your family tax free on your death.

Phasing can be applied to either flexible or capped drawdown but bear in mind that once you hit age 75 there is no saving, because even those funds which have not been moved into drawdown would be subject to the 55% tax.

CASE STUDY: HOW AN ANNUITY COMPARES WITH DRAWDOWN

An annuity

If you are a 60 year old with a £100,000 pension fund (after taking tax-free cash), and the GAD rate is 5.9%, a single-life annuity will provide you with a level income of £5900 per annum for life.

If you died at age 86 (average life expectancy) this annuity would have paid out a total income of £159,952. There would be no capital left for your family or heirs – any remaining capital in the fund would pass to the annuity provider. It is possible to add options such as a spouse's pension to enable the annuity to continue after your death, but this would reduce the annual income you receive from the annuity.[39]

Drawdown

A drawdown plan would also provide you with a maximum starting income of £5900. This maximum income is variable; dependent on investment returns and gilt yields.

Assuming gilt yields remain the same and you achieve 5% annual return (after charges) on your drawdown funds, if you die at age 86 you would have received total income of £164,906 from your drawdown plan (assuming you always draw the maximum). You would also still have £34,037 left in the drawdown pot. This sum could be used in its entirety to provide a pension for a spouse or dependent, or it can be paid out as a lump sum to a beneficiary of your choice, minus a 55% tax charge. If taking this option £15,317 would be paid out after adjusting for this tax. No inheritance tax would be due.

When choosing a drawdown plan you should shop around for the best provider. There is a wide variation in what providers charge; the difference could well add up to thousands if not tens of thousands of pounds over the course of the plan.

A compromise between annuity and drawdown

Given the risks of drawdown, and the relative restrictiveness of annuities, a compromise between the two arrangements might be the answer to producing secure income in retirement. Investors are increasingly choosing to blend the different retirement solutions rather than opt for a single product. One strategy is to use the 25% tax-free cash lump sum which you are permitted to take once you start drawing your pension to buy an annuity while leaving the rest of your pension fund invested via a drawdown arrangement.

The approach of mixing and matching will typically see an annuity delivering your core income to cover essential expenditure such as day-to-day living

[39] Calculations based on a 4% gilt yield which is the yield that is used to calculate new drawdown plans starting in April 2011.

costs while the drawdown arrangement is used to deliver a more flexible income on top of that.

Another option, instead of choosing to put part of your capital into an annuity and part into a drawdown fund, is to look at a flexible annuity, which we will examine next.

THE BIRTH OF SIPPS

Drawdown arrangements are typically written on a SIPP basis. SIPPs (Self-Invested Personal Pensions) were introduced in the UK in 1989 by then UK Chancellor, Nigel Lawson, in his sixth and final Budget.

The biggest attraction of SIPPs is their investment flexibility. A SIPP allows you to use your pension fund to build your own bespoke investment portfolio, enabling you to invest in assets which other pension funds can't, such as commercial property, gold bullion and private equity. Or you can invest in a full range of unit trust funds and shares, which is where most SIPP investors put their money.

Investments, as with other pension funds, grow free of income or capital tax, and tax relief is paid on any contributions made into the SIPP. A SIPP also allows you to pass on some or all of your pension money when you die. Should you die before taking any benefits, the full value of your fund goes to your heirs and won't incur any inheritance tax.

The cost of a SIPP will depend on the type of SIPP you buy. Off-the-shelf, generic SIPPs typically offered by execution-only stockbrokers and fund providers are lower cost and while these allow much greater investment choice than your average life company pension, they will be confined to the fairly conventional asset classes. Examples of providers offering these types of products include Hargreaves Lansdown (Vantage SIPP), sippdeal (e-SIPP), James Hay (iSIPP) and Fidelity's FundsNetwork SIPP.

A *full* SIPP will charge more but will allow you much greater freedom and flexibility to hold specialist investments beyond the traditional asset classes, including more alternative investments ranging from burial plots to football stadiums, royalties, high-cost telephone lines and website domains. Full SIPPs are offered by a variety of smaller or specialist SIPP providers such as, Rowanmoor Pensions, IPS Partnership, Mattioli Woods and Suffolk Life.

Investors favour SIPPs as a way of taking control of the investment reigns of their retirement money, and often use SIPPs to combine and consolidate different pension pots from different employments.

Flexible annuities

There are various pension solutions that seek to bridge the gap between annuitisation and drawdown, such as a flexible annuity (often referred to as the *third way*). The main advantage of a flexible annuity is its malleable income options. A traditional annuity, once set up, cannot be changed even if your circumstances should change but a flexible annuity will allow, as the name indicates, greater flexibility. You can alter the level of income taken, while also benefiting from greater investment control and a choice of benefits to pass to your heirs at the time of your death. However, these products are typically only available (and suited) to investors with larger pension funds of around £100,000 or more.

Under a flexible annuity arrangement, investors can take varying amounts of income between an upper and lower limit as calculated and set by the product provider. These limits are then reviewed every three to five years, depending on the annuity structure. Flexible annuities also allow a much greater level of investment control as you have a choice of risk-graded strategies and a broad selection of funds depending on the provider of the flexible annuity. Examples of flexible annuity offerings at the time included Canada Life's Annuity Growth Account (AGA), MGM Advantage's Flexible Income Annuity (FIA) and Sun Life Financial of Canada's I2live annuity.

The biggest advantage of a flexible annuity is that it allows you to draw an income to meet your needs while not being a permanent decision like buying a fixed-term annuity. A flexible annuity can be a good option for those investors who do eventually want to buy an annuity but who wish to bide their time before making this purchase. It could also be good for those who want to invest in equities and are prepared to accept the higher risk that goes with this in return for the potential for future income growth. For example, a flexible annuity can be bought while investors wait for annuity rates to increase to higher levels. In addition, over the life of a flexible annuity your health might have changed and you may qualify for an impaired annuity which will pay out considerably more income than an annuity bought earlier.

Flexible annuities are not without risk, the most pertinent being investment risk. There is also no income guarantee – income may rise as well as fall. These are usually quite complex arrangements and fees can be high. One way of managing these risks would be to buy a fixed annuity together with a flexible annuity. The money within the flexible annuity will remain invested in equity funds for the longer term giving you exposure to the markets, while the fixed annuity will provide you with an income guarantee. In this way you spread the risk and continue to benefit from investment opportunities and any rise in the market.

If neither an annuity, whether flexible or fixed, nor drawdown appeals to you, there might be another option: a scheme pension.

Scheme pensions

A scheme pension allows the investor to control the investment strategy and asset allocation within the fund, similar to the way in which they would with a SIPP. The investor controls what investments are held and when they are bought and sold – they might invest in commercial property, shares, funds, gilts, etc. It is not necessary to purchase an annuity alongside the scheme to ensure a secure income, as scheme pensions make a commitment to provide an income for the life of the retiree.

A handful of specialist SIPP providers, generally those that offer the full range of SIPP investment options, offer scheme pensions. These providers include:

- Hornbuckle Mitchell.
- Rowanmoor Pensions.
- AXA Winterthur.
- James Hay.

The annual income from a scheme pension is not fixed for the life of the scheme as it would be with an annuity and it is not capped based on GAD rates as it would be under income drawdown. Instead, it is the job of the scheme's actuary to determine how much income can be withdrawn from the fund each year, basing their calculation on three main factors:

1. Size of the pension fund.
2. Expected returns.
3. Life expectancy.

The maximum income that can be taken from the scheme pension is reviewed by the actuary at least every three years, perhaps more regularly. The actuary's aim is to actively manage down the capital in the fund during the member's lifetime so that it is at zero when the investor dies. In other words, you can be assured that you will obtain the full benefit from your pension savings during your lifetime.

If the investments held in a scheme pension perform well then the maximum income that can be taken would be increased by the actuary, and vice versa. In the same way, scheme pensions are beneficial if a deterioration in health reduces the life expectancy of the investor as the actuary may then, with medical evidence, increase the level of income payments.

A scheme pension may also be granted with a payment guarantee. So, if you are granted a scheme pension at age 75 with a ten-year guarantee, you will be assured that full benefit from your pension fund will be received either by you, or by your dependants should you pass away earlier than expected, over the next ten years.

PRACTICAL CONSIDERATIONS WITH SCHEME PENSIONS

- A scheme pension may be a useful option for pension investors who are not able to secure the £20,000 of pensions income necessary to enter a flexible drawdown.
- Scheme pensions are offered on a fixed-fee basis (the only additional cost is the regular actuarial review) whereas life offices charge an ongoing percentage with drawdown. However, given that a scheme pension is only available in high cost SIPPs, it can be an expensive option and is usually better suited to those investors with large pension pots.
- Once your funds are in a scheme pension they can not be transferred into any other kind of pension.

HOW A SCHEME PENSION COMPARES WITH CAPPED DRAWDOWN

Table 12.4 presents the maximum annual income that can be taken from capped drawdown compared to a scheme pension if beginning the arrangements at different ages and health. The capped drawdown income is based upon a GAD rate of 4%.

These figures show that a scheme pension will generate 18% more income per year (£7835) than a capped drawdown (£6600) for a 65-year-old man in good health. If the man was in very poor health at the time of taking the arrangement then the scheme pension would pay 50% more income per year (£9917/£6600 = 1.5).

Table 12.4 – a comparison of capped drawdown and scheme pension arrangements

	Male: £100k pension fund			Female: £100k pension fund		
Age	65	75	85	65	75	85
Capped drawdown maximum income	£6600	£9000	£15,400	£6200	£8300	£13,900
Scheme pension maximum income						
Good health	£7835	£9885	£16,155	£7686	£9432	£14,917
Fair health	£7996	£10,344	£17,097	£7798	£9772	£15,680
Poor health	£8230	£10,952	£18,218	£7949	£10,221	£16,583
Very poor health	£9917	£14,242	£22,768	£9090	£12,675	£20,349

Source: Hornbuckle Mitchell

How to increase your pension income

Your pension income will not just be a function of the pension vehicle you choose, whether this be an annuity, drawdown or some other arrangement. You can also influence the income you get in retirement by making use of different retirement strategies such as:

1. Opting to defer your state pension.
2. An immediate vesting personal pension.
3. Using employment to top up your pension.
4. Building in inflation protection.

We will not look at these in turn.

DEFERING YOUR STATE PENSION

You don't have to stop working or claim your state pension when you reach state pension age. You can put off claiming your state pension or, if you have already claimed it for a period, you can choose to stop claiming it. If you put off claiming your state pension you can either earn extra state pension or benefit from a one-off lump sum payment.

Under the Extra State Pension scheme you can earn an increase to your weekly state pension of 1% for every five weeks you put off claiming. This works out at about 10.4% extra for every year you put off claiming. The extra state pension will be paid to you with your state pension when you start to claim.[40]

If you put off claiming your state pension continuously for at least 12 months (which must all have fallen after 5 April 2005) you can choose to receive a one-off lump sum payment and your state pension paid at the normal rate. The lump sum payment when you claim it will be based on the amount of normal weekly state pension you would have received, plus interest added for each week. While this will be taxable, the income received cannot push you into a higher-rate tax bracket. Should you die before taking the lump sum, it can be paid to a surviving spouse or civil partner or form part of your estate.

If you have not yet claimed your state pension and you want to put off taking it up, you need not do anything. If you are already getting your state pension, but would like to stop claiming it to earn extra state pension or a lump sum payment, you need to contact your pension centre. The telephone number will be on any letters you have received from your pension centre.

Deferring a state pension should not affect rights to certain state benefits but it may not be advisable if a married woman can obtain a bigger state pension based on her husband's National Insurance Contribution (NIC) record.

AN IMMEDIATE VESTING PERSONAL PENSION

If you have reached retirement age, a way to generate a higher income is via an immediate vesting personal pension. As with an annuity, this is a contract providing you with a pension for the rest of your life: you receive a pension payment once a year until you die.

---

[40] **www.direct.gov.uk/en/Pensionsandretirementplanning/StatePension/DG_179966**.

A quarter of the total fund can be taken as a tax-free lump sum, while the rest is used to purchase an annuity. The first income payment will be made as soon as the plan starts which means you receive a whole year's income immediately. The amount of income you receive, much the same as a traditional annuity, will be based on annuity rates at that time, your age, gender and the options you choose, such as providing a spouse's pension or inflation-proofing your annuity income.

The attraction of an immediate vesting plan lies in the combination of tax relief on your contributions, tax-free cash and income from the annuity. The drawbacks are that you lose your capital completely and once you have bought the immediate vesting personal pension it can't be changed. Neither can you change it to another provider or temporarily stop receiving payments. There are very few providers offering these products, Standard Life being the main one, so the annuity payment rate might not be as good as that of a normal annuity.

Investors with small pension savings – no more than 1% of the lifetime allowance (the maximum amount of money you can save into a pension in your lifetime, currently set at £1.8million) – can draw the entire amount as a lump sum rather than take it as a pension. Up to 25% will be tax-free but the rest of the lump sum will be added to an investor's income for the year and is taxable.

USE EMPLOYMENT TO TOP UP YOUR PENSION

If you are employed there are two ways in which you can up your pension:

1. Salary sacrifice.

Salary sacrifice involves giving up some of your salary in exchange for payments into your pension. This will not only increase your pension contributions and overall pension fund but can also make you savings on income tax and national insurance. You also receive tax relief, depending on the tax band you fall into. Unfortunately not all companies offer salary sacrifice. It is also worth remembering that a reduction in your salary will reduce benefits linked to your salary such as jobseeker's allowance and could also impact your ability to secure a mortgage as banks and building societies use income to decide on loan eligibility.

2. Company share pensions.

Those who hold *shares in company or saving employer share schemes* can place these within a SIPP and benefit from the tax relief. You can either sell the shares and invest proceeds into your SIPP or move the shares into the SIPP. It has to be a SIPP because standard personal and company pensions are not allowed to accept direct investment of shares. Once the shares are transferred into a SIPP any future growth and dividend payments will be tax-free. It is worth consulting a financial adviser qualified in pensions because if you make a mistake the transfer might not be deemed as a contribution and hence not qualify for tax relief.

INCORPORATING INFLATION PROTECTION

If you are still saving for retirement, it is important that you keep increasing the amount you pay into your pension each year. If you don't, inflation will mean that your monthly contributions are worth less every year.

If you expect inflation to rise it is worth investing your pension fund in higher risk assets such as equities as rising inflation will eat away at the more cautious investments such as cash, fixed interest and low risk funds. You will have to take into consideration how many years it will be before your retire and whether you can afford to take the risk of investing in these assets.

Once you reach the point of retirement, you can inflation proof your income by opting for an inflation-linked annuity, although these usually have a low starting level of income. Alternatively you can look at utilising a strategy whereby you combine a level annuity with an escalating annuity.

13

TAX

Tax is an unavoidable fact of life and a major concern to the investor. However, if you arrange your investments in a tax-efficient manner and make use of careful tax planning you can shield your investment income from being subject to more tax than is necessary. Employing tax mitigation strategies – such as ensuring all reliefs and exemptions are claimed – and using tax-efficient investments – such as Individual Savings Accounts (ISAs) and pensions – you will be able to retain a higher percentage of the income generated by your investments.

Another reason why taxes are an important part of an investor's portfolio management dates back to the damage caused by the global financial crisis of 2007-2009. Following this downturn the UK was left with large debts and shortfalls in their budget. To get this debt back to a manageable level, the UK government needs to cut spending and increase revenues. Governments typically increase revenue by raising taxes. Tax hikes and spending cuts started in 2010-11 and are expected to become more severe from 2011-12 onwards. With tax likely to be a defining characteristic of the financial landscape going forward, it is as important now as ever to get your tax planning in order and ensure you don't pay more tax than you should.

Having said this, it is also important not to let tax considerations be the driving force behind your investment choices. Your investment decisions should first and foremost be based on your risk profile and in the interests of creating a diversified portfolio. Once you have achieved this you should then look at how to arrange your investments to be as tax efficient as possible.

Tax bands and rates change almost every tax year, with amendments typically announced in the preceding year's Budget. To avoid the risk of becoming redundant by future government Budgets, this chapter will not focus on the numbers and percentages attached to the different tax rates and bands as these are bound to change. The focus will instead be on the tax vehicles likely to remain part of the UK's investment landscape, discussing how best to utilise these to ensure you hold on to as much of your investment income as possible.

Before we do this, it is important to set out the difference between tax evasion and tax avoidance.

TAX EVASION AND TAX AVOIDANCE

There is a very clear distinction between *tax avoidance*, which is legally limiting how much of your income you pay to the taxman, and *tax evasion*, which is deliberately not paying tax. Louise Somerset, tax director at RBC Wealth Management explains this as follows: "Tax evasion involves breaking the law. Tax avoidance is arranging one's affairs in order, legitimately, to reduce the tax burden."

In recent years tax authorities such as HMRC have increasingly required individuals and businesses to disclose tax avoidance schemes. This has led to heightened concerns that those using such schemes are at risk of a challenge by the tax authorities.

It might be that a further distinction is needed in tax planning between straightforward tax mitigation – ensuring that all available reliefs and exemptions are claimed – and tax avoidance schemes. George Bull of tax experts Baker Tilly advises caution:

> If you are looking at routine tax mitigation the message is to pay attention to getting the details right: all too many tax mitigation plans that are perfectly acceptable in principle fail because they are not implemented correctly. And even greater care is needed where a more esoteric tax avoidance scheme is considered, such as one whose aim is to create a tax loss in circumstances where HMRC would say that the arrangements are such that the investor is not genuinely participating in a business or incurring a commercial risk.

You should always have a clear understanding of the relevant issues: the amount of tax you might save must be set against the costs and the potential risk attached to your chosen approach. Consulting an independent tax expert on these matters is therefore advisable.

The range of UK taxes

There are several ways in which the government can raise money from taxes. These include income tax, National Insurance (NI), council tax, VAT and corporation tax (CT). Given our focus on income, we will concentrate on taxes that directly impact investment returns. These are:

- Income tax
- Capital gains tax
- Inheritance tax
- Stamp duty

We will now look at these in turn.

INCOME TAX

Income tax was introduced in 1799 as a means of paying for the war against the French forces under Napoleon and is today levied against people's earnings. This will include income from employment, interest earned on your savings, rental income, pension income and dividend income from shares. While there are a number of allowances and reliefs which can help you reduce your tax bill, no one earning income is exempt from paying income tax.

The UK has three main income tax bands:

- A basic rate band of 20% tax.
- A higher rate band of 40% tax.
- A band of tax at 50%, known as the additional rate.

These are the percentages of income that have to be paid to HMRC and applied to all earnings, except earnings from interest paid on your savings (which is charged at a starting rate of tax) and income tax on dividends. The income levels at which these three tax rates apply will vary from year to year.

How income tax is calculated

Income tax is calculated by taking your taxable income (income less reliefs and allowances) and multiplying it by the appropriate rate(s) of tax. So:

```
taxable income = income - reliefs - allowances
```

then:

```
income tax = taxable income x the rate(s) of tax
```

Where:

- *Income* is made up of what you earn plus any other income you receive from investments and pensions, as well as certain capital payments, such as returns on insurance bonds, which are deemed to be income for tax purposes.
- *Reliefs* are amounts which you pay out, for example donations to charity or topping up your pension fund, and on which you then get tax relief from government.

- *Allowances* are tax breaks you are entitled to because of your personal circumstances such as your tax free personal allowance, a blind person's allowance, etc.
- *Taxable income* is the figure on which your tax bill will be based.

Income tax planning points

- If you have forgotten to claim a relief or allowance, you can go back to correct this and claim a refund of tax overpaid but you must generally make a claim within four years of the end of the relevant tax year. (This is a recent change and people who did not submit a tax return for the year 2005-06 may also be able to claim a refund.)
- Your employer or pension provider uses a tax code to determine how much tax you should pay. This code is determined by HMRC. If you are on the wrong code or a temporary code you could be paying too much tax and can be due a refund. To change your tax code, contact your local tax office.
- Making pension contributions or giving to a charity (known as a gift aid donation) will qualify for income tax relief.
- If a relative has died within the past two years a rearrangement of their estate could mean a saving on tax by putting income into the hands of family members whose income level is below the higher income tax band.

CAPITAL GAINS TAX

Capital gains tax (CGT) is defined by HMRC as: "a tax on the profit or gain you make when you sell or dispose of an asset." CGT can apply to a range of assets including investments such as stocks and shares, a second home, high-value possessions such as paintings, jewellery and antiques, and business assets. It is important to remember that it is the gain you make and not the amount of money you receive for the asset that is taxed.

CGT rates differ depending on whether you are a basic rate taxpayer or a higher earner. While the average taxpayer is unlikely to pay CGT and there is a long list of assets on which gains are tax-free, for those susceptible to CGT it is important to make use of the annual tax-free allowance for CGT. Referred to as the annual exempt amount this is the amount of gains you can make in any one year without incurring CGT. Other occasions when there is no CGT to pay include assets passed on at death, gifts between a husband and wife or between civil partners, and gifts to charity.

How CGT is calculated

To find out whether you are liable to capital gains tax when you sell an asset you need to determine whether you have made a gain or a loss on the disposal of your assets. The calculation for this is:

```
final price (of the asset) - initial price - allowable ex-
penses = capital gain/loss
```

Where:

- The *final price* is the amount at which you sell the asset.
- The *initial price* is the amount at which you bought or acquired the asset.
- *Allowable expenses* are acquisition costs such as the money paid to accountants and solicitors, any money spent improving the asset and disposable costs which are similar to acquisition costs.

On improvement costs, George Bull of Baker Tilly says:

> To be allowed as a cost for CGT purposes an expense must not have been deductible for any other purpose (e.g. as a repair on let property) but also the cost must be reflected in the price of the asset when sold. So an expensive reconstruction of a property to suit the owner's personal tastes and preferences but which does not increase the price the asset can be sold for may not be allowable.

CGT planning points

- If you have suffered capital losses in the past, on shares for example, these could be offset against a later year's gain. Losses must first be offset against any capital gains made in the same tax year. Since the 1996/1997 tax year it has been necessary to report a capital loss to HMRC if you want to be able to use it to offset against capital gains in future years. Losses must be reported within four years of the end of the tax year in which you made the loss.

BED-AND-BREAKFAST STRATEGIES

In the past, it was possible to realise a gain equivalent to the CGT tax-free allowance on the last day of a tax year, and then buy exactly the same investment back again at the start of the new tax year. This so-called *bed-and-breakfast* loophole was closed in 1998 and investors must now wait at least 30 days before they can buy the same investment again.

However, bed-and-breakfast has been replaced by a plethora of other strategies which can be useful ways to realise a tax-free gain (or loss). These include:

- *Bed & ISA*: The investor realises a gain by selling the shares or funds and then immediately buys them back within an Individual Savings Accounts (ISA) wrapper as a contribution, taking advantage of the fact that the 30-day rule does not apply to ISAs.
- *Bed & SIPP*: Here the investor sells the investment then buys it back within a Self-Invested Personal Pension plan (SIPP) as a contribution with the added benefit of receiving tax relief from the government.
- *Bed & Spouse*: Move investments into your spouse's name before encashment and use their annual CGT allowance as well as your own.
- *Bed & Spread*: You can't buy the same investment back within 30 days, but you could buy a similar one. For instance, you could sell a holding of BP shares and buy those of Shell, or sell Invesco Perpetual High Income Fund and buy the Artemis Income Fund.

INHERITANCE TAX

Inheritance tax (IHT) is paid on an estate when somebody dies. On death, everything you own – your home, possessions, savings and investments – goes into your estate. Debts such as outstanding mortgages and the costs of your funeral will be deducted from the total value of the estate.

IHT can also be payable on trusts or gifts made during your lifetime. Typically, the executor or personal representative pays IHT using funds from the deceased's estate while the trustees are usually responsible for paying IHT on assets in, or transferred into, a trust.

Not everyone pays IHT. It is only due if your estate – including any assets held in trust and gifts made within the seven years prior to death – is valued over the current IHT threshold, also referred to as the nil rate band. Married couples and civil partners have a transferable allowance – this means when one partner dies the other can add what is left of the deceased's allowance to their own annual allowance.

How to calculate IHT

To calculate IHT, take the rate of IHT and multiple it by the amount at which the deceased's total estate exceeds the nil rate band. So if the nil-rate band is £325,000 and an individual's total estate is £350,000, IHT is payable on: £350,000 - £325,000 = £25,000.

If IHT is levied at 40% (as was the rate in March 2011) then the tax bill will be:

```
40% x £25,000 = £10,000
```

IHT planning points

- If you are planning to leave some of your investment income to your heirs, estate planning is necessary to avoid IHT taking a nasty chunk out of the inheritance your benefactors receive. There are a number of IHT efficient investments such as farmland, forestry and business assets – provided these meet your income investment needs they could be a useful addition to your portfolio to mitigate IHT.
- Shares in unlisted trading companies can qualify for business property relief from IHT and for this purpose AIM companies are regarded as unlisted. The share will only qualify for IHT relief after it has been owned for two years and if, on death, the company still meets the trading company criteria for IHT purposes.
- If you have excess retirement income which you do not need for your spending requirement, you can make gifts from it that will be immediately tax exempt. The proviso is that the income should be

regular or habitual and should not affect your standard of living. You do not need to give away the same amount to the same person every year but it is advised that in the first year you do it, you write a letter to the person you are giving it to saying you may not always give it to them and it may not be the same amount each year.

- Assets gifted more than seven years before death escape IHT, provided the donor does not benefit from the gift. For example, gifting shares to a son or daughter who uses the annual dividend to pay for repairs to your home will not qualify, as the parent would be deemed to still own the shares for IHT purposes.
- It was announced in the 2011 Budget that IHT will be reduced by 10% for those estates leaving 10% or more to charity.

STAMP DUTY AND STAMP DUTY LAND TAX

- Stamp duty applies mainly to purchase of shares in UK companies. The rate of tax is charged at a fixed rate except for special transactions usually entered into by overseas investors. This tax is not collected directly, although payment is required to cancel an equivalent tax on agreements to transfer shares.
- Stamp duty land tax (SDLT) applies to the purchase of residential or commercial property over certain amounts. The rate of tax charged is tiered and varies depending on the purchase price. SDLT has become a significant cost to purchasers of property, especially high-value residential property.

Shielding income from tax

Tax-efficient investment vehicles can be used to reduce the tax charged against your income, provided they fit with your investment strategy. The vehicles we will cover are:

- ISAs
- Pensions

ISAS

An Individual Savings Account (ISA) is a tax free wrapper in which investments can be held without incurring income tax or capital gains tax. You don't even have to mention this income on your annual tax return. There are two main types of ISAs:

1. Cash ISA.
2. Stocks and shares ISA.

A *cash ISA*, as the name indicates, is essentially a savings account with a bank or building society which allows you to hold cash deposits and earn interest on these free of tax. A *stocks and shares ISA* is based on stock market investments. In these you can build a portfolio of investments in shares, gilts, corporate bonds and funds without having to pay tax on the dividends or capital growth to HMRC.

For each type of ISA you have an annual allowance, which is a limit on how much you can put into the ISA for a given tax year. You need not hold your ISAs with the same provider and depending on whether the provider allows this you should be able to transfer ISAs between providers with relative ease. But once you have used up your annual allowance, that is it for the year. While your entire ISA allowance can be held in a stocks and shares ISA, only half of the annual allowance is allowed to be held in a cash ISA.

The FSA (**www.fsa.gov.uk**) and the HMRC (**www.hmrc.gov.uk**) websites provide details of stocks and shares ISA providers, but for many people the best platform on which to run one is a fund supermarket, which enables you to keep all your investments in one place and benefit from a wide spread of investments.

ISAs are a useful vehicle for building up an income – if you used your full cash ISA allowance every year since ISAs were first introduced (in 1999) you would have built up a fund of over £40,000 by the end of 2010. Had you made use of your full stocks and shares ISA allowance every year since they were first introduced – £7000 from 1999 to 2007, £7200 from 2007 until 2009, and £10,200 in 2010 – you would have sheltered savings totalling £87,600, even without any investment growth. Similarly a couple investing both their full allowances into a stocks and shares ISA since their launch would have a nest egg of £175,200.

ISAs are not without their limitations though. Unlike a pension there is no government top-up or tax relief on the money put into an ISA. An ISA is not free of inheritance tax (IHT) whereas a pension fund sits outside your estate for IHT purposes, which means if you leave your ISA savings to your family on your death these could suffer a significant tax charge.

ISA planning points

- Stocks & Shares ISAs are typically provided by execution only stockbrokers such as Hargreaves Lansdown and TD Waterhouse and fund platforms such as Fidelity FundsNetwork. Minimum investments will depend on the provider but usually investors have a choice between making a lump sum investment or regular contributions. If you wish to make a withdrawal from your stocks & shares ISA you will have to give your provider notice usually by filling out a form online.
- Cash ISAs in turn are provided by high street banks and building societies. The rates available on these will depend on the account restrictions. For example, a cash ISA tying up your cash for five years will pay a higher rate than an instant access ISA. The type of ISA will also determine whether you can withdraw your cash at any time. An instant access ISA (for example) might allow this while with a fixed term ISA you might incur fees or penalties for early access.
- There is no limit to the amount of ISAs you can have as long as you remain within the annual ISA allowance. The annual ISA allowance for the 2011-12 tax year is £10,680. This can be held entirely in a Stocks & Shares ISA or half of the allowance (£5340) in a cash ISA. It is intended that the annual allowance will be increased in line with inflation every year.
- A couple making regular use of both their yearly ISA allowances can accumulate a sizeable pot which could be used to supplement their retirement income later in life, but remember that unused ISA allowances can't be carried forward.
- If you need to access your income immediately and can't risk it shrinking in value, a cash ISA will be the better option. The most important factor to consider when choosing a cash ISA is the rate of interest on offer.
- For those looking for higher growth of their income over a longer period and willing to contend with the risks that their investment can go up and down, a stocks and shares ISA is more suitable. You can invest double

that of a cash ISA and if the market goes your way you are likely to get significantly higher returns.

- You can start with a cash ISA and then switch money into a stocks-and-shares ISA later but the reverse is not permitted.

PENSIONS

Pensions, particularly Self-Invested Personal Pension plans (SIPPs) with their broad choice of investments, can be useful vehicles in which to grow your investments, and build up a significant income portfolio. To encourage people to save for their retirement, the government offers tax incentives on contributions made into a pension scheme, whether this is an employer's occupational scheme or your own personal pension plan. This means that your pension contributions (subject to the limits set up by the government) are up-weighted by the percentage amount of your income tax bracket. Examples of this are shown in Table 13.1.

Table 13.1 – examples of how pension contributions are up-weighted by tax bracket

Tax rate	Investment	Tax relief added to pension	Maximum additional tax rebate
Non-earner	£2880	£720	£0
20%	£10,000	£2500	£0
40%	£10,000	£2500	£2500
50%	£10,000	£2500	£3750

Any contributions made by your employer into your pension fund are tax free. Taking advantage of this tax subsidy could boost the income return from your pension fund significantly. Money invested into a pension receives tax relief at least at the basic tax rate. The table above shows the tax relief that will be added to any pension contributions. So a non-earner can contribute up to £2880 to a pension and receive a top-up from the government of £720 in the form of tax relief, pushing the total pension contribution up to £3600.

Another attraction of pensions is that your investments will grow free of tax which means if you sell an investment within your pension, there is no capital gains tax payable on any profit. There is also no income tax to pay on interest and dividends received.

There is no limit on the value of pension benefits a scheme can provide but you do have a lifetime allowance, which is the total value of all your personal and work pensions. It does not include any state pension, which you can build up in your lifetime without paying extra.

There are some drawbacks to pensions. Once you begin to take income from your pension, you will need to pay income tax. Also remember that unless you have reached the state retirement age, you cannot take funds from a pension. Even then, you won't get access to all the funds. You can only take 25% of the value of the fund as a lump sum, while the remainder will need to be drawn down via an annuity or drawdown plan.

The restricted access that comes with a pension can be a sticking point for the investor who wants ready access to their income, however it does help to impose discipline, stopping you from dipping into your pension fund prematurely.

Pension planning points

- Age can play an important role in choosing between an ISA and a pension. ISAs are useful investment vehicles for young investors who are starting out at the investment game and are keen to build up an income pot with ready access. A pension on the other hand might be more suited to those individuals approaching retirement. One strategy would be to build up funds in an ISA and then later transfer these to a SIPP or other pension plan. Of course, there is no reason why you can't hold both vehicles.
- Many taxpayers are higher earners when contributing to a pension, but basic rate payers when they start withdrawing from a pension. This can make pensions a particularly useful tax planning tool – as you can receive tax relief at a higher rate on your contribution but pay a lower rate once you withdraw income in retirement.

VENTURE CAPITAL TRUSTS

Venture capital trusts (VCTs) are a type of investment trust listed on the stock exchange which invests in small, higher risk UK companies. When investing in VCT shares your money will be spread across a portfolio of these start-up businesses. The tax relief available on VCTs comes in three forms:

1. Income tax relief on the initial investment in a new VCT launch or share issue.
2. Tax-free dividends.
3. Tax-free gains on exit.

The attraction of a VCT for income investors lies in the tax-free dividends. Whether you take your dividend as cash, or reinvest these, you will have no income tax liability. There is also no capital gains tax on profits made within the VCT (provided you hold them for five years) and no lifetime limit on how much you can invest. VCTs can be an enticing way to generate income that is largely free of tax.

You must be at least 18 to buy VCTs and you must invest when they are issued.

There are a number of different types of VCTs which invest in different areas and in different ways ranging from generalist VCTs to AIM (Alternative Investment Market) VCTs. It is important to know what you're investing in and the rules and caveats to each. A good source for information on VCTs is the Tax Efficient Review available online at: **www.taxefficientreview.com**

VCT planning points

- VCT shares can also be bought in the secondary market. There are currently only three market players who provide this service Singer Capital Markets, Matrix Capital Markets and Winterflood. Note though that you do not get income tax relief. The attraction of the secondary market is that you can buy shares at a discount to net asset value (NAV) which could mean a lucrative income payout, as older VCTs are more likely to be able to make dividend payouts as their investments come into their own.
- Unlike annuities, you can bequeath VCTs to your heirs, although they will incur inheritance tax if together with the rest of your estate the total amount is more than the nil-rate band.
- The tax breaks available on VCTs make these an attractive investment proposition, especially for tax payers who fall into the high and additional tax bands. But remember these are high-risk investments and

should ideally not account for more than around 5% to 10% of your portfolio. Never substitute a pension with VCTs – rather use VCTs as a tax-efficient complement to your overall investment income.

ENTERPRISE INVESTMENT SCHEME

The Enterprise Investment Scheme (EIS) is a higher risk investment focused on smaller, unquoted companies offering generous tax breaks for the investor. You can get 30% income tax relief on a qualifying EIS investment up to £500,000 a year, and provided you hold the shares in the unquoted company for a minimum of three years you can sell these completely free of capital gains tax.

EIS investments are exempt from inheritance tax if you hold them for more than two years and provided the company is still a trading company when the IHT charge arises. If an EIS investment fails, it is in part mitigated by income tax and CGT reliefs which may reduce the effective cash loss to as little as 40p for every 100p invested. If you are connected with the companies involved, such as being an employee or director or owning more than 30% of shares, you won't get income tax relief on the investment but may still be able to claim loss reliefs.

There are EISs that comprise a single company investment as their underlying holding rather than a portfolio of companies. Given the lack of diversification, these tend to be higher risk and unless you are very familiar with the single company's business, it is usually better to construct a portfolio of EISs. Also as EISs are not quoted companies, the shares will not be traded on the main market, as VCTs are, so unless the company is on AIM, or subsequently moves onto AIM, being able to sell your shares and exit the investment may depend on the company being sold or floated.

There are a number of types of EIS available. It is important to ensure the fund you choose meets the necessary requirements as any fund that is found not to comply with the EIS criteria – to provide finance to early stage trading companies – will have the tax benefits removed. As this is a changing market, you should check to see what is on offer at the time you decide to invest. Good sources of information on EIS include stock broker Clubfinance's website, **www.clubfinance.co.uk**, and the Tax Efficient Review website at **www.taxefficientreview.com**.

If you can afford the minimum EIS investment, which typically ranges between £5000 and £50,000, with a small portion of your portfolio (5% to10%), and this fits with your broader income investing strategy, an EIS can provide further diversification and some tax benefits unavailable to VCTs.

EIS planning points

- If you have not invested in an EIS in the previous tax year, you can carry back up to £500,000.
- An EIS investment can allow you to put off paying capital gains tax (CGT) on other assets. This deferral of CGT can be a major plus: if you have any assets that have risen in value (like a second home), you will be able to shelter your gains from HMRC by investing them in an EIS. To qualify for this relief, you must reinvest any proceeds from selling the asset in question within one year before and three years after the date of disposal.
- EIS funds can be categorised either as an *approved fund or an unapproved fund*. An approved fund allows investors to claim initial tax relief in the year the fund closes. However, to get approved status it has to invest 90% of its assets in the 12 months following launch, whereas an unapproved fund does not have this restriction. An unapproved fund can potentially be in a better position as it has longer to choose its investments and build a more diversified portfolio. Such a fund also gets its income tax relief on the date of each investment, provided it qualifies. When choosing an EIS, you will have to balance certainty of tax relief with the potential for better returns.

TAX-FREE INVESTMENTS

There are certain forms of investment income that are completely free of tax. These include:

- Interest and bonuses on SAYE (Save As You Earn schemes).
- Prizes from premium bonds.
- National savings and investment (NS&I) certificates.
- NS&I Children's Bonus Bonds.
- Dividends on shares in VCTs.

- Savings gateway interest and maturity payments.
- ISAs are sometimes considered to be tax-free investments but tax credits on dividends cannot be recovered. For individuals who pay income tax at the basic rate it means ISAs are on a similar footing with other equity-based investments.

Tax allowances and reliefs

There are a number of statuary reliefs, allowances and annual exemptions that you can make use of to lighten your tax load. Usually allowances are increased each year in line with inflation as measured by the Retail Price Index (RPI) in the previous year. Below are the ones most often used within an investment context:

INCOME TAX RELIEF

Everyone has a tax free personal allowance.

- *Planning point*: If one spouse is not a higher rate taxpayer or does not work, income producing assets can be transferred to that spouse or civil partner. He/she can use their personal tax allowance and basic rate band to reduce the joint income tax rate.

CGT TAX ALLOWANCE

All taxpayers, including children, have an annual amount which is exempt from capital gains tax (CGT).

- *Planning point*: Spouses and civil partners each have a tax-free allowance and it is worth reorganising assets and investments and holding them jointly to ensure each spouse's CGT allowance is used. Even if an asset is only put into joint ownership the day before it produces income, that income will still be split equally between both owners.

PENSIONS TAX RELIEF

When you put money into a pension, the government adds upfront tax relief in line with your tax band which can boost your pension pot significantly. You get relief even if you are a non-taxpayer or pay tax at the starting rate.

- *Planning point*: If you were to contribute £2880 each year (£240 per month) to a Self-Invested Personal Pension (SIPP) for your child, Alliance Trust calculates that the child could end up with a pension pot well in excess of £2m at age 65 thanks to the tax relief added by government.[41] See Table 13.2 for more on how this could work. Provided these payments come from your income they will not be liable to inheritance tax. The drawback of course is that your child will not be able to access the income in the Sipp until they reach retirement age.

Table 13.2 – how a pension fund grows by age 65 based upon various monthly contributions

Monthly contribution	Gross payment after tax relief has been added (£)	Pension Fund at age 65 (£'000s)
£40	50	458
£80	100	917
£88	110	1,009
£120	150	1,375
£160	200	1,834
£240 (Maximum payment that will attract tax relief before child reaches 18.)	300	2,750

Source: Alliance Trust

Notes: Based on basic tax relief figures in 2010.

TAX SHELTERING INVESTMENTS

There are various tax sheltering investments which allow you to defer your tax liabilities until a later time as well as sometimes giving you a tax-free element. These investments usually roll-up free of all taxes until they are encashed. Two examples are:

1. Offshore insurance bonds.
2. Maximum investment plans and endowments.

[41] Alliance Trust Figures. Assumes an annual growth rate of 6%. This is the FSA's mid projection rate of 7% minus 1% for investment charges. It assumes that basic rate tax relief is available at its current rate until age 65. Figure rounded off to the nearest thousand.

Offshore insurance bonds

If you invest via an offshore investment bond the investment return can grow tax free until you encash the bond. UK-based insurance bonds will have their investment income and growth taxed at a rate of between 15% and 20% per annum.

You can also withdraw tax free cash each year up to 5% of your original investment and if this allowance is not used in any one year it can be carried forward.

Maximum investment plans and endowments

Maximum investment plans and endowments are regular premium insurance policies. Provided premiums are paid for at least 75% of a ten-year term and they do not vary within specified limits. Tax is limited to insurance company rates of between 15% and 20% and there is no further higher rate tax to pay on encashment.

Tax summary

Tax planning is important so that your income is not subject to more tax than is necessary. But where do you start?

The first thing is to do your homework: tax rules change rapidly and continually. As closely as you study the investment market, you should study the tax market. Make sure you have a good grasp of the different taxes your investments might be vulnerable to and knowledge of the allowances and reliefs and the vehicles best suited to you.

Once you've done the groundwork, you can start with the simple things such as using your basic allowances, and setting up an ISA or a SIPP. Then you can get advice from a tax expert on more complex and risky matters such as VCTs and EISs.

Consulting a tax expert can help you to get your timing right. Investors often think about when to sell and buy, but may not consider the tax implications of timing. For example, if you sell an asset at a profit on 5 April 2011 you have to pay your tax bill on 31 January 2012. Delay your sale by a day to 6 April and you have another 12 months to pay your tax bill (until 31 January 2013).

Finally, always maintain flexibility. Tax legislation could look very different when your investment comes to fruition than it did when you made the investment. It is important to adapt your tax planning to fit with these changes.

INDEX

J

N

O

P

T

U